PHILLIPPE HALSMAN

Challenging Years

THE AUTOBIOGRAPHY OF

Stephen Wise

G. P. PUTNAM'S SONS   NEW YORK

Manufactured in the United States of America

VAN REES PRESS • NEW YORK

To

LOUISE WATERMAN WISE

*whose inspired and blessed comradeship
has done most to make this
tale worth telling*

CONTENTS

ILLUSTRATIONS

A BIOGRAPHICAL NOTE

OUR father wrote this autobiography during the last year of his life. He wished to set down a record of the events through which he lived, the causes in which he labored, and the beliefs which impelled him to action. As the reader will find, however, he described the major issues and struggles he had confronted with a minimum of emphasis on his own life. Thus the omission of even the dates and places of his personal history was deliberate, and grew, as his foreword indicates, out of a strong distaste for conventional self-discussion and revelation. Had he lived longer, he would have edited this volume in final form. He might even have consented to supply enough personal data to form an adequate biographical framework. In any case, we feel that this brief outline of his life is now both necessary and justified.

Stephen Samuel Wise was born in Budapest, Hungary, on March 17, 1874; he delighted always in the coincidence of his birthdate with that of Ireland's patron St. Patrick. His father, Rabbi Aaron Weisz, was himself the son of a distinguished chief rabbi of Hungary, Joseph Hirsch Weisz. Famed alike for orthodox piety and political liberalism, this grandfather was reputed to have had legendary gifts of prophecy and a tempestuous way of exercising them. He was an adherent of the great revolutionary, Kossuth, and after that leader's defeat, was forced to flee his home for a time.

Aaron Wise adopted the simpler spelling of his last name when he immigrated to America in 1875 to prepare a home for his wife and children. Possessed of an imaginative mind and gentle nature, he served as rabbi of Temple Rodeph Sholom in New York. To the last days of his life, Stephen Wise spoke of his father as the most inspiring teacher and older comrade he had ever known.

Upon Sabine, the mother of Stephen Wise, fell the task of caring for the four children she brought to this country in 1875 and the three who were born here. In doing so, she reflected the vigor of the stock from which she came. Her father, Moritz Fischer, had founded the porcelain industry in Hungary and attained both wealth and artistic success. Emperor Franz Joseph II honored him first by knighting and then by raising him to the rank of Baron. The exquisite Herend China pieces that the family factory produced are still treasured by collectors.

The Wise family established its first American home on East Fifth Street, New York. With his brothers and sisters, Stephen attended public school a block away, and from his boyhood impressed teachers and friends alike with a serious and earnest will to learn and to achieve. The prizes that he won in those early days are still in the family's possession, and later when he went first to City College and then to Columbia University, he attained distinction as a Latin and Greek scholar.

But it was the field of English letters that first won and always held Stephen Wise's affection as a student. The very fact that English was not his mother tongue—German being the first language of his home—determined him to master it. He pored over the writings of the British poets and prose stylists. Shakespeare and Milton, Matthew Arnold and Wordsworth were as familiar to him as Isaiah and Amos and Hillel.

From earliest youth, Stephen Wise decided upon the ministry for his life's work. Proudly determined to be an American in the fullest sense, he felt the call to be a servant and teacher of the Jewish people and its interpreter to the world without. Thus, while he was growing up as an American, he studied with his father in order to become a rabbi.

After graduating with honors from Columbia University in 1892, he went abroad, first to Vienna, where he was ordained under Chief Rabbi Jellinek, and later, to study and do graduate work at Oxford. Upon his return to the United States, he became assistant to Rabbi Henry Jacobs at Temple B'nai Jeshurun, New York, better known as the Madison Avenue Synagogue. His congregation was of the Conservative tradition which suited Stephen Wise, whose later religious liberalism never conflicted with his reverent love of traditional Jewishness.

Shortly after he began his ministry in B'nai Jeshurun, Rabbi Jacobs died, and after considerable debate as to the wisdom of electing so young a successor, Stephen Wise was chosen rabbi. He delighted in the story that after his trial sermon had made a deep impression on the Congregation, one of the trustees protested to the president that the sermon must have been written by Stephen's father and only delivered by him. The president replied that if their young rabbi had sense enough to preach one of his father's good sermons instead of his own bad one, this only proved how fit he was for the post!

It was during his pastorate at B'nai Jeshurun that four events occurred which profoundly affected his fate and future.

The first of these was the sudden death of his beloved father a few hours after preaching the Passover sermon in 1897. Still in his twenty-third year, Stephen Wise became the economic support and moral stay of his family. His youth was ended.

The second was the wave of Jewish persecution in Czarist Russia and the Dreyfus case in France, both of which cast a pall over the Jewish world. Stephen Wise came to realize then that the process of Jewish liberation was to be arduous, not automatic, and that its consummation was still far off.

The third was the advent of Theodor Herzl and modern Zionism into Jewish life. Almost alone among the younger American Jews, Stephen Wise recognized and rallied to his leadership. He founded the first Zionist Federation in New York on July 4, 1897, and journeyed a year later to the Second Zionist Congress in Switzerland, where his personal friendship with Herzl began and his compact with Israel's destiny was sealed.

The fourth event of those years was the meeting in 1898 of Stephen Wise and Louise Waterman. Two years later they were married. Thenceforth they were united until her death in 1947, by love so rooted in all their mutual aspirations, so tender and sustained, that their lives were and are one.

An artist by temperament and a painter by avocation, Louise Waterman knew little of Jewish laws and lore. But she had a passion for justice and mercy, and a pride in her people's past, which was kindled by her marriage to a flame of Jewish and human service. The great works that she undertook in later years, the founding of the first Jewish Child Adoption Committee, the caring for refugees from Hitlerism, the enlistment of American women in the battle against fascist tyranny—all these lay in the future.

But those first married years confirmed her faith in Stephen Wise and what he would achieve in the prophetic tradition. That faith never wavered and her children best know how in dark hours it upheld and renewed her husband's spirit.

Shortly before his marriage, Stephen Wise received a call to Temple Bethel in Portland, Oregon. Despite the counsel of friends and family that he would be burying himself so far from the center of Jewish life, he accepted the call. He felt that he needed to know more of the United States than New York City if he was to serve his country and his people in the fullest sense. Moreover, he wished to utilize the comparative quiet of a smaller city in order to read and study and write—luxuries denied him, since his active ministry had begun before he was twenty.

His decision to go West was abundantly rewarded. In Portland, he found a congregation responsive to the increasingly liberal views that were bringing him from Conservative to Reform Judaism. Here he enjoyed the opportunity to complete his thesis for a Doctorate of Philosophy, and to engage for a time in the creative Jewish scholarship he always loved, and which the stress of later life was to deny him. Here he prepared articles for the Jewish Encyclopedia and translated the Book of Judges for the Jewish Publication Society's edition of the Old Testament.

The beauty of the West became an indelible part of Stephen Wise's life. Here, in Portland, he made his first home, and here his two children, James and Justine, were born. Here too he made enduring friendships, precious throughout his life.

But his ministry in Oregon, for all its peaceful aspects, foreshadowed the battles that he would wage in the years ahead. On the civic front, he threw himself into the "Good Government" fight in state and city politics. In 1903 he was appointed Commissioner of Child Labor for the State of Oregon.

In Portland, Stephen Wise first began to preach at the invitation of Christian ministers and to interpret the Jewish faith and people to their congregations. Unconsciously he founded the interfaith movement in our country. His reputation grew not only as a brilliant orator but also as a man who had something to say and was not afraid to say it. He was invited to address civic audiences of every kind on the political and social problems before the American people.

In 1905, Temple Emanu-El, New York's Cathedral Synagogue, invited him to become its rabbi. His refusal of the call because the pulpit was "subject to the control of the Board of Trustees," is told in detail in this volume. Here it need only be added that the idea of founding a Free Synagogue in New York was conceived and developed by Stephen Wise in Oregon; that when he left the lifetime contract, at an unprecedented salary, which his Portland congregation begged him to accept, he had thought out what he was undertaking and knew the risks involved.

Returning to New York in 1906, Stephen Wise invited a group of like-minded laymen to join him in forming a synagogue whose pulpit would be free, whose pews would be equally open to

rich and poor, and which would minister to the social needs of
the whole community as well as to the religious needs of its
members. And the Free Synagogue grew in numerical strength
and communal influence from year to year.

Having founded it and its social-service division, Stephen
Wise plunged into related Jewish, civic, and social fields. As
the impact of his personality was felt first in New York and
later throughout the country, demands poured in from churches
and colleges and Chautauquas, from Zionist groups and community forums, that he visit and address them. For forty years,
he traveled up and down America speaking as often as five times
a day, preaching to Jews and Christians, pleading for progressive causes, beseeching contributions for the upbuilding of
Palestine, for relief abroad, for the needy at home. In spite of
the illness he suffered for the last fifteen years of his life, no one
ever found him unwilling or unable to answer any call that was
made upon him.

Yet, paradoxically, he did not spread himself thin. He chose
only such causes as seemed significant, and his efforts on their
behalf became related parts of his whole life. This underlying
unity was perhaps clearest to those in his own home. No husband was ever more devoted and adoring; no father closer in
loving comradeship. To his home he brought his rich full life
outside; with his family he shared its battles, its triumphs, its
defeats, its hopes, its problems.

A significant part of Stephen Wise's life was the summer home
he and his wife made on Buck Island, Lake Placid. It was in
1908, long before Lake Placid had become an internationally
known resort, that they bought a few acres of land and planned
the home to which they came back year after year for peace,
for inspiration, and for family togetherness. Here in Camp
Willamette, named for the Oregon river he loved, Stephen Wise
read and studied and wrote his sermons and addresses. Pulpit
Rock across the Lake, John Brown's grave some four miles
away, and the sentinel-like Mt. Whiteface that dominates the
Adirondack scene, became an integral part of his life.

Of his battles for American liberalism and for justice to all peoples, of his leadership in the democratic organization of Jewish life, of his embattled resistance to Hitlerism, of his paramount service in the achievement of Israel's statehood, *Challenging Years* is the record. It need only be added here that in writing this autobiography Stephen Wise deliberately refrained from stressing differences between him and the World Zionist leadership throughout the years. He held that these differences were less important than the overriding need for unity in behalf of a Jewish state, which might have been weakened had he revived or underscored them. It may further be stated that such differences had diminished, and that he worked closely with Dr. Weizmann during and after World War II. Finally he had absolute confidence in Israel's future under the leadership of Prime Minister Ben-Gurion and his Government.

He lived to see the establishment of the State of Israel— though like Moses, he was not destined to set foot in the nation he had done so much to bring into being. His wife died on December 10, 1947, and with her going his health and strength ebbed swiftly. On his seventy-fifth birthday, he received the loving and grateful tributes of men and women of every race and faith and station the world over who knew and loved him, or knew and loved what he had been and had done. In acknowledging these tributes, he reaffirmed the truths by which he lived—his dedication to the Jewish faith and fate, his loyalty to American democracy, his devotion to man's freedom everywhere, his belief in the oneness of humanity, and his final affirmation that peace, not war, could and must distinguish the future from the past.

A few days later, the illness that he had endured so heroically forced him to undergo a major operation. He rallied from it only briefly. Stephen Wise died on April 19, 1949. The Jewish people had lost its leader, America a great preacher and citizen, mankind a friend who had done justice, loved mercy, and walked humbly with his God.

JUSTINE WISE POLIER
JAMES WATERMAN WISE

ACKNOWLEDGMENTS

We are deeply indebted to Dr. David Petegorsky for his generous help in preparing Challenging Years *for publication. We also wish to express appreciation to Leona Schwartz and Florence Eitelberg, Dr. Wise's secretaries, who, together with Evelyn Linwood Abramson, transcribed the manuscript.*

J.W.P.
J.W.W.

FOREWORD

T HERE are Autobiographies and autobiographies. A fine difference obtains between the two. The former is egocentric; the second is heterocentric. In the former the writer sees the world and its life in relation to self. In the latter the writer sees himself in relation to the world. In the former one chronicles the facts of life, however far reaching, as if one were their author and creator. In the latter one becomes confessedly an accessory to and participant in the facts of which one's life is a phase. Mine is to be autobiography without the capital A.

Any autobiography, to be worth while, must give a man's relation to and participation in the events and movements of some critical or stirring time. As for my own, I have lived throughout nearly half of my country's history and have beheld immeasurable gains, alas, not without grave political and spiritual loss. I have been witness of a great epoch, an epoch that began with peace, freedom, and security. After two world wars this epoch may rise again to peace and freedom or culminate in the war to end peace and freedom—if not humanity.

As for another side of my life, I have looked upon and been related to the unbelievable tragedy that has befallen a great people. As an American citizen and rabbi and as one who helped to organize my fellow Jews in order that they might face and overcome their grievous woes, I have seen and shared deep and terrible sorrow. The tale might be less tragic if the help

of men had been less scant and fitful. I write these lines in
the midst of the Cardinal Mindszenty trial and tragedy. I cannot avoid the sorrowful reflection that the world never permitted itself to be equally disturbed over an infinitely graver
tragedy—the almost unchallenged slaughter of more than six
millions of my fellow Jews throughout the foul and brutal
Hitler years.

Though this be true, the record is far happier in relation
to my country's part in the most momentous hour of Israel's
history—an hour that beholds the end of centuries of homelessness for many Jews, the beginnings of hope for a people, an
incredible victory over the armies of massed nations, a generous
and forbearing peace under the leadership of Israel, the miracle
of Israel's re-creating itself in the land of its fathers under the
most glorious auspices.

I would not try to tell the story of these years if they were
to be nothing more than the story of one man's life. But in
truth these have been challenging years both from the viewpoint of my life as a Jew all my days and as an American
save for the first fourteen months of my life. I am enabled to
describe them as challenging on several grounds—restless curi-
osity, a capacious and I believe accurate memory, the calling
that chose me, plus a deep concern for every human interest
that, in a sense, I chose. All of these operated together to make
me a sharer in the large affairs of my country and my generation
and an active participant in the problems that developed out of
the all but overwhelmingly fateful tragedy of the Jewish people
in many lands.

I was born into the in-many-ways brave postwar liberalism
of the mid-nineteenth century of my adoptive country. I have
witnessed the glorious rise of that liberalism and the possibility
of what is awful to contemplate, liberalism's inglorious fall.
As for American affairs, I remain as I hope I have always been,
an unshakable liberal who, alas, has looked upon his country's
inevitable part in two world wars. In so doing, I have given

fullest support to two of America's great war presidents, Woodrow Wilson and Franklin Roosevelt. I refuse to believe, unless the forces of reaction and war evocation are to succeed in bringing down upon our heads the shame of avoidable war, that my country will abandon or forswear its tradition of liberalism, which I venture to call the Jeffersonian tradition of democracy, the rock and bulwark of our republic.

I was not more than seven years of age when a tragic epoch began for the Jewish people, the end of which is not yet. After several decades of fearless Jewish participation in the revolutionary movements against the Czarist government, the great exodus of Jews from Russia was decreed. Many years later, while I was preaching at Cornell, I enjoyed the privilege of a full and deeply informing talk with the university's great president, Andrew White. He who had been American minister at that woeful time confirmed the tale that the Czar's minister Pobodonosteff planned to solve the Jewish questions by dealing with Russo-Jewry, six millions in all, in the following way: One third of the Russian Jews were to be expelled; one third converted to Christianity; one third must be slain. The expulsion or exile proceeded according to his plans. He made a vast population homeless, uprooting and expelling hundreds of thousands.

Night after night as a child, I heard from my father's lips the tale of cureless suffering inflicted on a whole people. He was wont at the supper hour to tell my mother and us children the tale of what had been endured by the unhappy exiles who were then landing at Castle Garden. The most distressing of these stories moved us to tears of sympathy with the sufferers who at the instance of New York's leading Jews—such as Jacob Schiff, Felix Adler, Emma Lazarus, Joseph Seligman, Henry Rice—were being helped through the meager facilities of the United Hebrew Charities.

Reverting to Pobodonosteff's decree, one third of the Jewish population was not slain, but thousands were murdered in the pogroms, which were government ordered. As for that third two million, these were not converted inasmuch as there was no Russian Christianity to which to be converted, even if Jews had been ready for the great betrayal.

Such was my introduction to Jewish life. Today, after nearly seventy years, world Jewry still struggles with the major problem of the establishment of the Jewish State and the related problem of Jewish DPs—no longer to be considered Displaced Persons, but Destined for Palestine!

I have written the above at Montreux, Switzerland, where the World Jewish Congress has just held its second session after an interval of twelve Hitler and post-Hitler years. The spirit of the Jewish people, whatever its losses, remains unshattered. As I close these lines, I look upon the waters of Lake Geneva, and I take heart as I glimpse the Castle of Chillon. I remember that we were never, not even in our darkest years, like him who regained his freedom with a sigh. Jews are regaining their freedom with exaltation. We believe that such freedom will result in a nobler Jewish people—it may be in a more free and just and peaceable world.

Montreux, Switzerland
July, 1948

Challenging Years

THE AUTOBIOGRAPHY OF
STEPHEN WISE

I

Civic Affairs

MY interest in political affairs began at a rather early age, and I am tempted to add that it was uniformly bound up with the ethics of civic life. But, as I search my memory, I find that, difficult as it is for me after nearly seventy years to believe it, it was just five years after I was landed in the United States that I began, as a boy of six years and a few months, to take a keen interest in American political affairs—that is to say, the Hancock-Garfield election of 1880.

We children adored Hancock, and I carried a torch in Hancock parades. His name was resounding—Winfield Scott Hancock. He had been a Major General in the Union Army. He was very handsome. We were fed upon tales of his heroism in the Civil War, 1880 being only fifteen years after its close. We little ones could hardly be expected to take too seriously Hancock's classic answer to the question, "General Hancock, what do you think of the tariff?" to which he vigorously, though not astutely, replied, "The tariff is a purely local problem."

Through many a weary street I bore my torch and had the smelly kerosene permeate my youthful clothes. Election day came and I clearly remember the crushing blow I suffered. Soon after six next morning, beginning the habit of a lifetime, I went to a corner newsstand and got the morning paper. I had begun to read, and I was overwhelmed with sorrow. I must have been, for my parents often told me that I came into the house weeping copiously and shouting before seven in the morning, "What a shame! Hancock was defeated. Garfield is elected." My first election and my first political disappointment!

I remember clearly my early, childish disgust with certain things about elections in New York City. From the time I was six or eight I noticed how men were led to the ballot boxes by local party-precinct leaders of both parties. As the voter approached the shop or store in which the election was held, he was addressed and buttonholed by one or another or both of the precinct leaders. These had folded bills, ones, twos, fives, showing between their fingers. The voter was allowed to use the ballot given him by the politicians who held cash between their fingers. As he left the place, the voter was almost unblushingly handed the money reward that had been stipulated; his name and the amount he received were noted for reference in the next election and above all for report to the district leaders. This I beheld annually with an ever increasing sense of horror and shame. It all happened in the Eleventh Ward in which the synagogue of my father was situated. When I was thirteen we moved to an attractive home my father had purchased on East 30th Street within walking distance, except I must add during the day of the Great Blizzard, of the College of New York City, which my older brother Otto Irving Wise and I for some years attended.

The second presidential campaign that evoked my interest, as a child of exactly ten, was in 1884, the campaign in which Cleveland ran against Blaine. Again I made the wrong choice, or in any event, a mistaken choice, for my young friends and I were all for the Plumed Knight of Navarre, as Ingersoll named Blaine. Moreover the Jewish families of those days were Republicans chiefly because they associated the Republican party with the name of Lincoln.

I can still remember that I heard Blaine speak and was tremendously stirred by him. I think it was at the Polo Grounds, then at 110th Street and Fifth Avenue, that the great Republican demonstration was held, with Blaine as the chief speaker.

Had I known then what I know today, I would have supported
Cleveland in eighty-four. But at ten one does not think through
political problems, nor is one competent to pass upon the
validity of party platforms or of the merits of opposing candidates. I remember watching the Cleveland and Blaine parades
of 1884, hearing the Democratic paraders shout in derision at
Blaine, "Burn, burn, burn these letters!" This exclamation
had reference to a memorandum of Blaine in regard to the
Mulligan letters, which he should never have written. I remember too, as a Blaine devotee of ten years, having heard the Republican paraders, as they marched up Broadway, singing
scornfully with regard to Cleveland's dubious Civil War record:
"I cannot shoot, I will not shoot, but I can hire a substitoot!"
A number of circumstances, I need hardly say, united to defeat
Blaine. One was, as I recall it, the crookedness of the election
at Coney Island in New York State, where through stuffing
the ballot boxes Cleveland was given a slight plurality which
he needed to win New York and the national election.

I have always felt, remembering the Cleveland-Blaine campaign, that we who are parsons should be especially nervous
about presidential elections. I have never forgotten the little
less than tragic story of the incredibly unwise remark made by
the Reverend Doctor Burchard of one of the Fifth Avenue
Presbyterian churches. Speaking at a Republican reception he
used the fatal phrase, "Against you, Mr. Blaine, are arrayed
the forces of Rum, Romanism, and Rebellion." It was a superb
bit of alliteration, but in that moment Blaine was defeated. He
might and could have saved himself by a proper and immediate
retort. But he was too disconcerted by the idiocy of the remark.
He should have said, "Dr. Burchard, I deplore your remark.
There is no connection between Rum and Romanism, between
Rum and Rebellion, nor between Romanism and Rebellion."
Had he while on his feet made instant and overwhelming reply
to Burchard and squelched that blundering parson, he would
probably have won the election. Not even the Democratic
party of that day could have stuffed the ballot boxes of Coney

Island with enough votes to defeat him. But the deed was done. The fatally blundering remark of Doctor Burchard was telegraphed all over the country—and Blaine was defeated.

Such was the beginning of my interest in political contests. I might have gone even further back, that is to the election of 1876. In later years, that is to say after 1900, I had met and become the Oregon neighbor and friend of Judge George H. Williams who had been attorney general in the Cabinet of Grant. During an evening of exchange of neighborly confidences I asked Judge Williams, at that time the mayor of my then city, Portland, Oregon, what was the truth with regard to the charge that the election of 1876 had been stolen from Samuel Tilden and given to General Rutherford B. Hayes. His answer was astounding: "On the night of the election, when it looked as though Tilden might carry it with all of the disaster which his election and administration would mean to our country, Grant called us together and allotted different states to the members of his Cabinet. We were to go to those states which were in doubt and each of us was to see to it that the state was won, or recorded in any event, for Hayes. Grant did not say that the vote in the state must be honestly counted but that the vote of the state must be won for Hayes— of course he did not explicitly add, 'rightly or wrongly.'" In any event, Williams admitted to me with the utmost frankness that actually the election was won by Tilden but, as he put it, "The country could not afford to have a Democratic president at that time!"

One of the civic campaigns of my rather early years in New York I clearly recall, that of eighty-six with three eminent men as candidates for the office of mayor, Abram S. Hewitt, Henry George, and Theodore Roosevelt. It was hotly, even bitterly, fought with a result that will sound unbelievable after two generations. Hewitt, one of the finest of the elder citizens of New York, like his father-in-law Peter Cooper before him, was elected. I can recall that Henry George was second with 68,000 votes, all gotten on the single-tax program, which he, more

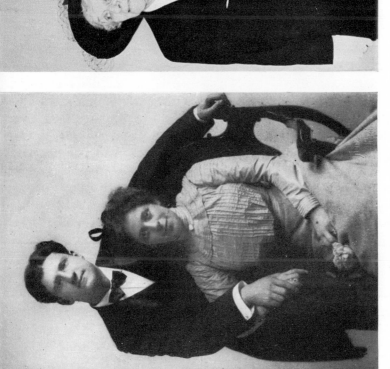

Rabbi and Mrs. Wise at the time of their marriage in 1900, and in 1946.

With his children, Justine and James, in Oregon, 1905.

than any other man, had brought to the attention of the American people. Theodore Roosevelt ran third and last with, as I recall it, 66,000 votes, the only time in his political life that he met defeat until Bull Moose Run. His career as police commissioner was to begin some years later.

My friends and I were ardent though still rather youthful supporters of Henry George. He won special support from Jewish citizens, many of whom followed him because of his classic utterance on Moses. The Pentateuchal program for the return of the land to its original owners Henry George held to be the forerunner of the single-tax proposal. A generation later, Joseph Fels, one of the most ardent disciples of Henry George, offered to give a goodly part of a considerable fortune if Lloyd George, very sympathetic at that time to single tax, would introduce it as a measure under the government to be established in Palestine by Britain as the mandatory power.

The fanatic devotion of single taxers was amusingly illustrated when we established the Portland, Oregon, Forum with the help of a group of distinguished civic leaders in 1902. The theme of the first meeting was to be religion versus science. One of the two speakers was to be J. D. Stevens, a one time Shakespearean actor. He never mentioned either religion or science. He held forth solely on the single tax. As chairman I found it necessary to say to him at the close of his single-tax disquisition, "But, Brother Stevens, have you forgotten the subject assigned for tonight was religion versus science?" The answer was priceless: "No, Mr. Chairman, I did not forget. I have limited myself strictly to the subject, for single tax is the science of sciences and the religion of religions." Was not my Oregon friend a typical single-tax devotee?

As rabbi in a relatively small city, Portland being under 100,000, I came into closer touch with the things out of which grew the lawless power of civic corruption. It was the union of gambling and liquor interests plus organized prostitution, which, in collusion with city officials and above all with the police department, poisoned and corroded the life of the city. The hold of these forces upon the city's life was fully known to the acquiescent and rather cynical population, which seemed to take it for granted that organized vice was entitled to no small part in managing the city and its affairs.

It was during my years in Portland that I was mildly tempted to seek public office for the first time in the United States Senate when it was felt by some of the Democratic party bosses that the state of Oregon was ready to revolt against the long-time Republican Party dominance, and for the second time when I took a very active part in the civic-reform movement under the leadership of Dr. Harry Lane, whom we succeeded in electing mayor. Upon his election Mayor Lane invited me to serve in his mayoral cabinet. I was tempted to accept, but despite my affection and respect for Dr. Lane, I declined the honor. I felt and still feel that a minister of religion should not, save under the most extraordinary and compelling conditions, accept public office tendered him under partisan auspices. The office of the minister is to awake and guide and lead to the end that civic life be clean and incorrupt. The moment a minister accepts public office at the hands of a political party, relations are established between him and the party that must inevitably affect his independence. In any event, such was my conviction as I faced alike the problems of Portland and the question of a minister's greatest usefulness.

I must add that soon thereafter Mayor Lane became a United States senator and later ended his political or public career by voting with two great senators, LaFollette and Norris, against President Wilson's Declaration of War against Germany. He may have been mistaken—I thought at the time he was—but I knew Lane well enough to realize that he acted out of the deepest convictions. Such was the story of the man's whole life. He had something of the quizzical humor of Will Rogers, whom he facially resembled. Like Rogers, he was part Indian by race.

Very early during my residence in Oregon, where my family and I lived from 1900 to 1906, I had a striking experience in connection with the gambling and prostitution in Portland. An extraordinary superstition obtained, which, according to Reverend Doctor Thomas Lamb Eliot, the spiritual father of the Northwest, resulted from Portland's retaining the mood of a pioneering community. The superstition ran that business prospered when gambling, drinking, and prostitution went unchecked. In truth it arose as a result of the fact that when the pioneering towns were prosperous, drinking, gambling, and prostitution followed in the wake of such prosperity. All these were beggarly dependents and lecherous invaders of the community and its prosperity, never in any sense the creators of that prosperity.

A few months after I had joined Dr. Edgar P. Hill of the First Presbyterian Church and other ministers in a crusade against the lawlessness of gambling and prostitution, the head of the gambling combine of the city went to the president of my congregation. The latter, Solomon Hirsch, was a thoroughly good and fine man who had served as United States minister to Turkey under President Harrison. His visitor began to complain to Mr. Hirsch concerning what he called "Dr. Wise's disgusting activities." He concluded his arraignment with a query to Mr. Hirsch, "Can't you do something to stop Dr. Wise?" Mr. Hirsch did me the honor of replying, "I cannot and I would not try to, but perhaps you can. Why not go and see him and do what you can with him?"

I never saw the gentleman until one day in a Turkish bath I heard a voice in an adjoining booth speak in the bitterest and most maledictory fashion about "Dr. Wise." I could not help hear rather than overhear the raucous remark, "If I ever get near that ⸺ ⸺ ⸺ I'll shoot holes through him." In view of the circumstance that I lay on a slab in a booth adjoining that from which these pleasant oaths had come, I did not linger unduly in the bath. I dressed and hastened to my home to congratulate my wife on the fact that my would-be assassin carried no gun with him at that particular moment when he might conceivably have recognized me, even though I had never had the pleasure and honor of meeting him.

Returning to New York from Portland in 1906 was to move from a garden smudge to a prairie fire, and I was touched by Mayor Seth Low's welcome to its civic life at a Cooper Union meeting. Within a year announcement was made that "King Richard" Croker, the former boss of Tammany Hall, was about to return from his exile to Ireland and its turf pleasures. I might have viewed the announcement with entire unconcern had it not been followed by the statement that a great public welcoming dinner was to be tendered Croker in honor of his return to New York. The dinner was held and was attended by a dozen or more of New York Supreme Court judges plus District Attorney William Travers Jerome, elected to office on an anti-Tammany revolt ticket.

The following night I had occasion to speak at a dinner of the Ethical Social League, founded and led by one of New York's finest citizens, the head of Cooper Union, Professor Charles Sprague-Smith. I felt that I must speak out against the shameful exhibition of the night before. In simple and frank terms I spoke of Croker's dinner as "New York's night of shame" and, with especial vigor, of the degradation of the city involved in the representatives of the judiciary uniting to do honor to one with a completely dishonorable record. The "night of shame" was made the theme of a series of brilliant cartoons in *The Mirror and Express* by the famed cartoonist, Homer Davenport, who waged such a fight as only a brilliant and daring cartoonist knows how to wage.

In comment on my address, *Life* in December, 1908, noted:

> Of course, the judges went to the Croker dinner. A good many, if not all of them, owed their nominations to him, we presume, and how can the stream be expected to rise above its source? . . . Nobody doubts, we suppose, that gamblers, liquor-sellers and disorderly houses paid tribute to somebody for protection in Croker's time, as they have done more or less since that time,

and that police captains got rich, and that all that was a part of the Tammany system of government. Nobody doubts, we suppose, that the public franchise corporations settled with Croker for what they wanted, and that plans for the improvement of the city were made to enrich persons who made them or knew what they were to be. That Tammany, and the men who managed it, had an immense rake-off in Croker's time at the cost of the people in what was done in the name of the people, we presume no one doubts. That it still gets a rake-off on anything it can, is equally believed. That Tammany 'works for its own pocket all the time,' through possession of political power and traffic in it, is universally admitted. All that is shameful, and Croker cannot possibly escape such shame as belongs to him as a notable head and profit-taker of a shameful system. . . .

So, the judges were right in dining with Croker, because it would have been an affectation not to. And Rabbi Wise was right in saying that it was a shameful night for New York.

Tammany Hall at that time meant more to me even than a political organization based on the protection and support of gamblers, liquor sellers, and disorderly houses or the shameful dependency of judges. I was well aware of the role that Tammany had played in every area of social and public life and of its long history of evildoing and of the close relation between civic corruption and the opposition to social justice.

As I pointed out in November, 1905:

In the thirties, the city of New York, the headquarters of the American Anti-Slavery Society, had not a place for Garrison to lay his head except the cotton-loft in the third or fourth story of a Wall Street storehouse, the hospitality of which was offered by a Negro. In 1833, Clinton Hall was closed to an anti-slavery meeting, which was compelled to adjourn to Chatham Street Chapel by a Tammany Hall mob. Seventeen years later, another Tammany Hall mob, led by a typical Tammany Hall leader, Isaiah Rynders, interrupted and finally broke up an anti-slavery meeting, in the Broadway Tabernacle. How well Tammany sustains its character for zeal in ill-doing, its inspiration being ever the pious hope breathed by Bluecher as he looked upon London,

"Was fuer Plunder," with the difference that Tammany's works have been uniformly consistent with Bluecher's faith!

To me it was clear that just as Tammany strengthened and fed upon civic corruption and social injustice so I, as a minister, could not separate the battle for civic decency and the battle for social justice.

It was satisfying to have a temporary leader of Tammany Hall, Lewis Nixon, tell me after some years that the Croker dinner was meant to be a public purge of Croker with a view to his return to leadership of Tammany Hall, hence the appearance of the Supreme Court judges and District Attorney Jerome. "Your phrase, 'New York's night of shame,' and the public's reaction to it killed that plan," he said.

George B. McClellan, who, chiefly because of his name, became Tammany Hall's successful mayoral candidate in opposition to Seth Low, finest of public servants, proved doubly disappointing in public office. He never seemed to get his teeth into the difficult New York situation and was content to pursue his academically indifferent way in municipal affairs. After the murder of Rosenthal, the gangster, he was unwise enough to appoint Police Lieutenant Becker to "investigate the affair," although, thanks to District Attorney Charles S. Whitman, suspicion had almost immediately begun to fasten itself upon Lieutenant Becker.

I therefore turned to the citizens of New York to demand an investigation:

LAKE PLACID, N. Y.
JULY 18, 1912

To THE EDITOR OF THE EVENING POST
20 VESEY STREET
NEW YORK

MY DEAR MR. EDITOR:

The Evening Post is right in declaring that the Rosenthal murder constitutes a crisis in the affairs of the Police Department. The writer, however, begs leave to amend and to urge that this assassination is not so much a crisis as a proof of the critical conditions under the current police regime.

Will not *The Evening Post* suggest editorially the coming together of a group of dependable men and women in order to undertake the task of investigating the conditions of lawlessness which have reached abhorrent dimensions in our city? This Committee should not be awed nor yet subdued by any certificate of character touching the Police Department from its figure head or its actual and responsible head, the Mayor.

Is New York to rival a Nevada mining town at its worst—in respect of law-breaking with impunity? If so, then let us have our Vigilance Committee of unterrifiable citizens, moving within the limits of the law.

The situation demands not a little white-washing Waldo, such as is the present mayoral jest at the head of the Police Department, but a man with a man's power and a man's grit and a man's wisdom. The citizenship of New York must now demand an investigation—withersoever it may lead—not by the police but of the police.

FAITHFULLY YOURS,
[signed] STEPHEN S. WISE

A civic committee was swiftly formed to deal with the situation, and I was called from my camp in the Adirondacks to address a public meeting. Those of us who founded and worked on the Citizens' Committee that resulted from that meeting were not interested only in convicting the murderers of a gambler. We were determined that the blackmail and plunder, organized to a fine science under Croker and Van Wyck, under which the Police Department of New York collected revenue for Tammany and even employed murderers to enforce its thievery, should be revealed to the citizens of New York and so ended. In this work Charles S. Whitman, then district attorney, performed an inestimable service with courage and against the greatest odds. When the ugly matter was finished, he wrote me on June 2, 1914:

You are one of the few men of the City who really understand all that the Becker case means and many of its ramifications. I appreciate more than I can tell you your attitude in the matter.

The knowledge that men like you have understood and have supported me during the most trying experience I have ever known, has been of itself a real inspiration—and I shall never forget it.

New York, after a thoroughly dishonoring record of mayors, had a brief and happy interlude during which it was comparatively well governed by a gallant young Irish-American, John Purroy Mitchel. A Columbia University graduate and grandson of an Irish patriot of fame, Mayor Mitchel, in addition to his direct service during his years in office, did much, after the dismal civic years before him and after him, to prepare the way for the wonderful and most serviceably cleansing years of LaGuardia.

This is my evaluation of his services today as I look back, and it was my feeling when he completed his first term, although some of my colleagues who had been battling for a more decent city felt far from satisfied with Mitchel's achievements. One of those colleagues, my friend Amos Pinchot, disagreed and wrote to me in 1916:

> The spectacle of Mitchel holding down the mayoralty respectably and creditably does not enthuse me. I think there ought to be a law against men holding down jobs respectably and creditably, unless they stand for something real. All the interests want is to have people hold down jobs just that way, and leave them alone. They don't want help, they just want non-interference and Mitchel's administration has been a perfect model of intelligent, enlightened, Christian non-interference with the big grafters, i.e., the real estate ring and the public utilities ring, which form the strength of the bi-partisan machine.

Incisive, right thinking, cutting to the heart of the weakness of most reform movements and their candidates for office at that time and throughout the years—Pinchot's criticism is as valid today as in 1916 in one area after another. And yet, at that time, the personal integrity of Mitchel, the change of atmosphere in city government, and the beginning of the appointment of decent, responsible public servants as com- missioners, John Kingsbury for example, who was determined to establish better conditions for those citizens of New York and their children who needed public assistance (then known as charity), were important enough to make me feel Mitchel must be re-elected.

I knew and loved John Purroy Mitchel, but in some respects he proved a woeful disappointment, though in truth he was as incorruptible as a man could be. Sometimes he was unwise, but he was always straight and just and clean. I also admired Mitchel for the enemies he had made. Yet I cannot help men- tioning one serious limitation of John Purroy Mitchel. He chose to see much more of a very limited social and dancing set than he did of the people whose uprising had elected him.

I should not leave Mayor Mitchel without telling that one morning in the fall of 1914 I was called to the phone and heard the extraordinary exclamation, "Dr. Wise, this is John Mitchel. Where in hell is Armenia?" I tried to quiet the Mayor and briefly explained to him just where Armenia was. Breathlessly he added, "Some representatives of Armenia are coming to this office in a few minutes and I don't know where Armenia is and what these fellows want." I suggested that he put a good stenographer on the phone, and I dictated to her a short state- ment of welcome and congratulation to the gentlemen from Armenia, soon to appear, and who were welcomed in friendly and, I hope, eloquent fashion by the Mayor of New York.

By 1930 New York City was again cursed by the indifference of its citizens and the selfishness, greed, and cunning of those who cared solely for personal gain. In addition, an atmosphere of vulgarity had for long breathed through the life of the city. Men sworn to protect the honor of New York and the well- being of its citizens were treating their obligation as a jest, enriching themselves and their camp followers and again corrupting the very sources of law and order. The cheap jesting of a cabaret performer came to be extolled above the decencies and sobrieties and sanities of clean and honest government. I felt that the churches and synagogues of New York should be in the vanguard of a movement to cleanse the city.

I never had any personal feelings about or against Mayor Walker. Nothing ever happened except his conduct as mayor, which moved me to feel that he had brought deep disgrace to our city. The year came when it became possible and, as I felt, necessary to act with respect to the shame this gifted man brought to the people of the city. A magistrate of his choosing behaved in a most shocking manner, but the people of New York remained unshocked.

From my study at Camp Willamette, Lake Placid, I telegraphed to Governor Roosevelt in protest against the Mayor and the District Attorney of that day. I saw Governor Roosevelt shortly thereafter in his home. He said, "Rabbi Wise, it wasn't cricket of you to give to the press the telegram calling upon me to act upon the case of that magistrate and Mayor Walker."

But I had known perfectly well that if I had written or telegraphed and not given out my message to the press nothing would have happened. My telegram brought action from the Governor, however reluctant. Soon thereafter, the City Affairs Committee—John Haynes Holmes, its inspiring head, and Paul Blanshard, its extraordinarily effective secretary, together with myself as vice-chairman—sent a formal petition to the Governor to remove Mayor Walker, after a fair and full trial, from office.

The petition was based on a memorandum prepared by the City Affairs Committee. It pointed out that under the charter the governor of New York had the power to inquire into the conduct of the mayor, suspend the mayor, or remove the mayor for incompetence or neglect of duty on specific charges.

We submitted specific charges based on careful study. These charges showed among other things that:

1. The health and lives of the citizens of New York had been endangered and impaired by the bribery, corruption, and appointment of unqualified politicians in the Departments of Health and Hospitals.

2. Unemployed workers continued to be cheated and defrauded by private employment agencies subject to the regulation of the Department of Licenses, and the last Commissioner, a Bronx District leader appointed by the Mayor, himself, was a man whose incompetency if not actual dishonesty was a matter of public record.

3. Bribery, corruption, and special favors were the order of the day under the creatures appointed by the Mayor to administer the Board of Standards and Appeals.

4. The city and therefore the citizens of New York were being swindled out of millions of dollars each year by excessive condemnation awards when property owners were represented by "political" counsel.

As I go over the work we did in those days, I feel again how necessary it is to have citizens who care, who know, who will arouse the conscience of New York.

It would have saved Governor Roosevelt no end of trouble and would have been a great kindness to the Mayor himself if Governor Roosevelt had acted without delay on the petition of the City Affairs Committee. Instead of that the Governor wrote the sharpest and bitterest kind of reply to Dr. Holmes and myself, suggesting that we devote more attention to religion and less to politics. I must add that two or three friends of Governor Roosevelt spoke to him at once in terms of reproach about the way in which he had written to Dr. Holmes and myself. Regretfully and yet half laughingly, he himself confessed he never wrote the letter. He signed it after a long, hard, all-night family discussion. And he added the name of the writer of the communication, which generosity forbids me to mention.

It should be made perfectly clear that Mayor Walker was not a disease, perhaps not even a symptom. He was merely the registering of one of the symptoms of what I regard as a recurring disease in the city of New York. The City Affairs Committee, of which I was an officer, was not engaged in a manhunt. The coming or going of Mayor Walker was quite incidental to the general business of the city government. We have got to go much deeper and eradicate the attitude of the citizenry that makes possible the election of a Walker, unlimited support of him, tragic toleration of him by the press and so-called great organizations such as the Chamber of Commerce, and the feeling of New York that this kind of civic battle against corruption is a show, that people are witnessing a motion picture to which they have no real relation. I know the price of decent city government is eternal vigilance and only hope that some younger New Yorkers will care enough to insist that this city shall not slip back into the corruption of the thirties.

In lighter vein, I recall that in the course of Mayor Hylan's second term, somebody who should have known both of us better turned to "Red Mike" and insisted on presenting me to him. The Mayor's response, spoken in surly fashion and in gruff tones, was, "I ought to know Rabbi Wise. He has attacked me often enough." Humbly I offered the Mayor this apology, "Mr. Mayor, I may have attacked you often—but not often enough!" In rather more friendly and witty fashion Mayor LaGuardia once said, having reference to Mayor Walker's not unhurried trip to England, "When Rabbi Wise talks about mayors there is usually a run on Atlantic steamship accommodations."

In the struggle against the corruption of city government in New York City, I again found that those public officials, indifferent to their own honor, were inevitably indifferent to the welfare of citizens or the hardship they were suffering. The tragic suffering of the unemployed in the early thirties left public officials indifferent and hostile. Early in 1932 I therefore suggested to Mr. Blanshard that the City Affairs Committee ought not to let the Comptroller and the Mayor shuttlecock the so-called appropriation for relief. We decided to make clear what the real hitches were. We urged the city administration to provide (unemployment) relief for the 107,000 families needing it. To clarify and dramatize the desperate needs of these families, Paul Blanshard set up an Unemployment Jury of New York citizens to hold hearings on the facts and I agreed to serve as one of the jurors. We then demanded more adequate appropriations.

Even more shocking than the delay and indifference of politicians was the slowness and overpoliteness of organized welfare agencies, who knew the suffering of the people they were supposed to serve. We could not understand and dared to ask "why welfare agency leaders ask for a sum that they know to be inadequate. If their own children were hungry, they would be more bold." At this time persons on relief were getting thirty cents a day, and the heads of families employed by the City Work Commission had been reduced to $1.43 a day. Still the welfare agencies asked for a six-month appropriation insufficient to keep up these levels in view of the mounting unemployment. They waited month after month, talked about conferences, but failed to demand the steps necessary to alleviate acute misery.

It was about this time or a little earlier that a great city salary grab was threatened. As I recall it, there was a hearing before the Board of Estimate, made up of those who were planning largely to increase their own salaries, in the case of Mayor Walker from twenty-five thousand to forty thousand dollars per year. When on behalf of the City Affairs Committee I had spoken rather sternly about those who seemed hell bent upon raising their own salaries in the midst of the term of office for which they had been elected, the Mayor turned to me rather plaintively, saying, "I have not proposed that these salary raises be made. My associates of the Board of Estimate have done so. What could I say to them?" My reply was instantaneous. "Your answer, Mr. Mayor, should have been, 'Is thy servant a dog that he should do this thing?'" Soon thereafter the whole proposal was dropped.

In view of my repeated attacks upon Mayor Walker, a company of fellow Jews, under the leadership of a Tammany Hall beneficiary and officeholder, were cajoled into attempting to neutralize the effect of one Jewish citizen's attitude toward the Mayor by singling out for honor him who, with all his uncommon charm, ability, and gifts, knew not what honor was. And a heinous deed was done. It took the form, in the midst of the most extravagant laudation, of the giving to Walker of a Scroll of the Law.

After the Mayor had fled to Europe and after the "temporary incumbency" of McKee and O'Brien for a short period, a happier civic day dawned for New York. Its citizenship after unbelievable experiences with the Walkers, Van Wycks, and Hylans resolved to make our great city decently livable again. The man and the hour matched. Fiorello H. LaGuardia was elected. He enjoyed one great advantage over his several civic reform predecessors. He knew New York. He was New York. There was no snobbishness in him. Early in his first term, at breakfast in my home, he told me of his rule "never to accept a social invitation from anyone who had not invited me before I became mayor." He knew New York almost as well as that Assistant District Attorney of whom, after the election of McClellan over Low, I naïvely asked, "Did you expect any such majority as McClellan got?" The answer was rather meaningful. "The Hall thought 28,000 majority would look about right."

LaGuardia was not without faults—his childish impatience, his extravagant self-confidence, his complete incapacity for devolving the minor duties of his office, his overdramatic sense, his readiness to listen to certain groups who did not in the least share his concern with the common welfare! But over and beyond all these was his unlimited integrity, his vision of the greatest of cities, ministering to the well-being of its millions of population, his making public office unpurchasable—and this was equally true of his chief subordinates. And what a change from Tammany's method of government!

No reform mayor of New York has ever been re-elected, not Strong, or Mitchel, or Low. LaGuardia was elected three times and served throughout twelve years. His regime was and long will remain a landmark in American municipal history. I have often thought that LaGuardia was a perfect though perhaps limited answer to Lord Bryce, whose last book, dealing with Latin America, expresses the feeling that municipal misgovernments might almost prove the undoing of democracy. To Lord Bryce this was the one deep shadow on the fine picture of the democracy of the morrow. LaGuardia gave to city government a new hope and to the citizens of American cities throughout the land the faith that these could have honorable and incorruptible government if, truly caring, they chose such leadership as LaGuardia gave us.

With two interruptions up to the election of LaGuardia, New York had Walkerism for thirty years. This was possible because the voters did not care. There were those who did not care because they did not understand, who were duped and fooled for too long because no one helped them to care except for a handful of "cranks." No newspaper in New York—save for one—spoke out with courage. Pulpits were chiefly vocal in fault-finding with "sensation seekers," like Holmes and myself. For the most part the Bar was silent. There were others on top who did not care because they could control and manage the vast fiscal interests of New York so long as they could bargain and pay for this control. In New York the men of large affairs never said a word about the Walker administration, its shame or incredible infamy, until after the taxes became too high.

Yet when the people understood, Walkerism ended. I can only hope that the people will not again be lulled into a false slumber that permits the slow but steady return of Walkerism to the life of New York. I hope we will never take

the position that, because filth comes back to a city after cleaning, no cleaning is to be attempted. It may as well be said
that the city sewage system is not worth while because it
must constantly be renewed.

II

A Great Adventure Begins

AMONG the most fateful occasions in my life, none was more deep and challenging in its effects than my attendance at the Second Zionist Congress in Basle, Switzerland, in August, 1898, as a delegate of the Federation of American Zionists, which I had helped to found one month earlier. My Zionism I owed chiefly to my father. It may have been in my blood, but it was the tide of his devotion which bore it to the heart of my being. My father, without being strictly Orthodox as was his father, was an ardent Zionist, and his Zionism is one of the earliest and sweetest memories of my life. As very young children in our home, we got our first lesson in saving and giving in connection with the humble ambassadors from the land of Israel, into whose little tin cups we placed our scant savings, that these in turn might be given to satisfy needs in the Holy Land.

It was at that Congress that I first met Theodor Herzl, founder of modern Zionism. I stood before a young, bearded Jew of goodly stature, then somewhat under forty, who bore himself with the simplicity of a son of kings and prophets. I have said of him many times that he stood like a man before kings and that he looked and stood like a king among men. He looked less like an Austrian Jew—which he was—than like some ancient monarch of the Near East. At once, I felt a bond with him, apart from my unreserved acceptance of his

23

leadership. His epochal book of two years earlier, *The Jewish State*, had revealed what fifty subsequent years agonizingly confirmed—that his was the gift of prophecy.

The facts of Herzl's life need no retelling. Budapest born, he became a student at the University of Vienna, practiced law for a few years, became a journalist and a moderately successful playwright. While correspondent at Paris of the *Neue Freie Presse* of Vienna, the Dreyfus trial shocked him into his first awareness of the problem of the Jewish people, and soon the assimilationist Viennese became the leader of the Jewish people.

Few men may truly be said to be epochal. Within the last millennium of Jewish history, not more than four men may be so styled—Maimonides, Spinoza, Mendelssohn, and Herzl—and one of these four is epoch-making not in relation to Jewish life but in the things that concern the liberation of the mind. Herzl was epochal. Those of us who have lived alike in the pre-Herzlian and the post-Herzlian epochs know that this man's coming upon the Jewish scene brought another era into being. No epochal figure stands alone; other and lesser figures prepare the way. In the case of Herzl, even the minor figures were of major import—Hess and Kalisher, Smolenskin and Gordon. No epochal figure stands alone in yet another respect, for he has successors. Thus, there were and there are men who continue the work of Herzl, and yet he stands alone—unique, epochal, Sinaitic in so far as he reshaped the life of his people.

One cannot touch on all the factors in the scene of which he was central. The world without was hostile, its hostility taking many forms and all of them embittering, impoverishing, degrading. In the presence of all the facts of malice in the outside world, Jews had become irresolute, enduring all things not with high charity but with low and hopeless resignation. An index of the incalculable hurt that had been done to Jews everywhere by the ill will of the world was to be found in the 1870's and 1880's, before Herzl's day, in the attitude of the so-called cultivated and enlightened Jews toward anti-Semitism of one kind or another. In order to controvert anti-Semitism, Jews had set out verbally to deny the truth of their Semitism. Such denial, half imbecile and half insolent, was infinitely more provocative than any decent and courageous attitude would have been. After Herzl's day, Jews began no longer to deny their Semitism or to conceal their Jewishness. To the former they assented as a fact; the latter they affirmed as their distinction.

Unknowing of what some Jews in Eastern Europe had written or done, Herzl, after analyzing the nature of the Jewish problem, saw clearly that it could be solved only through the re-establishment of the Jewish nation in its own homeland. He recognized the essentially political nature of the task. Thus, he projected the Jewish problem for the first time as an international problem and gave a two-thousand-year-old dream its first major impetus to practical fulfillment. His real title to immortality, however, is the fact that he was the herald of a Jewish renaissance. His trumpet call reawakened the moribund Jewish consciousness. "Zionism," he had said, "is both a mournful necessity and a glorious ideal." By inspired word and high example, he made out of a mournful and tragic necessity a glorious and inspiring ideal. Herzl came upon Jews disunited, fearful, hopeless. He spoke, he wrought, he led; and when he left, the Jews to whom he had proclaimed a message of deliverance had once again become a people.

It is difficult, in this year of the establishment of the Jewish State, to realize how Herzl, in that far-off day, stood almost alone. Reform Jews in Germany and English-speaking lands would not hear him. Many Orthodox Jews denied his message because they were awaiting the divinely appointed Messiah who was to bring them deliverance. "Practical" Jews regarded his proposals as fantastically visionary. As soon as he had announced that the First Zionist Congress in 1897 would take place in Munich, the German rabbis united in moving the

Jews of Germany to keep the congress out of Munich. Thus they fought to establish their quasi-Teutonic or political orthodoxy by insisting that, far from being Zionists, they were "German citizens of Jewish faith." Herzl thus found no meeting place in Munich and the congress was held in Basle. But after twenty years another movement was to be launched in Munich, which was to find lodgment, even security, yea glory throughout two decades, culminating in the slaughter of more than six million Jews in the war in which the Nazis engaged against democratic civilization.

German and English Jewries failed Herzl. But he was thrice fortified by the instant and enthusiastic understanding of his cause by the Jewish masses. Nearly ten millions in Central and Eastern Europe turned to him with almost messianic fervor, following him fanatically throughout the few remaining years that were to be his lot. German Jews generally imagined themselves secure. But East European Jews were mournfully conscious of an insecurity that, as Herzl surely foresaw and bravely foretold, was to reach a tragic climax, after another generation, for East and West European Jewry alike.

At Basle I made a twofold discovery. Joseph, the Bible relates, said, "I seek my brothers." Without seeking, I yet found my brothers. It may be that I should qualify the words "without seeking," for I, a Zionist, consciously and with the utmost deliberation, had chosen to be a delegate. To that extent, it might be said that I sought my brothers out. Whether or not I sought them out, I found my brothers. I found not simply a collection of Jews bent on the high ends of Zionism but an assemblage of fellow Jews united by a single and exalted purpose—and my brothers.

Before meeting them, I barely knew that they existed save as a name, as a group with whom I had become closely associated, under the impact of the Zionist movement. Not only did I find my brothers, but by the same token I found myself.

I had lived part of the early years of my life in the Lexington Avenue, rather than the Park Avenue, ghetto of German-born and German-descended Jews of New York. I have always regretted—and have been not a little ashamed—that I barely knew or even touched the life of a much larger group of New York Jews, who had come to New York since 1881, the Eastern European Jews. My contacts with these as child and youth were few and limited, though I came to know their children in connection with the work of the Hebrew Free School Association and the Educational Alliance. After the publication of the *Judenstaat*, I came to know, to foregather with, and to work day by day with another group of Eastern European Jews. But save for books and through study, my personal relationships with Jews had been largely limited, as I have indicated, to the middle-class ghetto of New York. The fortunate among us, for the most part second-generation, German-speaking American Jews, had just begun to claim the privileges of a higher education. But our place as students and teachers alike in university life was definitely limited. To come, therefore, upon a gathering of Jews nearly all of whom were intellectually the equals of the best we knew in our country, many of them superior to such college professors and even presidents as we knew, and uniformly beyond compare with the intellectuals in American Jewish life, was nothing less than a revelation.

Herzl was not the only outstanding figure of this company. There was Max Nordau, already world famous as thinker and writer. In many ways he was a man of larger stature than Herzl as he was beyond peradventure of wider fame when he entered into the Zionist movement. But he proved his greatness not by seeking to rival the younger man, but with the wisdom of the sage and the generosity of loyal discipleship, sustaining his junior in years and lesser in fame. It was his intellectual honesty and spiritual courage that made him perhaps the most frank and forthright teacher of his generation. Evasion and circumlocution were impossible to him who may at times have seemed to indulge in the manner of exaggeration but who never failed to meet issues, however disturbing and challenging. Grimly in earnest about winning his people from the by-

paths of self-contempt and self-obliteration to the highway of
noble self-reverence, he abhorred every sham but none more
than the sham of those Jews who sought to lose themselves in
a world that misprized them.

Chaim Weizmann was present but too young to give promise
of a great career in the two fields of science and statesmanship.
There was Nahum Sokolow, as completely a Jewish personality
as the nineteenth century produced. Child of Eastern European ghetto, he was an amateur rather than a professional
scholar, first and foremost in the field of Hebrew journalism,
as well as its creator. His amazing vitality to the end and his
incredible versatility, these two were ghetto derived, for the
ghetto child was toughened by fate's sternness and could turn
his hand to any duty that claimed him. At the Congress in
1898, I recall that Herzl leaned heavily on Sokolow as mediator
between the conflicting groups. Others were Rabbi Ruelf,
revered figure of German conservative Jewry; Rabbi Samuel
Mohilever, alone among the Orthodox rabbis of Eastern Europe to give to the cause full-hearted support, his face beautiful
with the benignity of wisdom and tolerance; Mandelstamm of
Kiev, foremost among the ophthalmologists of his day; Professor Shapiro of Heidelberg, more than any other person the
proponent and furtherer of the Jewish National Fund; Nahum
Syrkin who did most to forge the bond between Zionism and
Socialism. And there were others: Wolfsohn, affectionately
styled "Litwak" by Herzl, a Jew from Russia who had settled
in Cologne; and Dr. Bodenheimer, the most eminent of the
German Jews.

In my ignorance, I had anticipated a glorified edition of the
long-drawn-out sessions of New York's unwearying East Side
Zionists. To my surprise, I found myself in the midst of a
parliamentary gathering, its membership and intellectual stature far above the Berlin Reichstag and Vienna Reichsrat, to
sessions of which I had been witness. Discussion was orderly
and on a high level. Its orderliness was a tribute to the restraint
of the delegates. This, in truth, was extraordinary, seeing that

three quarters or more of them came from lands in which their silence respecting Jewish affairs and their governments was compulsory. Far more significant than a handful of outstanding individuals was the quality of the entire body of delegates, their intellectual stature and the ardor of their devotion. England was rather inadequately represented by Sir Francis Montefiore and Dr. Moses Gaster, chief rabbi of the Spanish-Portuguese Congregation of England, a Rumanian by birth and upbringing. It must, in truth, be said that he bore himself as a rival of and competitor to Herzl rather than as his out-and-out supporter. And yet, in later years, his service to the cause, particularly in the days immediately prior to the issuance of the Balfour Declaration, became very great.

At the Basle Congress in 1898, two English-speaking secretaries were named: Jacob deHaas, long-time English Zionist and biographer in later years of Herzl and Brandeis, and myself, who must have been chosen as representative of the American dialect of the English tongue.

There were many thrilling moments. There was little or no oratory for the sake of oratory, though some of the participants in the debates will stand out in Jewish history. The eloquence of Herzl was unstudied and effortless. In the absence of Israel Zangwill at this congress, the Anglo-American group of delegates was undistinguished in public utterance, for the most part unable to speak adequately in Hebrew or Yiddish and, therefore, silent. The great orator of this and other Zionist congresses was Nordau. Master of the biting phrase, relentlessly mordant in denunciation of the foes of Zionism, he poured the lava of his wrath with nothing less than volcanic fury upon the *"protest Rabbiner."* These were the rabbis who by their attack on Zionism, as I have said, had prevented the meeting of the First Zionist Congress at Munich. He was devastatingly scornful and scathingly referred to the *"auch Juden und Bauch-juden,"* Jews of the most casual relationship to their people, identified with them, if at all, solely because of their preference for food delectably prepared in the Jewish fashion.

The congress did not limit itself to eloquent speeches and pious resolutions. It will ever be remembered as the congress that gave birth to the financial instrument of the movement, the Jewish Colonial Trust, without which much of the early economic development of Jewish Palestine could not have been accomplished. Its birth was attended by every manner of genial jest among the *accoucheurs.* Not the least of these were tales predicting that family-treasured phylacteries and exquisitely embroidered prayer shawls would be offered as complete and sole security for loans, however large. The jests happily proved unfounded, and the Jewish Colonial Trust, which has since become the Anglo-Palestine Bank, has weathered every financial stress and storm since its founding and stands today as strong as any financial institution in the Middle East. Herzl, the dreamer, author of the financial plans, was not so impractical despite all deprecation of him as a mere visionary and incurable idealist.

I was not a little surprised and greatly satisfied at an incident that occurred one day during the congress. Our banner, the Zionist banner, floated above the building in which our meeting was being held. A regiment of Swiss paraders was about to pass the building—it was August 17, I believe, a Swiss national holiday—when their leader ordered a halt. Taking off his hat, he pointed to our banner. His soldiers immediately saw the spirit of their leader and our banner was given a grand salute.

On my way to the congress, I had met a most distinguished American journalist, James Creelman. He learned with interest of my plan to attend the congress and invited me to report the sessions for the readers of the *New York Journal.* Upon the close of the congress, I hastened back to London and to Mr. Creelman's office, from which I cabled my report, prepared with no little help from him. This was the first cabled European report of a Zionist congress to an American newspaper. I recall that I commented in a burst of enthusiasm on the closing session. It concluded at about five in the morning. As Herzl finished his unoratorical but moving appeal to the delegates, day dawned, and Herzl shone in the glow of the rising sun. His was prophecy to be fulfilled, as he foretold, after fifty years. And what years of strain, and struggle, and hopes deferred, and bitter divisiveness, and above all tragic failure in the last years of the mandatory power these were to prove before the day of fulfillment!

If up to this time I have not mentioned the American delegation, it has been because the American delegation was even more sadly inadequate than the English, distinguished only by the appearance of Professor Richard Gottheil, historian of American Zionism. He was the son as well as the Zionist comrade of the honored Dr. Gustav Gottheil, first among all the Reform Rabbis of the middle nineteenth century to cast the hobgoblin of consistency to the winds. Without recanting Reform, he unfurled the banner of Zionism, to him the banner of the Jew, because of the depths of his loyalty to the great Zionist tradition of his people. It was not easy for Gottheil, rabbi of the "Cathedral Synagogue" (Temple Emanu-El) of New York, with its membership made up at that time almost wholly of sons and grandsons of the Jewish immigrants from Germany of the 1840's and 1850's, to seem to disavow a cardinal tenet of Reform Judaism, which had long before broken with the Jewish national ideal. Another fine American delegate was Mrs. Emma Gottheil, wife of Professor Gottheil. Born in Beirut, she was in after years to become one of the founders of Hadassah.

I have already referred to the profound impact of the congress on my life. I journeyed to Basle merely as a delegate to a conference. I returned home a lifetime servant of the cause in the name and for the sake of which the Congress was assembled. I caught the first glimpse of my people as a people, gathered from many lands, one and undivided, not in creed but in their human faith. This faith was that the tragic dispersal of Israel must end, that the miraculous survival of the Jewish people did not forever guarantee survival in an increasingly hostile world, and that the ancient home of Palestine could and must be rebuilt.

We were united by the faith that despite partial dispersion in
many parts of the world the survival of the Jewish people and
the revival of its creative genius could only come to pass in the
land of ancient glory, which needed to be awakened from its
centuries-old and enfeebling slumber. This newly gained conviction became and remained the lodestar of my life.

Zionism, I then came clearly to see, was the resolve and effort
of the Jewish people to reconstitute itself as a people in the ancient Jewish homeland of Palestine. Zionism meant the reunion
of the land that had too long been without the Jewish people,
with the Jewish people, which had for too long been parted or
severed from its historic home. That henceforth became the
message I sought to carry to my fellow Jews everywhere and to
the thousands of non-Jewish audiences I have addressed in almost every community of this country.

Few persons today can realize or recall the resistance that the
concept of Jewish national rebirth encountered in those years.
After the first Zionist Congress in 1897, for example, Rabbi Isaac
Mayer Wise, distinguished head of Reform Judaism in the
United States, gave a statement to the press, which read:

> The Jewish Congress which met in Switzerland in the latter
> part of August with the object of securing Palestine for re-
> colonization by the Jews has attracted widespread attention in
> this country and has given rise to much comment and specula-
> tion. The so-called Jewish Congress in Basle was, properly speak-
> ing, neither a Congress nor Jewish. It was really a convention of
> some voluntary advocates of a plan for the relief of the Jews in
> the Orient. It was not Jewish because it represented neither the
> sentiments nor the religious propensities of the Jews as a body.

In 1899, I wrote to Henrietta Szold, guiding spirit of the
Jewish Publication Society and translator of Graetz's monu-
mental history, suggesting the publication of a volume on Zionism by the Society. Miss Szold, later to achieve immortality as
the founder of Hadassah and till the day of her death in 1945
one of the most honored figures in Palestine, where she had

settled more than twenty years earlier, wrote to me on March 26, 1899:

> As for the other matter, the publication of Zionist literature by the Jewish Publication Society, I can say almost with perfect confidence, that the proposition would not be met with favor. So far as I know the temper, equally of the Zionist and the non-Zionist members of the Committee, a strong indisposition would manifest itself. The movement is, indeed, of the essence of the Jewish faith and race, as you write. I believe, moreover, that it is the only living thing in the Judaism of today. Reform and Orthodox squabbles, public Seders and Synods and all the rest of the palaver is on dead issues. And yet the Society cannot risk a book on Zionism.

One other example of the early opposition may be interesting. In April, 1904, a few short months before Herzl's tragic death, I was in Europe for a meeting of the Zionist Actions Committee. Jacob Schiff, the foremost American Jewish philanthropist, was traveling in Europe at the time. I was anxious for him to meet Herzl, hoping that the latter would convert Schiff to the Zionist cause. In response to my query, Schiff wired me to the Hotel Victoria in Heidelberg on April 20, as follows:

> Herzl has already inquired through Frankfurt friend about our travelling plans and is acquainted with these. If he wishes to discuss Zionism am unwilling to do so as with deepest attachment to my brethren in faith and race I am an American pure and simple and cannot possibly belong to two nations. I feel that Zionism is a purely theoretical and sentimental proposition and as a practicable one has no future.

> JACOB H. SCHIFF

A good deal had to be done and much had to happen before Zionism could hope to gain adherents among the ranks of German American Jews, whom Schiff represented. Up to the day of Herzl, there had been, as I have already hinted, a minimum of contact between Jews of German parentage and descent and Jewish immigrants of "later vintage," who came not so much to revive Zionism as to reclaim it. The latter came to our country under the most unfavorable conditions from Eastern Europe in the 1880's and 1890's. By this time, the German-descended Jews had begun to make a place for themselves in American life. Some families had achieved post-Civil War prosperity. The newcomers were almost uniformly poor, necessarily so because of their sudden expulsion from Russia. Through the German Jewish charities, these had for a time to become dependents upon and beneficiaries of the German Jews. Benefactors are sometimes forgotten as benefactors by beneficiaries. Beneficiaries are more rarely forgotten as beneficiaries by benefactors.

Language as well stood in the way of full understanding. The German Jews had become more or less versed in the English tongue, though many of them retained their German accent even over decades. The Yiddish of the newcomers was strange to the German stratum of Jewish life. Moreover, the newcomers had for the most part at first been religiously conforming, even Orthodox, whereas Reform Judaism was too often misused as a charter of escape, of inward alienation from the Jewish body politic.

All of which may explain why there was an utterly reluctant acceptance of Zionism for a quarter of a century or more on the part of German-descended American Jews. How could these poor, East European refugees of yesterday be imagined to have anything to commend to us, their onetime benefactors? To be an American Zionist in the last decade of the last century was to be the son or grandson of East European Jewish immigrants. One could count on the fingers of two hands the numbers of sons and daughters of Portuguese-Spanish and German Jews who were ready at the outset to avow themselves disciples and supporters of Zionism, as was for example, Josephine, the sister of Emma Lazarus.

After the 1898 congress, I corresponded frequently with Herzl. He followed developments in the United States closely,

BUREAU
DES
ZIONISTEN-CONGRESSES
IN
BASEL.

לשכת הועד
:=
הקונגרם הציוני בבזל.
∼∼∽

Nr. ....,   BASEL, am ‗22‗ August 1903‗.‗‗

Sehr geehrter Herr Collega !

Auch mir thut es herzlich leid Sie am Congress nicht begrüssen
zu können . Ich habe mich schon gefreut Ihnen persönlich meinen
besten Dank sagen zu können, für die guten Dienste, die Sie unserer Sache
geleistet haben . Ich muss dies nun brieflich thun .

Es würde mich sehr freuen, wenn Sie mich von den Erfolgen
Ihrer Agitationsreise auf dem Laufenden halten würden .

Seien Sie herzlich gegrüsst von Ihrem ganz ergebenen

getreuen.
Herzl

Herrn   Steephen S. W i s e , Rabbiner
          P o r t l a n d (Oregon)

          America

Most honored Colleague:

I, too, am very sad not to be able to greet you at the Congress. I had
already looked forward to being able to convey to you personally my deepest
thanks for the good services you have performed for our cause. Now I must
do this by letter.

It would please me very much if you would keep me informed of the
results of your campaigning trip.

Heartfelt greetings to you from your most devoted and faithful

HERZL

and we received frequent suggestions and constant encourage-
ment from him. Thus, on December 13, 1899, he wrote me from
Vienna:

> MY DEAR FELLOW-ZIONIST:
>
> With great pleasure, we take this opportunity of expressing to
> you our most heartfelt thanks for your great work which we are
> following attentively.

On April 25, 1902, Herzl wrote me about the plans for the
publication of his novel *Alt-Neuland*. "The purpose of today's
letter," he wrote in part, "is to inform you that I intend to dedi-
cate a proportionate part of the proceeds of the novel *Alt-Neuland* to the propaganda needs of our movement in America. I
have worked for three years on the book which describes the
future shape of our plan after realization." After discussing its
publication in Yiddish and English and the distribution of the
income from the book, he concluded: "If my author's feelings
do not deceive me—which of course is possible—the discussion
of our movement which has quieted down a little will receive
new inspiration through this book for a long time to come; but,
of course, I may be mistaken."

Years later, I had the intense personal satisfaction of trans-
mitting to the two men who did most to carry on Herzl's inspiration and to give fulfillment to his dream, tangible links with
Zionism's greatest figure. In November, 1933, on the occasion
of Justice Brandeis' seventy-seventh birthday, a group of his
devoted friends and disciples presented him with the manuscript of one of Herzl's memorable letters. At the time, I had
the privilege of writing to him on behalf of the group as follows:

> We know that you would not have us send you gifts, but
> something has come into our possession, which we offer you with
> renewed devotion to our friend and leader. It is, as you will see,
> a longhand letter of Theodor Herzl. We place it in the hand of
> him, worthiest of all living Jews on earth, to have it in his pos-
> session. It goes, as it were, from the hand of Herzl, through us

followers of Herzl and Brandeis, to him who in our hearts and in history, will have his place by the side of Herzl.

Almost ten years later, in 1942, a historic conference was held in New York City in the Hotel Biltmore at which American Jewry affirmed the establishment of an independent Jewish state as the major postwar demand of the Jewish people. At that time, as chairman of the American Zionist Emergency Council, I gave expression to the complete confidence that American Jewry reposed in Dr. Weizmann as leader of the Zionist movement. Turning to Dr. Weizmann, I said:

> I believe, Dr. Weizmann, it will be you who will gain from Britain, the United States and the United Nations at the Victory Peace Conference the Charter for the Jewish Commonwealth of Palestine.
>
> Some years ago, through the generosity of friends there was presented to me a ring worn till his death by the immortal founder of the Zionist movement, Dr. Theodor Herzl. Dr. Weizmann, at the Peace Conference, when presenting the claims of the Jewish people, I wish you to have on your finger the ring of your predecessor as President of the World Zionist movement, and I present you with this, the ring of Theodor Herzl, and place it in the hand which, under God, is to receive the Victory Charter for a Jewish Commonwealth in Palestine.

My unwavering faith that the Jewish State would be established was the legacy I had received forty years earlier from Herzl himself. I have oft told of my last conversation with him in April, 1904, at the meeting of the Zionist Actions Committee, a few months before his death at the age of 44 on July 3. Herzl placed his arm around me and said, "I shall not live to see the Jewish State. But you, Wise, are a young man. You will live to see the Jewish State." I thank God that it was given to me to live till that glorious day of May 14, 1948, when out of the centuries of Jewish suffering and persecution, of prayer and hope and labor, the prophecy of Theodor Herzl was at last fulfilled.

III

Zion: Homeland and Hope

MY earliest relations with Palestine may be said
to date from the 1880's. In that year my paternal grandfather,
Chief Rabbi Joseph Hirsch Weisz, died in Erlau, Hungary. He
had been the rabbi of that community for forty years. As one
of the curiosities of modern Jewish history, it is worth noting
that his successor, Rabbi Schreiber, chosen in 1881, remained
in office from 1881 until 1945 so that the two rabbis in succession together served the congregation for one hundred and two
years, 1843–1945. The latter might have gone on somewhat
longer, but in his nineties he was dragged away by his Nazi
captors. On his way to the concentration camp before the
first railroad station was reached, he died, and his body was
flung out of the train.

I may have more to tell later of this grandfather whom I
never saw, although he saw me in Budapest shortly after my
birth. His death brought sorrow to his revering son, my father,
who had not seen him since my birth. Once the week of
mourning (*Shivah*) was ended—during which, under the traditional regime, mourners spend their days in complete inaction and family retirement, save at prayer services and religious
study morning and evening—my father invited his mother to
join us in America and share our home. Again and again she
declined to the sorrow of all of us. It must have been with

tears that she wrote to my father, "I must go to the Holy Land." She added, "I go not to live there but to die there. There I wish to pray; and there to die, to be laid to rest amid the sacred dust of Jerusalem; to be buried on the slope facing the Holy of Holies." She sailed in one of three ships, which bore a goodly number of the devout to Jerusalem. As I recall it, the other two ships were lost. My father happily often had good tidings from and about her from one who acted for a number of years as the messenger of the Hungarian Jewish community of Jerusalem. He was a very fine person, Simon Judah Stampfer, who brought to our home not only welcome personal messages but, as early as 1883 when I was nine, moved us grandchildren to become concerned about Palestine, of which he told us the most wonderful tales. We became little emissaries and fund collectors for Palestine. Each of us children got a little red tin box, labeled "Jerusalem," in which we placed whatever funds we could get or give from our most limited childhood resources.

In 1892, just a decade after my grandmother Rachel Therese went to pray and to die in Palestine, my father resolved to visit her. All plans, which included my accompanying him, were laid. I had been fortunate enough—having just graduated from Columbia College—to secure a commission to write a series of letters or articles from Palestine for the *New York Sun.* I was privileged to meet its great editor, the famous Charles A. Dana, Lincoln's and Stanton's assistant secretary of war, who was in the midst of a Russian lesson when I went to him. We were to sail early in June. On the eve of sailing my father received a cable of, to him, heartbreaking words, "*Mutter gestorben,*" Mother died. It was a cruel and crushing blow to her son, and I have often wondered whether my father's death, at the early age of fifty-two, four years later, was not due in part to the grief and shock that struck him through his beloved mother's death under the circumstances I have mentioned.

I did not go to Palestine until 1913 when in the course of a sabbatical half-year leave my wife and I left our very young children in Munich and journeyed to Palestine. I learned at once what hardly surprised me, that my grandmother was still remembered after twenty years as the charitable and compassionate *Erlau Rabbanit,* rabbi's widow from Erlau, known and beloved throughout Jerusalem for her good works. Her charities were made possible only by living on very little while giving much to those in need of the generous allowance she received from my father.

As soon as we reached the port of Jaffa, we faced difficulties. The only letter I carried was one of warm friendliness from President Wilson. It did not help me much, as we immediately faced what I felt was the indignity of being compelled to accept and sign a document that bound us to remain in Palestine not more than some weeks. My soul rebelled against the necessity of signing a document under the terms of which I was pledged to leave the Holy Land of my fathers within a brief and limited time. I felt I should refuse to enter Palestine on these abject terms and that I must appeal to the State Department and its head, my friend Secretary of State Bryan, to avert this insult to me as American and Jew, but I was warned that no appeal for a change in the terms would be dealt with in less than a month or more. I perforce yielded or I would have been compelled to return to Europe without our setting foot on that, to us, priceless soil. I succumbed, accepting terms that were deeply painful, and I could not help feeling degraded as I yielded.

The mention of Bryan's name reminds me that, when Ambassador to Turkey Henry Morgenthau went to the Secretary of State for final instructions before leaving for his post in Constantinople, instead of giving detailed instructions to Morgenthau on the problems that had begun to loom on the Turkish and Middle East horizon, Mr. Bryan limited his instructions to the following: "Uncle Henry, you know a great deal about real estate. I wish you would do this for me. Get an option on the purchase of the mountain from which Jesus delivered the Sermon on the Mount." I think that Morgenthau has told the story in his account of his services as ambassador to Turkey. As I recall it, the land proved unpurchasable because it is in the possession of a religious community. I have the feeling, knowing Mr. Bryan as I did, that he dreamed of standing some day on the Mount of the memorable Sermon and repeating, for all the world to hear, the most famous of all his public utterances, "The Prince of Peace," a worthy enough purpose but slightly naïve—as Bryan was.

At that time, in 1913, Jaffa was little more than a squalid Arab port, and its next-door neighbor Tel Aviv was still in its earliest infancy. I remember its Mayor Disengoff, bringing us some delicious oranges and telling us he hoped that Jewish Palestine might export five thousand such cases of oranges in the course of the next spring. By 1937, the orange industry had so expanded, owing very largely to Jewish enterprise, that they exported nearly fifteen million cases. Tel Aviv was barely a city when first we saw it, and Disengoff remained its extraordinarily devoted mayor as long as he lived. His was a vision of the city that even the miracle of Tel Aviv has barely approached. When for the third and last time we visited the city in 1935 the Mayor gratefully accepted two portraits for its art museum, painted by my wife, one being a portrait of Judge Julian W. Mack, whose devotion to Palestine and Zionism was as unwavering as his services for nearly forty years on the Children's Court of Chicago and as United States Circuit Court judge. The second portrait was that of her husband, skillfully painted but not without partiality by Mrs. Wise, in fulfillment of the Mayor's request. In 1944, in connection with my seventieth birthday, Tel Aviv did me the honor of making me an honorary citizen or freeman.

Two impatient days at Jaffa included a visit to the Rothschild wine cellars at Petach Tikvah. This colony gave us a first glimpse of what Palestine could do for the Jew. We had come from Egypt, where the baksheesh hunters were no less importunate than the sand fleas. I remember having asked the American consul general whether in the event of presentation to the Khedive, his premonarchial majesty, too, would hold out a firmly suppliant hand. After being escorted through the amazingly spacious wine cellars, I offered our old guide a suitable *pourboire*. He turned upon me quietly, *"Aber, Herr Doktor, in Palestina nehmen wir ja nichts."* ("But, Dr. Wise, here in Palestine, we accept no tips.") The land of bondage was seen in a flash to be behind us!

We had another and still more inspiring experience after some days at Kerem Abraham, the Vineyard of Abraham, a sort of municipal stoneyard for the workless in the suburbs of Jerusalem, especially at that time for the refugees from Kishinef. A fine-looking youngish Jew volunteered to escort us about; he explained every point of interest beginning with the fascinating rock tombs. As the lunch hour passed, I apologized for detaining him from his midday meal. He laughed without bitterness, adding, "We have no noon lunch hour here." And when I learned that he and his family were living on the rather insufficient ration of coffee and bread for breakfast and tea and bread for dinner and that in America, where he had lived for some years, he had earned from fifteen to twenty dollars weekly in the Baldwin Locomotive Works of Philadelphia, I ventured to inquire, "Why endure starvation, seeing that plenty beckons from across the seas?" His reply was enlightening and even thrilling, as in Hebrew he spoke: "Ah, but you forget that we are living in the land of our fathers!"

I wonder whether any thrill quite equals that which comes to one who has long dreamed of Palestine, as the train begins to make the ascent from Jaffa to Jerusalem. Ordinarily a railroad ride is rather prosaic and unexciting but this was different. An Australian fellow passenger remained quite impassive as we waxed dithyrambic over the view of the classic Judean hills we were encircling. He interjected, "Nice enough country but what poor scrawny sheep compared with our own in Australia!" Happily for him, I had not the strength of Samson, though one of his weapons was close at hand!

Every approach to the Holy City has a fascination and glory of its own, whether rising from the east by the Mount of Olives, or from the south, Bethlehem way, so that one breaks out into, "I will lift mine eyes unto the hills," or from the desert north. But none quite matches the climb from the west as one catches the first gleam of the Golden City.

I need hardly tell that our first errand upon reaching Jerusalem on the eve of Passover was to visit the grave of my grandmother, which my revered father was, alas, denied the privilege of seeing. The warden of the Hungarian Jewish community of Jerusalem escorted us to the plot that had been accorded her as a grave of honor in the midst of the graves of famed and pious rabbi scholars. Her heart's prayer had been answered. Her grave faces the Holy of Holies. It was marked by a simple gravestone for which I felt privileged to substitute another, thus fulfilling my father's unspoken wish, by describing her as "the Mother of Aaron Wise."

Since I am writing of the Mount of Olives and the grave where this saint rests, I must tell a story of more than twenty years later, during our visit in 1935, when we were guests at the Government House of the High Commissioner for Palestine, Sir Arthur Wauchope. After dinner the women guests were invited to sit and chat, one by one, with the host. When Mrs. Wise was escorted to his side by an aide-de-camp, Sir Arthur chivalrously said, "Madam, make a request and it shall be granted to you." My wife, whose perfect idealism was not untouched by a sense of the practical, replied, "Yes, Sir Arthur, I have a favor to ask you. Dr. Wise and I today again visited the grave of his grandmother. As I stood there on the Mount of Olives I noted a funeral procession, and I saw how hard it was for the cortege to carry the dead over the rough stone road. Would it be possible for Your Excellency to have that road made a little less rough and uncomfortable for the mourners?" He smiled, saying, "Mrs. Wise, your wish shall be granted." We heard no more of this until some time later at the wharf at Haifa, just as we were about to embark, when a courier appeared from the office of the High Commissioner, presented his compliments to Mrs. Wise, and formally said, "His Excellency directs me to inform you before you leave Palestine that the work of improving the road to the Mount of Olives Cemetery has been begun."

Her intercession was more effective herein than on two other occasions I chance to recall. One hot noonday in April we had left our car and were walking through the Arab section of Jerusalem when we looked upon an arresting sight. Underneath a wagon, in order to escape the heat of the broiling sun, an Arab woman lay crouched with an infant in her arms. I might have passed on, but my wife exclaimed in manner half startled and half sorrowing, "Oh, see that poor baby." I did look, and to our common horror we clearly saw what Mrs. Wise, womanlike, had quickly perceived. The lovely little infant's closed eyes were rimmed and covered with flies. My wife at once took a dainty kerchief and handed it to the mother, saying through our Arab-speaking guide, "Please use this handkerchief to keep your baby's eyes clean. If you do not and permit these filth-bearing flies to rest on your baby's eyes, it may lose its sight." The woman smiled as she stowed away the kerchief and a bit of baksheesh, merely answering, "It is the will of God."

Among the Arabs and other Near Eastern peoples "the will of God" covers and seems to condone many practices that seem rather queer in the eyes of visitors. We were walking along the road from Jerusalem to Bethlehem when my wife and I together noticed a rather ungallant procession. A definitely stout Arab was riding a little donkey. Behind him trailed a woman, leading two little ones and evidently soon again to bear another child. My wife was so obviously shocked by this ungallant spectacle that, despite the mild protests of our Arab guide, she turned to the man on the donkey, asking, "Why don't you get off the donkey and let your poor, tired, pregnant wife ride?" To this he gave answer in a few words, "If I were seen walking beside the donkey on which my wife rode, I would be forever disgraced." And, by way of after-thought, added the now increasingly familiar, "It is the will of God."

These days in Jerusalem were Jewish days—even though nearly half of the population was non-Jewish. The Jew gave form and color to his environment instead of being formed and colored by it—for the first time as I saw it.

After the Passover days, the whole of the week being observed in holiday fashion, the Easter season was at hand. In common with many Americans, I wished to be present at the ceremony of the Holy Fire on Easter Eve, as it is called, actually Saturday morning. The English consul, acting in the absence of the American, not only refused to secure a permit for me, but warned me against the peril of going even in disguise. As, he added, he had warned Zangwill some years before, "Should the Russians, crowded together at the service, somehow discover that you are a Jew, they would rend you limb from limb." And this in the most plaintive tones, "If anything did happen to you, sir, it would be most unpleasant to me and my office."

I looked upon the aftermath of the Holy Fire from a nearby roof—the poor multitudes of Greek Catholics, for the most part Russian pilgrims, eagerly clutching at the fire with which they lighted the tapers ever after to be jealously guarded. Throughout my stay in Palestine, I got many glimpses of the Russian peasants pilgriming afoot throughout the land. Of one experience I have told but never written. We were at the Jordan—not much as a river but "liquid history," as someone called the River Thames to a group of Americans boasting on the terrace of the House of Commons about the Mississippi. I was about to dip my hands in the waters when a very old Russian peasant woman, who had been surveying me rather dubiously, shouted at me in her native Russian, "Zhid, Zhid, what are you doing

with your Jewish hands in my Christian River!" For a moment
I was disconcerted, after which I asked our guide to reassure
the vehement Russian lady that my fathers had bathed in the
waters of this river long before her Russian grandfathers had
ever taken a bath! Nothing more was said, though much was
looked and muttered, while I performed the pilgrim's office
of laving my Jewish hands in the waters of the Jordan.

At Bethlehem I looked upon something saddening, which
may since have been modified by the exit of the Turkish
administration. In the Church of the Holy Nativity we came
upon a troop of Turkish soldiers. These, we learned to our
horror, were stationed there in order to prevent Greek and
Roman Catholic, Armenian, and Copt worshipers and even
priests from slaying one another! A year or two before our
visit, a bloody and fatal melee had been started by reason of
the fact that the priests of one communion had touched lamps
in the crypt of the nativity that were supposed to be in charge
of another communion. How vain the hope of peace on earth
as long as there is no actual peace among those who profess
to be followers and priests of the Prince of Peace!

To one such warlike priest it fell to my lot to teach a lesson.
We were inspecting the crypt in Ludd (or Lydda) in which
according to legend St. George is supposed to be buried.
As we entered in the wake of a young Greek Catholic priest,
some native gamins followed us. They were sternly reproved
and dismissed by the priest. When we reached the crypt he
espied another group of ragged urchins, and he took from
his robe its encircling belt and struck at the lads, who fled.
Turning to him I asked, "Have you ever heard of a young
Jew who nineteen hundred years ago said of such as these,
'Suffer little children to come unto me for of such is the
Kingdom of Heaven'?" The priest's scowl softened just a little
as he muttered and crossed himself, "Jesus Christ."

Certain impressions stand out after an interim of thirty-five
years, most of all the unbelievable courage of the Palestine

pioneers. Dr. Weizmann once wittily said of Herzl, "He enjoyed the advantage over me of not knowing the land, its people, the Arabs, or their language." These incredible pioneers, to the honor of their names be it said, not only did not know the land, the Arabs, and their language, but many of them had not the faintest knowledge of the fundamentals of agriculture. Yet as early as 1913, within a generation after the beginning of resettlement, we were enabled to look upon the beginning of that miracle of development which was to be wrought. That miracle included, above all, the hardest work of every kind, which was to become the basis of the life of the new Palestine. There was no work, however burdensome, that the settlers did not or would not do. When we landed at the railroad station on the outskirts of Jerusalem, the little fiacre had no room for our one rather large trunk. A tiny Yemenite Jew took the trunk and bore it all the way to Fast's Hotel. When we gave him five francs, the equivalent of the cost in New York of transferring such a trunk, the hotel proprietor protested, saying, "You have given him more than a day's wages." I could only answer, "He has done more than a day's work."

This must be the answer to those who have, in ignorance or in ill will, protested against those provisions of Palestine life rather than law that debarred Jews from hiring Arab labor. There was back of such tradition the fear the Jews might purchase land, "settle and develop it with the aid of Arab labor rather than their own." This would have been fatal to the morale of the pioneer resettlers. The hurt to the Arab laborers was undesigned. It was bound, too, to bring about a larger development of the land, which, after years, made it possible to employ the services of large numbers of Arab laborers—that is, after the first, hard, grinding pioneering work had been done by the Jewish colonists.

My impression of things Jewish might have been summed up in 1913 in a few words. There had been a brave, a very brave beginning but little more. By 1913 Zionism had been in the field for more than fifteen years and how meager were the results! This is not meant to be a reproach to the Zionist organization but rather a defense thereof and an indictment of the Jewish people. What little there was in Palestine had been begun and developed before the rise of Zionism, and the little added was a testimony of dishonor to the Jewish people. Whether because of lack of imagination or because of morally searing fear, these had committed and were for a time destined to continue to commit the sin of leaving the thin line of Jewish outposts without those reinforcements which it was the part of collective decency, irrespective of theory, to bring to their heroic brothers.

One important thing I learned, somewhat to my surprise. I knew, of course, that Palestine was a Turkish dependency not an Arab kingdom or province. But I had not understood how completely Palestine was under the suzerainty of the Turkish Empire. One day while walking in Jerusalem we heard the most unearthly screams. I hastened to the building from which these came. There I beheld a sight that was sickening. A man was tied to the floor of a granarylike building. He was being mercilessly flogged or bastinadoed. I took it for granted that he must have been guilty of some great crime. Turning to my Turkish-speaking guide, I learned that he had committed the crime of not having handed in to the high authorities the right amount of the grain he had grown and reaped. I have had frequent occasion to allude to this instance when in discussion or debate I was told that the Arabs were masters of their land of Palestine until the Jews came. In truth they were the serfs of what, in World War I, I dubbed the Turkish assassinocracy.

The new Palestine is very old. But age old and sacred as the old Palestine was, as we journeyed up and down the land, we felt that the land is still the most informing commentary on the Bible. The Jordan River, the so-called City of Jericho, Mount Zion, Samaria, Bethlehem, Hebron, Beersheba, the Lebanon, the hillsides, the vineyard-terraces, camels, donkeys, goats, and goats' milk, which alone was drinkable!

In contrast to the old Turkish-dominated, Turkish-corrupted, and Arab-neglected Palestine, we got our first glimpse of the work of Hadassah and the Hadassah nurses. The most appalling thing about our visit was to find the great number of sight-dimmed and the blind. Even the few unconfined lepers, despite their hideous scars, were not as mournful a sight as the blind, young and old. Happily, Hadassah has had a real part in eliminating if not yet entirely overcoming the blight of blindness.

The Palestine of the immediate prewar year, 1913, was for the most part, save for spots where there were Jewish beginnings, a land of misery, disease, poverty, lawlessness, and ignorance. Jews had come to lay the foundations of education and even higher schools of learning, as might have been expected, for Jews cannot live without schools and education.

Upon returning to America I resumed my earlier activities in the Zionist movement, utilizing my newly gained knowledge of the land and its people to win adherents to the Zionist cause. It was not until 1922 that we again visited Palestine. In the meantime the American Federation of Zionists, bearing for a time the name Provisional Committee for American Zionist Affairs, had greatly increased its strength and influence, thanks especially to the leadership, which Justice Brandeis had been moved for a time to take on himself. In the meantime Palestine had become occupied enemy territory, and after 1922 it was to become mandated territory of Britain.

Contrasting the Palestine of the occupied enemy territory with the Turkish province of 1913, many things thrust themselves into view—the ease of travel by rail from Cairo to Jerusalem with only one change at Kantara on the Suez Canal; the use of Hebrew in all railway notices and tickets and shop signs, including those of Ford agencies; the obvious lessening of disease and misery, due in no small part to the superb services of American Jewish women rendered through the Hadassah and its medical unit reinforced by the Straus Health

Bureau; the deeper sense of security with which one moved about despite the myriad rumors of Arab uprising. And there was something not so palpable yet utterly pervasive—a new dignity of Jewish life, which if not wholly free from *chalukah* (charity doles) was unmarred by its spirit, which if not economically self-supporting had shaken off the taint of dependence.

If this new dignity leaned a little on the side of pride, truculency was not of it. For everywhere one noted the desire to make for complete comity with the Arab population, the only matter in dispute being whether this could be achieved through the humiliation of invertebrate assent to every fiat of extemporized Arab cabals or through the changeless front of dignified self-affirmation. A fine young Jew, gentle as a woman but a lion in defense of the oppressed and wronged, put it: "There is a world of difference between *Unter-drueckung* und *Voelkerkampf*," "between oppression by another people and struggling with them on the level of equality."

On the day of the signing of the San Remo Treaty we and Mr. and Mrs. Sol Rosenblum, of Pittsburgh, who had done much for the Hebrew University in Jerusalem, were, together with their and our children, the guests at dinner of Colonel Wyndham Deeds, now Brigadier General Sir Wyndham, then the civil governor of Jerusalem. He looked upon the assumption of the mandate over Palestine by his country or empire as a twofold blessing, alike to Britain and to Palestine. After dinner, though he was, I believe, a teetotaler, he offered a toast to all of us in these words: "To the disinherited Jews the world over, England has but two words to say—'Welcome home.'" We were thrilled over the sacred privilege of being welcomed after more than 1800 years to our ancient home and our historic hope.

Early on the following day, we brought the glad tidings of ratification to the colonies on the Jaffa Road. One might have expected that the day would be given over to holiday and rejoicing. Instead of which, the heads of the little com-

munity, after notifying all the families, reached the decision
that the day for which they had long and ardently waited
could most fittingly be observed by carrying on those common,
daily tasks which they felt meant the actual ratification of the
mandate.

If only Palestine through its mandatory years had remained
under the inspiration of such figures as Deeds, Allenby, and
Plummer, there would have been a happier story to tell, even
despite the un-English anti-Jewishness of Bevin! Britain, however, made the tragic blunder of filling the mandatory administration with colonial servants. Throughout succeeding years,
these brought to Palestine the mood and manners of the Colonial Office. They were sorely unsuited to a mandated territory
tenanted chiefly by urban Jews who were at least as literate,
not to say cultivated, as the ruling colonial officers.

The British mandate officials, for the most part, did not
appreciate this, and their sympathy and helpfulness went out
not to the driven and homeless Jews, seeking to rebuild their
life and their land, but to the Arab peasants living upon the
lowest economic, social, and educational level, who had not
done or had not been permitted to do anything for the land or
for their own lives.

It was this that may have moved Josiah Wedgewood, as
faithful and understanding a friend as Jews have known, to
take up the cudgels on behalf of Palestine as the "seventh
dominion." He hoped that dominion status would end the
strange disparity of treatment of Jews and Arabs and give to
Jews the place they merited within the British Empire.

In the course of our second journey we saw much more of
the Palestine that was to be, notably the budding colonies of
which we heard heroic tales. We noted with pride and gratitude the greatly augmented services of Hadassah, which within
ten years had grown to be an institution of highest value to
Palestine in the making. It was a voyage of rediscovery, and
the most rewarding discovery was the body of pioneers and

builders who were to prove the richest treasures of the land, patient, hardy, daring, undemanding save of themselves. They and above all the members of Histadruth (the labor movement) became the strength and bulwark of the Palestine of later years.

By 1935, the year of our third visit to Palestine, that land had ceased to be a home merely for the newcomers. Its dwellers thought of themselves more than ever before as pioneers who must prepare the way and make a home for the hapless ones left—alas, one must say, kept—behind by tragic circumstances. It was told us in the summer of 1935 that these veritable pioneers kept no money for themselves but were wont to send hundreds of pounds, their last possessions or its equivalent, to their people in Poland or wherever these were still reachable. I remember Jessie Sampter, American poet, who after years of toil and hardship wrote to us in November, 1933, and clearly described the situation in those early days of the engulfing Nazi horror: "I think it would be hard for you also—for anyone not actually here—to realize the spirit in the country today, the combination of resentment, vigor and determination occasioned by the large influx of German Jews, by our sense of power in being able to help them where no other help exists, and by the cowardly interference with this process which the government is setting up to quiet the false and falsely encouraged fears of the Arabs."

The ship that bore us from Trieste to Palestine carried some three hundred *chalutzim* and *chalutzot,* young Zionist pioneers who went to join the men and women who have borne the burden of colonization for more than a generation. These youthful pilgrims had the joy of homecoming—no sadness of farewell as they embarked. Our contingent chanced to be largely of the Poale-Mizrachi group, social liberals with a conservative religious viewpoint. Their crossing of the Mediterranean was but a stage of the pilgrimage, which begins with months of intensive training in agriculture and industry,

in what were known as the *hachsharahs,* camps that fit youth
for self-sustaining life in Palestine.

The days seemed to be divided between dancing and discussion. And such dancing and such discussion, both vital and
intense and endless! The Hora is not unlike the Virginia reel
of our youth—plus Oriental fire and Hassidic fervor. As
Emerson said to Margaret Fuller, in extenuation of his prolonged stay at an exhibition by a danseuse of their time, "This
is not dancing! it is religion." One felt that these young beings
were dancing out of the bondage of the ghetto into the freedom
of the homeland. Any excuse sufficed to start a dance—all
group or folk dancing, which made the sensual gymnastics
of the modern dance in the first cabin seem pale and vulgar.

When dancing flagged—and that rarely enough—discussion
began. I have not heard discussion on a higher level, or
carried on in a fairer and more sportsmanlike way, with plenty
of bantering and sheer fun and unimaginably keen dialectics.
It was in Yiddish for the most part, with not a little Hebrew
added, which had been acquired as a living tongue in the
training camps. The raillery and good nature throughout did
not blunt the sharp edge of controversy between two groups,
the Social Democrats who look upon religious precept as a
quasi-capitalistic device, and the Mizrachi workers, who aim
simultaneously at two kingdoms of heaven, the one purely
spiritual or religious and the other social economic or this-
worldly.

In the old days, the first thing that even a semipious Jew
did upon reaching Palestine was to recite a prayer of thanks-
giving. In the new day one's primary privilege or obligation
on touching Jerusalem, I was solemnly informed, was to enter
one's name in the Book of Visitors at Government House. Having done so, I went immediately to visit an old friend, Dr.
Arthur Ruppin, who looked like an owl and had more than an
owl's reputed wisdom. I came to him with a score of problems
pressing on my heart. His sage counsel was, "Forget problems
and see Palestine. Give yourself the joy of looking upon the

land and its people and their achievements and forget all problems until you return to America or at least until you reach the Zionist Congress." I followed his counsel. From that moment I tried to see Palestine not as a partisan nor yet as a critic nor yet, what was impossible, as a carefree tourist, but as a measurably dispassionate observer eager to see what, since 1922, had been wrought by our fellow Jews under the British mandate.

We were to be privileged to get a good, though in part hurried, impression of Palestine plus a glimpse of Syria. We were to look upon the indisputable miracle of Tel Aviv, to be thrilled by the splendor that is Haifa, with its explicable appeal to the artist in Herzl, who chose Carmel as his place of burial. We were to be fascinated by the utterly exotic charm of Damascus, which struck me as a Hollywood imitation of Jerusalem.

But Jerusalem still stands and will, I believe, forever stand alone. Best of all the city, which had trebled its population in a decade, had not lost its old-time loveliness. A myriad changes and additions had not affected its mystic uniqueness. The city set upon a hill still remains the standard by which to measure every other city of famed beauty, whether it be Italian Florence, or Spanish Toledo, or pre-Nazi Nuremberg, or Austrian Salzburg, or Galician Cracow, or Lithuanian Vilna. Anyone who can walk from Bethlehem to Jerusalem without lifting tear-dimmed eyes to the hills of Zion, whence help and salvation have come to humankind as from no other source, is made of sterner stuff than the writer.

At last, nearly twelve years after its founding, I was rewarded with a glimpse of the Hebrew University. I remember having heard it discussed at Basle in 1898 and even before that by one of the earliest of its dreamers, Israel Abrahams, at Cambridge. Here it was only a beginning but not without the dignity of lofty promise. From its summit one looks westward to the Mediterranean, the city of Jerusalem at its feet, and eastward to far-off lonely Moab beyond the Dead Sea.

Nothing in all Palestine touched our souls as did the sight of hundreds of little boys and girls, for whom lovely homes had been built in every colony. Young Jewish boys and girls out of Germany, after being exposed to shame and humiliation by the Nazi criminals, were at home amid the ennobling and exalting surroundings of that home toward which the prayers of seventy generations had been directed.

Nowhere in Palestine did I find a moment's forgetfulness of the central and primary truth, that the business of dwellers in and restorers of Palestine was to build a future, to make that future conform to the best in the Jewish past and create a new best and new nobleness in the Jewish future.

IV

A Rabbi Sides with Labor

M Y first contact with labor conditions and labor problems came as early as 1895. A street-car strike took place in Brooklyn, and some strikers were killed. The strike arose over questions of wages and hours. The following Sabbath morning in the course of my sermon I spoke on the evil of shooting down strikers who sought nothing more than the right to live decently and humanly. After the service I noticed a little group of officers of the congregation in excited conversation. The treasurer of the synagogue, a member of a banking and investment firm, approached me asking, "What do you know about conditions in that street-car strike in Brooklyn?" I answered that I had informed myself as well as I could with regard to living conditions of the strikers. "They are grievously overworked and underpaid." He grumbled and muttered inarticulately, and I seized on a moment's pause to say, "I shall continue to speak for the workers whenever I come to feel that they have a real grievance and a just cause."

I had no formal contacts with labor organizations in those days. But a little later in Oregon I was one of a small group, including Dr. Thomas L. Eliot, Thomas N. Strong, and Millie Trumbull, which, knowing of child-labor conditions in the fish canneries of Astoria and the Columbia River fisheries, brought about the introduction and ultimately the legislative adoption of a child-labor law. This created a State Child Labor Commission of which I became a member by gubernatorial appointment, serving on it until 1906 when I returned to New York.

What we struggled to achieve for children in those days now seems so pitiable that one can only wonder at the anger and opposition we met. Even after we secured the law and the State Child Labor Commission was appointed by the Governor, enforcement was extremely difficult. But the methods used to defeat enforcement were not altogether different from some of the methods now used to defeat the purposes of such new legislation as our state laws against discrimination in employment.

One intervention of mine in a strike difficulty proved to be serious and availing. The Los Angeles *Times-Herald* had long been a "hot spot" in the field of industrial relations. The *Times-Herald* building was wrecked in a dynamite explosion. Feeling ran very high in 1911–1912 against organized labor, on whom the burden of the violence of the McNamaras was placed. It was easy to whip up hysteria not only against the men involved in the dynamiting, but also against the labor movement and against those few friends who sought to explain why such violence was the inevitable result of the social conditions of that time and the treatment of workers who insisted on their right to organize and to be heard. In an address at Carnegie Hall at that time, I pointed out:

> As long as labor organizations are denied a hearing save just before election seasons; as long as they are treated with scorn and contumely; as long as they are cast out and denied, it is not to be wondered at that the leaders, finding themselves and their organizations outlawed, should in turn be guilty of outlawry; that being cast out, they should resort to the weapon of the outcast; that being denied a hearing after the manner of orderly and reasoning friends, they should make themselves heard after the manner of destructive and unreasoning foes.

At about the same time, John Haynes Holmes delivered an address in which he said:

> I would rather be in the McNamara cell than in the office of the President of the Steel Trust. . . . I say that there is more peril to America in the criminal corporation, than in the criminal laborer, and I say this also, that if I had to make my choice between being leader of the corporations or being sent to the dungeons of San Quentin, I would choose the latter.

Because of these addresses, Holmes and I were described as "the McNamaras of the pulpit" by *American Industries*. This journal of the manufacturers also published a delightful cartoon in which Dr. Holmes and I were depicted as the Dr. Jekyll and Mr. Hyde of organized labor. I was so outraged by this designation, which described Holmes and myself as two men guilty of violence and murder, or inciting to it, that I even questioned whether I should not bring a libel action and consulted my good friend, Benjamin Cardozo, who was then practicing law in New York City. He wrote in answer to my question:

> I think that the heading of the article, 'McNamaras of the Pulpit,' is a libel. I think that the statement that you have condoned or defended violence or assassination is also a libel.

His further advice was that

> Civil actions [in libel matters] are not expedient where the subject of the libel is criticism of the public utterance of a man occupying a public or quasi-public position, except in those cases where resort to the law becomes a real duty in order to vindicate a deep and not merely nominal injury to one's character and reputation. Here . . . the wrong consisted not in imputing a disgraceful act, but in an unjust—a cruel and unjust—interpretation of the meaning of your words, which, however, were quoted so that the injustice was manifest to anyone who took the trouble to read the article through.

I followed this advice not only at that time but always thereafter, feeling that my own actions and my own words must at all times speak for themselves. In this decision Holmes joined me in characteristic fashion:

> I had been filled more with amazement and disgust than any-thing approaching anger. I fear that I have become so used to being called names during the past few weeks that I have become callous to assaults of this nature.

It occurred to me that this labor war, as evidenced in the McNamara case, called for an impartial federal investigation. I discussed the matter with the editor of *The Survey*, Paul U. Kellogg, and subsequently with Florence Kelley, Lillian Wald, and Samuel McCune Lindsay. We called a meeting of a group, including those named and Jane Addams, and we resolved to unite in a request to the President to name a Commission on Industrial Relations. After some months of united effort to secure the appointment of such a commission under the chair-manship of Samuel McCune Lindsay and with special public-relations assistance from that uniquely valuable organ of the common welfare, *The Survey*, President Taft agreed to name a commission.

Although we had high hopes, we learned to our dismay that President Taft submitted to the Senate for approval a group of names who, in the words of one of our committee members, "consisted of appointees largely unknown; commission lacks weight; money wasted; better none." We, therefore, had to undertake a vigorous protest to the Senate to defeat the con-firmation of the commission as proposed. We urged that a commission be appointed which could, in the eyes of the public, command such respect as would meet the needs stated by President Taft himself in recommending the creation of the commission. He had said: "The time is ripe for searching in-quiry into the subject of industrial relations, which shall be official, authoritative, balanced and well-rounded."

In the light of this need and this promise, we could not accept a commission that included no well-known economist or social workers or adequate representatives of the public.

Happily, after President Wilson took office, the work of the commission was strengthened by the appointment of Frank Walsh of Kansas City as chairman, in September, 1913. The commission studied the problem over a period of months and under the excellent and resourceful leadership of Walsh made a constructive and significant report to the President. In a sense it was the first formal attempt of the government to concern itself with facts and threats in the field of industrial relations.

In 1911 I was invited to speak—for the first and last time— at the annual banquet of the New York Chamber of Commerce. I welcomed the invitation because it gave me the opportunity to face some of America's greatest captains of industry and finance. Present that night among others were Andrew Carnegie, James J. Hill, J. P. Morgan, Charles Schwab, George Baker.

I knew that this was a critical occasion, not for the Chamber of Commerce but for me. I could ingratiate myself with this august assembly and lose my soul; I could displease them and keep it. Suffice it to say that when I sat down the only comfortable man in the room was Admiral Peary—seasoned to subarctic temperatures!

> Mr. President and Gentlemen of the Chamber of Commerce— I must say to you tonight that which I have said about you upon many other occasions,—flattering you with that frank truth-speaking than which I could offer you no sincerer tribute.
>
> When I have read from time to time of religious noonday meetings held in shops and factories for the wage-earners, I have ventured to observe that the important thing is not so much to bring religious ministration to the daily toilers,—the soldiers of the common good,—as to bring it to the captains of industry and commerce, which you are. For the conscience of the nation, after all, will be that which you make it,—yours is the high and solemn duty not only of registering, but in large part of determining the character of the conscience of the nation. . . .

Not only ought the barter or trade side of business be completely moralized, but we need to ethicize what might be called the processes of creating and production, of distribution and consumption. No business order is just nor can it long endure if it be bound up with the evil of unemployment on the one hand and over-employment on the other, the evil of a man's under-wage and a child's toil, and all those social maladjustments incidental to our order which we lump together under the name of poverty. Let us not imagine that we can shift to the shoulders of over-worked charity the burdens that can be borne only by the strength of underworked justice. Yes, the stricken ask not the occasional tonic of charity, but the daily meat and substance of justice. We are never to forget that ours is a democracy, that a democracy, in the words of a high servant of the commonwealth means "the use of all the resources of nature by all the faculties of man for the good of all the people..."

The conscience of the nation is not real unless the nation safeguard the workingman, safeguard him from the peril of overwork, as well as from the occasional accidents of industry. The conscience of the nation is not vital unless we protect women and children in industry, and protect them with half the thoroughness and generosity with which, for many decades, we have protected infant industries. We have not the right to speak of the importance of conserving the opportunity for initiative on the part of the individual as long as masses of individuals are suffered to perish without the opportunity of real life. The aim of democracy is not to be the production of efficient, machine-like men in industry. The first business of democracy is to be the industry of turning out completely effective, because completely free and self-determining, citizens.

It was about this same time or a few months earlier that the terrible fire, commonly known as the Triangle Fire, occurred in a factory in New York City. Many girls were burned to death because the doors had been locked so that no goods would be removed by any of the employees, and when the fire broke out they were unable to escape. The hideous tragedy led a few of us to seek to arouse the community to face the necessity of demanding that there be legislation to protect workers against such catastrophes. We therefore called a citizens' committee meeting at the Metropolitan Opera House on Sunday, April 22, 1911, at which I said:

This ought to be a fast day of the citizens of New York, our day of guilt and humiliation. Let it not become a day of unavailing regret, but let it be a day of availing contriteness and redeeming penitence.

It is not the action of God, but the inaction of man that is responsible. I see in this disaster not the deed of God, but the greed of man. For law is divine, and this disaster was brought about by lawlessness and inhumanity. Certain calamities man can do no more than vainly deplore,—such calamities as the San Francisco earthquake and the destruction by volcano of Martinique. But this was not an inevitable disaster which man could neither foresee nor control. We might have foreseen it, and some of us did; we might have controlled it, but we chose not to do so. The things that are inevitable we can do no more than vainly regret, but the things that are avoidable we can effectively forestall and prevent.

It is not a question of enforcement of law nor of inadequacy of law. We have the wrong kind of laws and the wrong kind of enforcement. Before insisting upon inspection and enforcement, let us lift up the industrial standards so as to make conditions worth inspecting, and, if inspected, certain to afford security to the workers. Instead of unanimity in the shirking of responsibility, we demand that departments shall cooperate in planning ahead and working for the future, with some measure of prevision and wisdom. And when we go before the Legislature of the State, and demand increased appropriations in order to ensure the possibility of a sufficient number of inspectors, we will not forever be put off with the answer: We have no money.

This meeting is not summoned in order to appeal for charity on behalf of the families of the slain. What is needed is the redress of justice and the remedy of prevention. The families of the victims ought to be beyond the reach of the need of charity. Having denied them the justice of physical security, we ought at least be willing to give their survivors the justice of economic redress. They need justice, not charity. It is we who need charity, for dare we face inexorable justice? . . .

We know that we cannot and should not take away property without due process of law. Neither may we take away life with or without due process of law. Alas, for another one of a multitude of proofs that we regard property as sacred, and are ready to suffer a violation of the rights of life as if these were not sacred but violable, and violable with impunity.

This consuming fire will have been nothing more than a flash in the pan if other evils are suffered to go unchecked and uncorrected,—evils not less terrible because less swift and less sudden. It is just as necessary to protect women workers from the industrial and occupational diseases as it is to protect them from industrial accidents. We need to provide not only for security from accidents but security from the incidents of the industrial regime. I would have women workers safeguarded in every way, —safeguarded from the economically, physically, morally and spiritually disastrous consequences of over-work and under-pay and under-nourishment and insanitary housing, which seem to be the inevitable accompaniments of things as they are today. . . .

If the church and the synagogue were forces of righteousness in the world instead of being the farces of respectability and convention, this thing need not have been. If it be the shame and humiliation of the whole community, it is doubly the humiliation of the synagogue and of the church which have suffered it to come to pass. We may not be ready to prescribe a legislative program nor devise an industrial panacea, but we must demand and demand unceasingly an ever-increasing measure of social equity and social justice.

The hour has come for industrial peace. It must be peace with honor,—say some. But it must be more than peace with honor. It must be peace with security as well. We would have no peace with honor for some, and, at the same time, deny security to all. The issue at stake is not the open shop but the closed door, which shuts out the toilers from safety and justice.

The lesson of the hour is that while property is good, life is better, that while possessions are valuable, life is priceless. The meaning of the hour is that the life of the lowliest worker in the nation is sacred and inviolable, and, if that sacred human right

be violated, we shall stand adjudged and condemned before th
tribunal of God and of history.

As a result of the response of the community and the ver
hard work of some young citizens who were deeply moved b
this disaster, including Abram I. Elkus, Belle Moskowitz
Frances Perkins, and a young man later to become known a
"Al" Smith, we organized a permanent group and began th
battle for adequate safety legislation for factory workers.

In 1912, I found myself engaged in what was a new kind o
work for me, which helped me to understand more intimatel
the conditions of workers at that time. As a result of a lockou
in some textile mills in Pennsylvania, it was agreed by th
employer and employees that I should hear both sides and see
to mediate the dispute. As I go over the notes of my first media
tion case in 1912, I find the following list of salaries:

winders	$4.75
doublers	4.75
reelers	4.25
lacers	4.25
1st-time spinners	4.75
2nd-time spinners	6.00
bobbin boys	4.50
openers	4.75
shakers	4.75
learners	3.00 to start

They were not daily but *weekly* wages. It was through thi
experience that I became intimately aware of the condition
in our textile mills. I found that a large proportion of the em
ployees were children, that the actual wages were averagin
two and three dollars a week, and that the forelady was receiv
ing six dollars a week for fifty-eight hours of work. Seriou
complaints were submitted by the workers that the superin
tendent cursed and even struck some of the women and chil
dren. At that time the situation of one child was brought befor

ne, which I shall never forget. This boy at first attempted to
work in the mines, where he had earned $1.10 a day, but had
been forced to leave because of the legislation against children
working in the mines, only to be forced to work in a textile
factory for many hours for fifteen cents a day. The strike had
been brought to a head, and the employees had demanded
one dollar a day. At this point, the employer told them to pack
up and leave. Even my most earnest effort to secure the most
limited improvement of these conditions failed, because the
employer would concede practically nothing, and it was only
after a strike that certain concessions were forced upon him.

Throughout this experience, I was struck by the degrading
conditions of the workers, including small children, their inability to win even the most modest wages, which were not
sufficient to buy the merest necessities of life. I was also deeply
challenged by a letter that had been addressed to the employer
from a board of trade in a neighboring community, which suggested the employer move to its town so as to avoid labor
troubles. That letter stated, and I quote:

> We have made a canvass of the town and find there are ninety
> girls over fourteen years of age who would be willing to work in
> a properly conducted silk mill and they are of a class above
> the ordinary, in which the spirit of labor unions do not prevail.

It had become increasingly clear to me from my work on
behalf of children in Oregon, from the conditions that preceded
the acts of violence of the McNamara brothers, from my intimate contact with the workers in the silk mills, and from the
attitude of employers and boards of trade that no basic change
could be made in the life of workers until they had won the
right to organize and bargain collectively. I had seen during the
years the development of the corporate control of industry, with
its substitution of directors representing scattered, absentee
shareholders for the personal employer of bygone days. I had
come to realize fully that confronted with an organization on
the side of the employer, like the then billion-dollar steel trust,

the individual worker was indeed helpless. I had seen that legislation forbidding employers to discharge employees on the
ground of their membership in labor unions had been repeatedly held unconstitutional by the courts and that, unless
America expressed itself through support of labor's struggle
to organize, we would have increasing violence as well as the
continuation of intolerable industrial conditions.

It was, therefore, inevitable that in October, 1919, I felt
impelled to face the obligation to speak out concerning the
smear campaign then developing in our country against workers who sought the right to organize. The chief objective of
the assault by the employers was the organization of the workers. The employers by and large felt that if these could be
broken down "inordinate claims" would no longer be made by
the workers. Their share in war profits seemed incredibly irk-
some to many masters of industry. Nowhere was this more true
than in the steel industry, where, as I recall it, more than half
of the employees of the United States Steel Corporation were
still working twelve hours a day and where the employers had
resorted to the use of the black list and the labor spy as
weapons in their industrial war upon their own workers. Not
satisfied with this, they had also employed secret-service agencies to instigate civil war among workers. One circular at that
time, addressed by an agency to one of its operatives, reveals
these methods:

> We want you to stir up as much bad faith as you possibly can
> between the Serbians and the Italians. Spread data among the
> Serbians that the Italians are going back to work. Call up every
> question you can in reference to racial hatred between these two
> nationalities.

I came to see that as between Judge Gary and Samuel Gompers there had arisen an ethical, social issue of deepest concern
to the whole American people. At that time, too, there were
heard the first, shall we say, grumblings or mumblings about
the endangering Bolsheviki. I felt the absurdity of lightly and

naïvely using the word Bolsheviks as a term of reproach and scorn for anything or any person unapproved. If there were groups in American life guilty of repression and suppression, it was such a group as the United States Steel Corporation under the leadership of Judge Gary. It was not the workers demanding their right through organization to share in the American way of life but the heads of the United States Steel Corporation who, through rejection of unionism among the workers, sought permanently to deny them that basic and inalienable right.

On June 18, 1919, I therefore wrote to Samuel Gompers and told him that I learned with great pleasure that the American Federation of Labor, under his direction, would attempt to organize the steel workers, and that I wanted him to know that if I could be of any help, I was at his command. I was naïve enough to add in that letter:

> Surely the heads of the steel industry will not be idiotic enough to attempt to withstand the organization of their workers. I cannot believe, despite their record, that they will be so Bourbonish.

I was wrong and in the following strike months every form of violence and economic pressure was used by the steel industry against the workers who were on strike. As I followed the strike during the summer months—the violence practiced against women and children, the denial of the right to meet, the corruption of local public officials, and the indifference for the most part of Church and press alike—I felt that I must speak out. I therefore announced that the subject of my first sermon before the Free Synagogue, at Carnegie Hall, after the High Holy Days, would be: "Who Are the Bolshevists at Home and Abroad—How Shall We Know Them?"

Before going to Carnegie Hall that Sunday morning, I said to my wife, "My sermon of this morning will light a million-dollar blaze." As she smiled incredulously, I explained that the synagogue building, for which we had gathered large sums and which was to cost more than a million dollars, would not

be built because of the cancellation of large gifts sure to follow
upon my sermon. It all happened as I predicted—only more so!

In opening my address, I reminded my congregation that
I knew that some of the members might refuse to lend their
help in the building of the synagogue home as a result of
what I was about to say but also again made clear that, while
it might not be necessary for them to build a synagogue, it was
necessary for me to speak the truth as I saw the truth on great
issues. I then turned to the subject of the steel workers in
America.

> The war ends, the war was ended and it was won just as much
> by the workers in the steel-mills of Pennsylvania and Ohio as by
> the American soldiers in France. And now immediately after
> the war, partially because of the feeling of reaction that follows
> upon the moral stimulus of a great undertaking such as the war,
> the heads of industry—and I think it is true of the heads of a
> great number of industries in America—have set out to reverse
> Government sanctioned, in any event, Government recognized
> standards and to undo the work of the war as far as the gains
> to the workers are concerned.
>
> The men in the iron and steel industry are striving for a funda-
> mental right of industry, at least so I conceive it;—the right to
> organize and to deal organizedly with their employers. I don't
> like the term, "collective bargaining," because it is misunderstood.
> I use simpler English, the right of the workers to organize and
> organizedly and unitedly to deal with their employers.
>
> Now, to urge, as it is urged and all the time urged, that Union-
> ism makes for abuses is to state the veriest commonplace. But has
> it ever occurred to you that terrorism and outlawry do not breed
> nice manners?
>
> For fifteen years the men in the steel industry worked twelve
> hours in the day, seven days in the week, and I would ask some-
> one among you to be good enough to point to anything that Judge
> Gary and his gallant associate defenders of the liberty of the
> workers said during those fifteen years with regard to the freedom
> of men during all that time. Things would still be as they were
> up to five years ago in the steel industry if Judge Gary and his

associates could have averted the pressure of public judgment, of public wrath and of public contempt. The Steel Corporation granted nothing voluntarily nor will it ever.

As for the so-called freedom of the workers, which Judge Gary considers so sacred a theme that he would not discuss it with the United States Senate, how can the judgment and the will of the workers be ascertained? They have never been free to organize. Mr. Gary and his associates,—in profound and American solicitude for the rights of the majority, tell us that a minority controls a majority. Well, the fact is that a minority always leads, precedes, and liberates a majority. Moreover, some fifteen or twenty-one men, who meet in Hoboken annually, talk about maintaining the freedom of the majority, and at the same time that they are fooling you and deluding the nation, refuse to meet in conference with the representatives of a great number of workers.

I charge Mr. Gary with having made it impossible for me as an American citizen to know what the thought and what the will of the workers in the steel industry is. They never have been free to utter themselves. They are not free today.

I charge the United States Steel Corporation with resorting to every manner of coercion and even of violence. If I am stating that which is untrue, if I am libelling the heads of the Steel Corporation, they have the power of redress. I am a responsible person and can be found at any time. I charge Judge Gary and the men associated with him with resorting to every manner of coercion, intimidation, and violence ... in order to avoid the organization of the workers.

The press reported the address rather fully. Letters of approval from men whom I deeply respected, and letters of violent disapproval came together. I was advised that a previous invitation to Pittsburgh would not be cancelled, but that I should know that in view of my remarks on the steel strike, the rabbi felt that I should be made aware "that the Gentiles are putting us in a bad light as a result of Dr. Wise's talk and that it will hurt the Jewish cause in this section." I advised the gentleman that I regarded the invitation as withdrawn. A Mid-Western rabbi, Dr. Silver, sanctimoniously advised his congregation that a minister was justified in attacking evil but not evildoers. A so-called minister of religion in New York preached a vituperative sermon in which he charged that I was playing politics in the pulpit and prostituting the pulpit for "personal notoriety and sensationalism."

Within twenty-four hours resignations had begun to pour in. I immediately answered each member who resigned, advising him that owing to comment in agreement and disagreement with the address, I had resolved to give a second address on the same theme the following Sunday, under the title: "How Ought the Pulpit Deal with the Industrial Situation?" and that I should be glad if he could be present and hear the address, adding that the letter of resignation would be acted upon by the membership committee, unless after the following Sunday the member wished to rescind such decision.

Incidentally, I might observe that one special type of piety I uniformly evoked from the membership of the Free Synagogue—the piety of resignation! At the risk of punning, I must admit that time and time again a sermon on any theme of current interest was followed by one or more resignations. One of the foremost Jewish financiers of the country led the procession by resigning from the synagogue's Executive Council, also a large employer of labor whose industrial plant, after thirty-five years, is still nonunion. The synagogue's first treasurer resigned. This time the resignations came in such large numbers that for the first and only time I felt the matter should be put to the test of a congregational decision.

I did the thing which I have always believed a minister or rabbi should do. When a congregation seems ready in goodly numbers to dissent from or protest against the word or deed of its minister, he must offer his resignation and the congregation must be left free to accept or reject such resignation. The Executive Council met under the temporary chairmanship of an old and honored friend, Oscar Straus, the first member of the Jewish community to attain Cabinet rank as secretary of commerce. My resignation was presented to the

Executive Council and was refused in friendliest terms with the dictum that the principle of the Free Synagogue stands— the pulpit is free, but the rabbi speaks not *for* but *to* the congregation. It was the only time in the history of the Free Synagogue, now in its forty-second year, that the ideal of pulpit freedom was put to the test—and the ideal was sustained. But the building was lost.

The central and basic principle of the Free Synagogue, however, has enduringly been maintained, throughout my lifetime in any event, and will be continued throughout the lifetime of my successors if they choose, as they will choose, to be equal to the test, beginning with my disciple and comrade, friend and successor, Rabbi Edward E. Klein.

I cannot close my reference to the steel strike without speaking of the Inter-Church World Movement. Shortly after the founding of the Inter-Church World Movement in October, 1919, when I made my address, a committee on the steel strike was appointed to investigate the facts. This committee consisted of the Bishop of the Methodist Church, the Bishop of the Episcopal Church, one of the secretaries of the Presbyterian Church, and a number of other earnest, thoughtful, conservative people. The first thing they did was to offer to mediate between Judge Gary and the men on strike. The men accepted; Mr. Gary at once refused the tender. The strike went on for a while and then was lost, and the men returned to work. In the meantime these men representing their churches went on with their investigation. In April, 1920, they submitted a typed report. Every effort was made to suppress that report because the findings were against the United States Steel Corporation, although temperate in spirit and couched in conservative fashion. After a delay, a handful of men demanded the right to publish the report and it was printed. From that moment on the Inter-Church World Movement was dead.

One might ask who killed the Inter-Church World Movement? At the time someone wittily suggested to me that "a steel splinter got into its eye." The fact remains that the publication of the investigation report killed the movement of the Protestant Churches in America that was created and designed to bring about the union of the religious and church forces in America.

We were still in a period when men not only believed but admitted that the public utterances of ministers should be supervised and restricted by church officers. I remember the comment of various ministers concerning the struggle of a Christian minister with his congregation regarding his right to speak on any subject which he believed his congregation should know about. Some ministers supported him while others held that a pastor's domain was the Bible and biblical subjects and that when a minister interfered with current politics he was exceeding his ecclesiastical authority.

During this controversy, some ministers still took the position that if the minister were tactful he would not get into trouble, others that the minister should preach only the gospel, and still others that "the pastor should be governed by the officers of his church, and the officers should be the governing body to decide on all public utterances of the pastor." One minister even went so far as to say of himself in answer to the question on this subject: "I am employed by a community of people who pay me my salary. They give me their pulpit and their following. If I have the gift of free speech so much that I can say what I please regardless of who or what is involved, I am dishonoring my position." Although I have frequently been attacked for speaking the truth on many issues, I was never attacked more viciously than for speaking out in regard to the rights of workers and making my attack specific against the exploitation of steel workers and the denial of their right to organize.

The word sensationalism was used over and over again to discredit me, and more important to discredit what I had said. I said that Judge Gary had Cossackized the steel industry. The term may have sounded sensational but it was nonetheless true because graphic and vivid. The later Inter-Church Steel Report proved that Judge Gary used the spy system and that there

Working as a shipyard laborer in Stamford, Connecticut, during World War I.

New York Chamber of Commerce banquet, 1911, addressed by Rabbi Wise. On the dais left to right: Thomas A. Edison, Stephen Wise, Bishop David H. Greer, George F. Baker, J. P. Morgan, Governor Emmet O'Neal of Alabama, Rt. Hon. James Bryce, British Ambassador, President Hosburn of the Chamber of Commerce, Governor John A. Dix of New York, Mayor

had been a system of terrorism within the industry for years.
This is Cossackism. As I look back, I recall a man in the Jewish
pulpit who called me a sensation monger at the time. He dealt
with the steel strike shortly after I did and justified Judge Gary.
I was sensational only in that I dared to speak the truth as I
saw it, and he was unsensational in that he did not see the
truth or, if he saw it, he did not have the manliness and the
decency to speak out in a place dedicated above all things to
truth-speaking.

If a man wishes to avoid the appearance of sensationalism,
the only thing he need do is what most men in the pulpit do—
tap social wrongdoers on the wrists without, of course, mentioning their names. The fact is that my business as a teacher
of religion and moralism is not to call attention to wrongdoing
in such fashion that people shall not really know what I say,
but to make it clear that certain wrongs are being done by certain people. In arguing this point I was once reminded that
Nathan, the Prophet, did not hold a meeting when he wished
to speak to David but went quietly into his chamber and said,
"Thou art the man." The implication of much of the criticism
leveled against me at that time was that public speaking against
the wrongdoer, as well as for the wronged, was not in keeping
with biblical tradition. I still wonder whether some of the
gentlemen who thought of this excuse for not speaking out with
courage, and who claim to believe in Nathan's method of in-
fluencing others while refraining as they do from pulpit utterance touching the man who does wrong, find and avail
themselves of opportunities to go to that man's banking office
or counting house or shop or factory and say to him "Thou art
the man."

There are things that are absurd and sensational and vulgar
in the pulpit, but that is no reason for confusing the vulgarian
in the pulpit with the man who makes people think and feel
aright. I for my part have found that the term sensationalist or
sensation monger is oftenest applied to the men in the pulpit by
those of their colleagues who have a peculiar genius for leaving

their congregations undisturbed in their weekly church or synagogue slumber.

Startling is another name for or an interchangeable term with
sensational. Do not men need to startle? Are there not times
men require to be roused, when they must be awakened out of
the depths of their slumber? It was said of Tolstoy that he
stabbed men awake. There are times when men need to be
dynamited into wakefulness.

I have never felt the need of defending myself against the
charge of sensationalism for I have known my own motives. In
a world of shame, the truth bravely uttered is bound to sound
sensational. I have sought the truth and aimed to further the
sovereignty of righteousness among men. Within my limited
powers, I have purposed to magnify the ideal of justice, and I
have spoken and speak for the sake of these things and only
for them.

From the earliest days of the Mooney case, I was convinced
that a grave injustice had been done and therefore concerned
myself with his defense and later with helping to secure the
pardon to which he was entitled but which was denied time and
again by the governors of California. Because I had had
the advantage of living in the Western part of the country, more
or less as a neighbor of California, from 1900 to 1906, I was in
touch with the atmosphere out of which the war on Mooney
grew. I knew that gang of thieves and looters—though they
happened to be millionaires—who were in control of the United
Railways in San Francisco. The whole Mooney case went back
to their determination to destroy a man of Mooney's type. I
studied the Mooney case for years. I discussed it with some of
the ablest lawyers in the nation, and I came to hold the firmest
conviction that Mooney was the victim of something that was
half hysteria and half conspiracy and that there was never the
slightest evidence of his guilt in relation to the case.

Feeling as I did about it, believing that a great wrong was
being done by California to Mooney and Billings, holding that

he was the victim of a nefarious plot on the part of certain powerful, ruthless groups in California. I could not be silent. Again and again I spoke my mind touching this great wrong and did what I could to have it corrected. The walls of opposition, conspiracy, and evil, which together, as much as the walls of San Quentin, kept Mooney a prisoner year after year, was again revealed when the Honorable Matt I. Sullivan, appointed adviser to Governor Rolph on this case, dared to state in November, 1932: "I am too old a man to be reading any more Mooney reports." It was in the light of this background and this quotation that I sent the following letter to the Honorable Matt I. Sullivan and at the same time gave it to the press:

DECEMBER 7, 1932

HON. MATT I. SULLIVAN
SAN FRANCISCO, CALIF.

SIR:

The San Francisco *Daily News* of November 28 quotes you in the following terms: "I am too old a man to be reading any more Mooney reports. I won't read this latest attack." You thus say of yourself, "I am too old a man to be reading any more Mooney reports." We have known that for some time. We tried to indicate in our earlier statement that you could not with intelligence and without prejudice have read the documents submitted to you by the Governor of California in the Mooney case.

We have no quarrel with you, as a bitterly vindictive old man, lacking the decency squarely to face the issues of a case which involves the honor of your State and of the nation, a case which is at the center of the world's moral interest. The case, we concede, should never have been submitted to you. Our quarrel must be with Governor Rolph, who entrusted so great a responsibility to one as injudicial as you have proven yourself to be. In truth you did not report on the Mooney case. You did nothing more than recapitulate the biases and prejudices and passions which have been accumulating under the regime of lawlessness in your community. As an officer of the law, you were entrusted with a task to which you have contributed nothing save the rehearsing of ancient spites and unspent venom.

If remembered at all in the Mooney case, your name will be a symbol of the degradation to which men may fall when they forswear reason and conscience in order, for one reason or another to serve injustice. We must assume, in justice to you, that you were not and are not a free agent, that you were under the compulsion of acting as you did, and that the masters who employed you demanded nothing less of you than the report which will endure as the epitome of all that so-called law and lawyers can do at their basest.

With pity rather than contempt we turn from you to the Governor whom you have ill-served. He should have been discerning enough not to ask you to serve as adviser....

We can do no more than hope that some day the manhood and womanhood of California will make themselves felt despite every influence which has shackled one California Governor after another, to the end that not only shall Mooney be freed, but that California be freed from the shame that has too long rested upon your State.

With deepest sorrow that a great cause should have come under the necessity of being entrusted to such hands as your own,

VERY TRULY YOURS,
STEPHEN S. WISE

Powerful though frightened and angered interests were determined to resist the development of a strong labor movement and the enlargement of the rights of workers during the early decades of this century. Hence, the Mooney case, like the Sacco-Vanzetti case, represented not only a serious misuse of our judicial system but indicated how far civil rights and judicial rights could be denied in substance when individuals came to be symbols.

Of all the many labor situations and strikes in which I became concerned from time to time over the years, one more may be worth mentioning, namely, the Passaic strike of 1926. On finishing college my daughter had gone to work in 1924 in the textile mills in Passaic with another young friend, Bertha Paret, to learn at first hand about the working conditions in the textile mills. They brought to me intimate reports on the low wages, the night work for women, and perhaps most significant the organized system of terror, which made workers fearful to talk to one another. During this period their home was entered, their books and papers were gone over by a labor spy, who subsequently came to me and confessed what he had done.

I also saw how here, as in the steel industry, powerful employers had banded together to use and increase the hostility of one foreign-born group against another in the hope of avoiding the organization of the workers or united demands for decent living conditions and the right to organize. It was therefore natural that, when months later in January, 1926, a strike was called, I made every effort to secure a peaceful and decent outcome in the Passaic mills. During the strike, the denial of the right to meet, violation of all civil liberties, the corruption of local police officials by the textile owners, and the cry of Communist leadership against the workers were all invoked. On this last point, it is interesting to note that Senator Borah, to whom I brought the matter in the hope of securing a senatorial investigation, and who became deeply interested in the situation at Passaic, wrote to me on March 26, 1926:

> At this time in this country when anyone has any views to express or takes action along any lines not in accord with the established order of things, he is immediately charged with being a Communist. The charge of being a Communist is coming to be the shield and protection for almost every kind of human exploitation. There would be no Communism in this country that anyone need be disturbed about if conditions were what they ought to be and if justice were meted out as it should be.

Despite efforts by Senator Borah and final assumption of some responsibility by the American Federation of Labor, after a year strikers were temporarily defeated and remained unorganized until after the passage of the National Labor Relations Act and the development of the CIO.

In passing, I would like to add that in this strike, as in many other cases in which social justice for workers was involved, I had the privilege of working closely with Sidney Hillman for whom I came to have an admiration and affection that lasted throughout his life.

In the Passaic strike, the steel strike, and in other situations, I had come to see the absolute necessity for the organization of unskilled workers on an industrial basis if there was to be any protection of their rights as Americans, any substantial improvement in the conditions under which they worked, or any equality in their bargaining power essential to sound labor relations in America.

It was for these reasons that I hailed the development of the CIO, which from the outset showed concern not only with those workers who belonged to skilled crafts, but with all workers, regardless of their skill, their trades, or their national origin. It was for these reasons also that I hailed the CIO for seeking to help workers in every industry to respect fellow workers not only by eliminating from trade unions discrimination of race, religion, or national origin, but positively by embarking upon a program that would seek to eliminate such un-American thinking and action in every area of the life of our country.

And so it was natural that I should accept the honoring invitation from Philip Murray to address the CIO Convention in Atlantic City in November, 1946. There I summed up the thinking of forty years and more on the relation of organized labor to the battle against anti-Semitism:

Mr. President and gentlemen, I take it that your invitation to speak before you this morning, is owing in part to the circumstance that in mid-July of 1946 it became my sorrowful duty to preside over the service in farewell to a great labor leader, a man who was indeed an industrial statesman. For many years I

knew him. I honored him and I cherished him as a friend. As Jew
and as Rabbi, I was proud of the service of this foreign-born
Jew, this great labor leader, to our beloved country. Now that the
bitterness has in some degree died away, it has become possible—
even for his enemies, and he was great enough to have won many
enemies, including would-be Presidents of the United States—
it has become possible to appraise justly and decently the character of a great American. I proudly and reverently speak of this
great Jew, this truly great servant of his country, this truly great
comrade of Franklin D. Roosevelt, Sidney Hillman.

The invitation to address this convention meeting on anti-
Semitism reveals a profound understanding on your part of the
significance of this problem. I feel that you did not invite me
chiefly as President of the American and World Jewish Congress,
nor even as a representative of millions of the victims of anti-
Semitism—6,200,000, according to Mr. Justice Robert Jackson—
in order that you might express your deep and unfeigned sympathy with my brother Jews. Your invitation implies that you
grasp the relation that obtains between resistance to anti-Semitism
on the one hand, and, on the other, your own faith in the invin-
cible and inviolable democratic processes.

I was most happy to read this morning as I came here of the
admirable resolutions that this convention has already adopted.
I call anti-Semitism anti-democratic. What could be more anti-
democratic than racism, the thing that you are going to combat
in your great enterprise in the southern states, a conflict which
will remain to the honor of the Congress of Industrial Organizations, whether you succeed or whether you fail. "Not failure but
low aim is crime," said the poet. To fail to go to the southern
states and make the fight that you are resolved to make, that
would be a crime, but not failure in the carrying out of that
truly American enterprise.

Anti-Semitism stems from the madness of racism. This is its
origin but not its end. First implicitly and later explicitly, as
in the rise of anti-Semitism, racism utterly denies the fundamental
premises of democracy. Racism is of course the antithesis of
democracy, for democracies deny the validity of racism, the
truth of racial superiorities or inferiorities. Democracy means
justice to all, from all, and utterly denies the imagined or spurious

claims of racism. But anti-Semitism, a most common form of racism, does not stop even there; it denies, and it ultimately sets out to invalidate the foundations of democracy, economic and social.

The assault by Nazism upon my people was the greatest hurt and the greatest honor which ever befell us.

For once, yea twice, Hitler judged rightly. He understood, criminal madman though he was, that he could not conquer the world for enslavement of the human race, for injustice, for war, unless he first destroyed my people. And, alas, he all but succeeded. And if he had won the war, Jews everywhere would have been marked for slaughter and destruction, even as we did lose more than six million. Subconsciously, he paid this tribute to the Jewish people: "As long as Jews live the world cannot be enslaved, for Jewish history, virtually began with the cry of Moses to Pharaoh, 'Let my people go.' So Jews must die before I can create a universal sovereignty over and enslavement of the human race."

But he paid you a similar compliment—though you were second, and not first as we were, in the receipt of that compliment—the moment he gained power. On the hideous 5th day of March 1933, he abolished labor unions, he stole their millions and millions of marks, he imprisoned and slaughtered their leaders. From this point of view, he was right, right for the second time—a world cannot be enslaved as long as organizations like the Congress of Industrial Organizations exist.

My people are the classic people of resistance to injustice and enslavement, and you today are becoming a mighty organization under a great and wise leadership.

I, as an old American—for I lived 71 of the 72 years of my life in this country—I, as an old American, summon you to the great task, though you require not my summons, of resisting any and every attempt, on the part of any political or industrial leaders in America, to march backward. I have a simple formula. We are not going to surrender the gains for democracy—political, social or economic—achieved under the peerless leadership of Franklin Delano Roosevelt.

Do battle, I beseech you, against every form of racial and religious prejudice. Fight those forms of racial and religious prejudice which maintained that iniquitous anachronism supported by Bilbo and Rankin—the poll tax. Help to establish a permanent, nation-wide FEPC, and, above all, build up and strengthen a program which does not merely in negative fashion discourage anti-Semitism, but seeks to deepen the sources of understanding sympathy and to further every possible method of tolerance and brotherliness in American life.

I have had the privilege in a long and full life of speaking before many and varied groups of men. I have never spoken to any group of men before whom this privilege has made me happier and prouder than it has through meeting with you and addressing you this day.

It was for the same reasons that I opposed the Taft-Hartley Act from the day of its inception, because I regarded it as a Congressional strong-arm attack on those rights of labor that are part of the basic structure of democracy. It must, it will be repealed.

V

Founding The Free Synagogue

An episode which changed the whole course of my life occurred in 1905 when I was still the youngish rabbi of Temple Beth Israel of Portland, Oregon. Out of a clear sky came the lightning of an invitation to give a number of sermons and addresses at Temple Emanu-El of New York, known as the Cathedral Synagogue of the country. Its pulpit was vacant after its long-time occupancy by two distinguished figures. The former of these was Dr. Samuel Adler, who had been called from Alzey, Germany, a most learned scholar. After Adler came my learned friend and teacher, Dr. Gustav Gottheil, who pioneered self-respectingly in the field of Christian-Jewish relations.

Leaving Oregon, I said to intimate friends, chief among them the former president of Oregon University, Dr. Chapman, and Richard Ward Montague, highest type of citizen and jurist, "I am going to New York to preach some trial sermons at the Cathedral Synagogue. They will call me to be their rabbi. I somehow feel that I will have to decline their call. If I decline it, as I believe I shall have to do, I will go back to New York from Oregon to found a Free Synagogue." That proved to be an accurate prediction of what was to happen.

One who preaches trial sermons lays himself open, as no man with self-respect should, to harassing experiences. After five years of free and independent preaching to a most friendly and indeed forbearing, as well as generously appreciative, congregation, I was greeted after preaching at Emanu-El by men and women, meaning to show their approval, with such exclamations as "We were very much impressed," "We were very well pleased," as if I had wished to please, when in truth I had sought solely to awaken. For the first time I came to understand the term trial sermons, as I had to listen to such expressions as "Doctor, it was a fine sermon." It was my soul that was tried; I had poured it out in earnest and unafraid appeal to these people to be single-minded and greathearted Jews. They responded to me as if I had been delivering a high-school prize oration. I was chilled and disheartened to the last degree. Above all, it prepared my spirit for the great refusal, to which I was inexorably bound to rise after some days.

Negotiation began at once after my address by the president, James Seligman of the then famous banking firm. A committee consisting of a majority of the Board of Trustees of Emanu-El came to me. I name them for the record: James Seligman, M. H. Moses, Daniel Guggenheim, Isaac Spiegelberg, and Louis Marshall. Marshall, honorary secretary of the temple, was so much of a master or dictator in Emanu-El that Dr. Emil G. Hirsch, the greatest preacher of the American Jewish pulpit, once said, "Temple Emanu-El lives under *Marshall* law."

Marshall began by asking me with such geniality as he could muster for the performance of an uncongenial task, what would be my conditions in accepting the proposed call of Emanu-El to be its rabbi. I had carefully and self-searchingly considered what my reply would be to such an inevitable query. "Gentlemen, I name two minor conditions and one major. I must have part in the religious service, participation in which is precious to me, and I am accustomed to have the service of a private secretary." The answer was there could be no objection to these conditions, though both sounded novel to the committee, the congregation being accustomed to have the service chanted wholly by its cantor, and no previous rabbi at Emanu-El having asked for a secretary.

Thereupon I spoke in simple and earnest terms, "You are call-

ing me to be the rabbi of Emanu-El. I am not a preacher or
scholar of note, but you have heard that I have gained for my
temple, Beth Israel, my people throughout Oregon, and their
rabbi, the respect and for the most part the good will of the
entire Northwest community. If I have achieved that, it has
been because in my inaugural sermon at Beth Israel, September,
1900, I declared: 'This pulpit must be free'."

Mr. Marshall, perhaps to his credit be it said, without a
moment's hesitation and without even the faintest pretense of
consultation with his colleagues, said rather testily, as was his
wont, "Dr. Wise, I must say to you at once that such condition
cannot be complied with; the pulpit of Emanu-El has always
been and is subject to and under the control of the Board of
Trustees". My answer was clear, immediate, unequivocal: "If
that be true, gentlemen, there is nothing more to say".

And that would have been the end had not one of Mr. Marshall's colleagues, all of whom seemed surprised by the finality
of Mr. Marshall's statement and the immediacy of my reply, interposed the question, "What do you mean by a free pulpit?"

I replied fully and deliberately, putting my worst foot forward, "I have in Oregon been among the leaders of a civic-
reform movement in my community. Mr. Moses, if it be true,
as I have heard it rumored, that your nephew, Mr. Herman, is
to be a Tammany Hall candidate for a Supreme Court judge-
ship, I would if I were Emanu-El's rabbi oppose his candidacy
in and out of my pulpit." I continued, "Mr. Guggenheim, as a
member of the Child Labor Commission of the State of Oregon,
I must say to you that, if it ever came to be known that children
were being employed in your mines," having reference to his
presidency of the famous copper mines, "I would cry out against
such wrong. Mr. Marshall, the press stated that you and your
firm are to be counsel for Mr. Hyde of the Equitable Life Assurance Society. That may or may not be true, but, knowing
that Charles Evans Hughes's investigation of insurance com-
panies in New York has been a very great service, I would in

and out of my pulpit speak in condemnation of the crimes committed by the insurance thieves."

I added that I could not and would not under any circumstances accept a call to be the rabbi of a congregation under such, as I saw it, humiliating conditions. The interview terminated though not before one of the deputation made clear, to Marshall's obvious irritation, that "any recommendation we may make with regard to your election as our rabbi would be accepted by the congregation." I arose, not however before saying for the last time, "If Mr. Marshall be correct, I would not under any conceivable circumstances accept the call of Emanu-El." The committee left. My mind was made up. My prediction seemed near to fulfillment. My wife, bravest and finest of spirits, waiting for me in the adjoining room, met me with a simple but infinitely heartening greeting: "You had no other choice."

But there was no finality. In the course of a week, before we could leave for Oregon, I had three visits, two of them from members of the committee that had come to extend the call, Messrs. Seligman and Guggenheim, president and treasurer respectively, who urged me most earnestly and generously to reconsider my decision, each maintaining that I was not to take Mr. Marshall's dogmatic assertions too seriously. A third and unexpected visitor was Jacob Schiff. After some talk, which was a renewal of the urging of the others, he asked me to accompany him as he walked to the Montefiore Home of which he was founder and president. Again and again he asked me to reconsider. When I complained of Louis Marshall's intolerable suggestion, Schiff said: "But he is like that—what the Germans call *ein Krakaeler*, the best possible rendering for which is a *forninster*." Finally, in the course of the long and exhausting walk, I asked him point blank, "Would Dr. Parkhurst," and I named him because he was the outstanding clerical figure of New York in that day, "accept a call to a Christian church on the Marshall terms?" Mr. Schiff's answer made my decision final and unalterable: "That would be different. Dr. Parkhurst is a Christian minister and you are a rabbi." Nothing more could be said.

I hurried home and sought out Professor Felix Adler, whose father, Samuel Adler, as I have already pointed out, had been a rabbi of Emanu-El. Dr. Adler strongly supported my position, saying with real feeling what I later embodied in my epistle on the "Freedom of the Pulpit," that the position of Marshall was an insult to the memory of his father, who would never have consented to stand in such a muzzled pulpit. Professor Adler approved of a brief note which I sent to Mr. Marshall before leaving New York.

That might have been the end of the tale. But more happened. Rumors of the call to Emanu-El's pulpit had preceded my return to Portland. I preached on the first Sabbath eve thereafter, told the full story in unvarnished, withal strictly accurate, terms and announced that I would more than carry out the terms of my arrangement with the Congregation of Portland, remaining its rabbi till September, 1906, and then go to New York, there, in the largest Jewish community of history, to found a Free Synagogue.

The report of the sermon was telegraphed to New York, and Mr. Marshall at once saw fit, instead of dealing with the larger issue that had been raised, virtually to ignore it. He took refuge in what at best was a technicality, namely, that there had been no call and that there could not have been a call inasmuch as no congregational meeting had been held. How fair such quibble was it has become rather too late to debate. What alone troubled others and myself was that Mr. Marshall should have been willing to destroy the reputation of one as young as I then was and, what was even worse, that no member of the Board of Trustees, which had dealt with me, was ready to tell the truth and by so doing brave Mr. Marshall's wrath. Many years later, having invited Mr. Marshall to give an address before the Free Synagogue, I introduced and welcomed him as "the inspirer of the founder of the Free Synagogue," without evoking from him even a reluctant smile!

Assailed as I was, my veracity and integrity questioned, I prepared with utmost care the epistle on the freedom of the pulpit, and in this I had the help of two friends, Felix Adler and Richard Ward Montague, whom I have already named. It was carefully reasoned and clearly stated, remaining unanswered, and, I venture to believe, unanswerable, as a plea for pulpit freedom—not only the Jewish pulpit but the pulpit of religion! Few things in life have given me deeper satisfaction than to have ministers of Christian churches, as well as my rabbinical colleagues, throughout more than a generation speak gratefully of the battle I fought for the freedom of the pulpit.

Because this open letter marked the turning point of my life and served as the introduction to my ministry in New York, I include it here:

AN OPEN LETTER

PORTLAND, OREGON
JANUARY 5, 1906

To THE PRESIDENT AND MEMBERS OF TEMPLE EMANU-EL,
    NEW YORK, N. Y.

GENTLEMEN:

On the first of December I received a communication from Mr. Louis Marshall, chairman of a committee of the board of trustees of Temple Emanu-El.

NEW YORK, DECEMBER 1, 1905

DEAR DOCTOR:

At your request, I am formulating the substance of what was said to you last evening by the committee of inquiry appointed by the Board of Trustees of Congregation Emanu-El.

The committee waited upon you, for the purpose of ascertaining whether or not, in the event that it should be concluded by the board of trustees and the congregation, to extend to you a call to occupy our pulpit, in conjunction with its present incumbent, Rev. Joseph Silverman, such call would be accepted.

In making this inquiry it was stated to you by the committee, in view of the traditions of the congregation, and out of consideration of the church polity which had always prevailed therein, it was considered as a necessary condition, applicable to any incumbent of the office of rabbi in the congregation, that the pulpit should always be subject to and under the control of the board of trustees. This was considered to be particularly important, in view of the circumstances, that the requirements of the congregation were such as to render it essential that there should be two incumbents of its pulpit, of equal rank and performing identical functions.

It is fair to say, that this announcement of our congregational law, is not a mere figure of speech, or an empty formula, although in the past it has never led to any friction between our rabbis and our board of trustees. It does not mean that the board of trustees will call upon any incumbent of our pulpit to sacrifice or surrender his principles or convictions.

The converse of the proposition is equally important—that the board of trustees shall not, and will not, sacrifice or surrender the principles or the convictions which it officially represents. The logical consequence of a conflict of irreconcilable views between the rabbis and the board of trustees is that one or the other must give way. Naturally, it must be the rabbi. It goes without saying, therefore, that at such a juncture, he should have the privilege of resigning. His failure to exercise that option necessarily implies an acquiescence by him in the views of the board of trustees.

Our insistence upon the phraseology which I have employed, and which is a mere adoption of the terms in which the unwritten law of the congregation is couched, is based upon the idea, that it is but fair to the rabbi and to the congregation that both shall understand at the outset the nature of the contract which exists between them, and that the former shall enter into the pact with his eyes open, so that he may never have occasion to complain, should a difference ever arise, that he was placed in the position of either sacrificing his principles, or of becoming a martyr to what he may possibly describe as the intolerance of the board of trustees.

The committee likewise believes that, without in any way detracting from the dignity of the rabbis or of the congregation, both of co-equal importance, whatever understanding is reached between them, should be perpetuated by some form of writing, whether it be by correspondence, memorandum or formal agreement. The very fact that in our several conferences there has arisen the necessity of defining the language used by the respective conferees indicates the wisdom of such a course.

With best regards, I am, very truly yours,

LOUIS MARSHALL.

Dr. Stephen S. Wise.

On December third I addressed to him the following reply:

MR. LOUIS MARSHALL,
 CHAIRMAN OF COMMITTEE OF BOARD OF TRUSTEES,
  TEMPLE EMANU-EL.

DEAR SIR:

If your letter of December first be expressive of the thought of the board of trustees of Temple Emanu-El, I beg to say that no self-respecting minister of religion, in my opinion, could consider a call to a pulpit which, in the language of your communication, shall always be subject to, and under the control of, the board of trustees. I am,

YOURS VERY TRULY,
STEPHEN S. WISE

While my position in the matter under question is thus explained in unmistakable terms, I feel that it is become my duty to address this open letter to you on the question of the freedom of the Jewish pulpit.

I write to you because I believe that a question of supereminent importance has been raised, the question whether the pulpit shall be free or whether the pulpit shall not be free, and, by reason of its loss of freedom, reft of its power for good. The whole position of the churches is involved in this question, for the steadily waning influence of church and synagogue is due in no small part, I hold, to the widespread belief that the pulpit is not free, and that it is "subject to and under the control" of those officers and members of the church or synagogue who, for any reason, are powerful in its councils. The question, therefore, "Shall the pulpit be free or shall it not be free?" is of infinitely greater moment than the question of the occupancy of your pulpit by any man whosoever, and it is the deep conviction that this is so that has impelled me, now that any thought of a direct relation between us is definitely set aside, to address you in earnest language as men equally concerned with myself in the well-being and increasing power of our beloved religion.

When a committee of five, constituting a majority of the board of trustees of the congregation, came to me, for the purpose of ascertaining whether a call to occupy your pulpit would be accepted, and, if accepted, upon what terms, I stated that I had but one stipulation to make with respect to the terms of such call, and that I was ready to leave everything else to the judgment of the board of trustees and the members of the congregation, merely adding that a written contract ought not to be deemed necessary between a congregation and its minister. The one stipulation I made in the following words: "If I am to accept a call to the pulpit of Temple Emanu-El, I do so with the understanding that I am to be free, and that my pulpit is not to be muzzled." I made no other stipulation; upon this I insisted. Counsels of prudence, which were urged upon me, suggested that I should have taken this freedom for granted, but viewing the manner in which my stipulation was met by the members of the committee, I deem it most fortunate that I anticipated the situation which has arisen. . . . It was indeed held by some members of the committee that the phrase, "the pulpit shall always be subject to and under the control of the board of trustees," was "an empty formula," or "a mere figure of speech," which interpretation, however, the chairman of the committee at once emphatically disavowed. Even though this phrase were admitted to be an empty formula, I would still be under the moral necessity of refusing to maintain a fiction, of making a compact in terms of falsehood to teach in a place dedicated to truth. But how can a form of words so threatening to the liberty of a minister of religion be regarded as a mere figure of speech? The very fact that it was insisted upon is evidence that it was not intended as a formula, and, if it be intended seriously, as it clearly is, I have only to repeat that no self-respecting minister of religion could consider a call to the pulpit of a church or synagogue on such terms. Such a formula, taken under any construction that may be put upon it, is not chiefly humiliating to me, who unequivocally reject its terms, but much more humiliating to the congregation in the name of which such terms are offered. . . .

It is not said that in the event of a conflict of irreconcilable views between the rabbi and a majority of the members of the congregation the rabbi must give way, but that the acceptance of the terms "the pulpit shall always be subject to, and under the control of, the board of trustees, implies acquiescence on the part of the rabbi in the views of the board of trustees in the event of a conflict of irreconcilable views between him and them, or the necessity of exercising the "option" or "privilege" of resigning. The board of trustees thus assert for themselves in the last analysis the custodianship of the spiritual convictions of the congregation. . . . Stated more simply, the rabbi, whose whole life is given to the study of and preoccupation with religion and morals, must always hold his views subject to revision or ratification at the hands of the board of trustees, or of any number, howsoever small, of the members of the congregation having sufficiently formidable influence with the board of trustees. In other words, the mere fact that a certain number, not necessarily a majority, of the members of the congregation or certain members of the board of trustees, might object to his views is to compel retraction, silence or resignation, without the slightest guarantee that reason and right are on the side of the objectors. The mere statement of the case is its own severest condemnation. . . .

The chief office of the minister, I take it, is not to represent the views of the congregation, but to proclaim the truth as he sees it. How can he serve a congregation as a teacher save as he quickens the minds of his hearers by the vitality and independence of his utterances? But how can a man be vital and independent and helpful, if he be tethered and muzzled? A free pulpit, worthily filled, must command respect and influence; a pulpit that is not free, howsoever filled, is sure to be without potency and honor. A free pulpit will sometimes stumble into error; a pulpit that is not free can never powerfully plead for truth and righteousness. In the pursuit of the duties of his office, the minister may from time to time be under the necessity of giving expression to views at variance with the views of some, or even many, members of the congregation. Far from such difference proving the pulpit to be in the wrong, it may be, and oftimes is, found to signify that the pulpit has done its duty in calling evil evil and good good, in abhorring the moral wrong of putting light for darkness and darkness for light, and in scorning to limit itself to the utterance of what the prophet has styled "smooth things," lest variance of views arise. Too great a dread there may be of secession on the part of some members of a congregation, for, after all, difference and disquiet, even schism at the worst, are not so much to be feared as that attitude of the pulpit which never provokes dissent because it is cautious rather than courageous, peace-loving rather than prophetic, time-serving rather than right-serving. The minister is not to be the spokesman of the congregation, not the message-bearer of the congregation, but the bearer of a message to the congregation. What the contents of that message shall be, must be left to the conscience and understanding and loyalty of him in whom a congregation places sufficient confidence to elect him to minister to it.

In the course of the conferences held between the committee and the writer, it was urged that the pulpit has no right to demand exemption from criticism. The minister in Israel does not regard his utterance as infallible. No minister will refuse to correct an opinion—though he will take the utmost pains to achieve correctness in substance and form before speaking—when reasons are advanced to convince him of his error. Nor will he fail to welcome criticism and invite difference of opinion to the end that truth may be subserved.... To declare that in the event of a conflict of irreconcilable views between the minister and the board of trustees, it is the minister who must yield and not the board, is to assert the right not to criticise the pulpit, but to silence its occupant, and, above all, to imply that the board of trustees are always sure to be in the right, or else that the convictions of the board of trustees shall stand, whether right or wrong, and that the minister must acquiesce in these convictions, right or wrong, or else exercise the "option" and "privilege" of resigning.

The Jewish minister, I repeat, does not speak ex cathedra, and his views are not supposed to have a binding force upon the congregation to which he ministers. He is to express his convictions on any subject that comes within the purview of religion and ethics, but these convictions do not purport to constitute a creed or dogma to which a congregation must in whole or in part subscribe. But the board of trustees asserts the right to define and to formulate the views in which the rabbi must acquiesce, or, failing to acquiesce therein, resign. . . . Not only is the rabbi expected to sign away his present independence, but to mortgage his intellectual and moral liberty for the future. Stated in briefest possible terms, the rabbi is asked to subscribe to a statement of present and future convictions of the board of trustees. The demand is put forth that he subscribe to a blank page the contents of which are to be determined, not on the basis of his understanding of and loyalty to the teachings of his religion, but by "the views of the board of trustees." This is indeed to attempt to rob the pulpit of every vestige of freedom and independence. I am asked to point the way, and my hands are tied; I am asked to go before and my feet are fettered. . . .

If I could bring myself to accept a call to the pulpit of Temple Emanu-El upon such terms, and this is unthinkable, the board of trustees would never find it necessary to call upon me to surrender my convictions, for assent on my part to the stipulation, "the pulpit shall always be subject to, and under the control of, the board of trustees," would involve such a sacrifice of principles as would leave me no convictions worthy of the name to surrender at any subsequent behest of the board of trustees. It is equally meaningless to declare that "in the past this has never led to any friction between our rabbis and our board of trustees." Where a rabbi is reduced to the choice of acquiescence in views, right or wrong, because held by the board of trustees, or of silence, friction is impossible. The absence of friction in the past between the rabbis and the board of trustees of Temple Emanu-El proves that either the pulpit has been circumspect or that it has been so effectually muzzled that even protest was impossible on the part of an occupant who had subscribed to such conditions. A third possibility obtains—that the board of trustees has had the forbearance of the angels with the occupants of the pulpit insofar as they have not abused the power which they claim as their own. As for the forbearance of angels, which has possibly been theirs, I wish to make clear that I would not deliver my conscience into the keeping of the angels. My conscience is my own.

Finally, to hold that the subjection of the pulpit to, and its control by, the board of trustees is a written or unwritten law of the congregation is to maintain that the pulpit of Emanu-El never has been free, and this, I am sure, does not accord with the memories that still remain alive in me and in others of high-minded, independent, revered teachers who have occupied that pulpit. One of the former occupants I have intimately known, and were he living today he would repudiate the claim that he had for many years been the occupant of a pulpit which was not free.

I have sought to do you the justice of helping you to realize the seriousness of the situation which you face. This situation, I believe, you have not planned; into it you have, however, permitted yourselves to drift. That this appeal to the spirit of my people at its highest shall not have been made in vain is my hope, for the sake of our religion, which a free pulpit alone can truly serve.

I am,

> FAITHFULLY YOURS,
> STEPHEN S. WISE

Only two things remained, in a sense equally difficult: To take leave of Oregon with all its precious associations and memories was the first. That was most difficult, for in the six years of residence in Oregon I had come to love the state and its people. The second was to move on to New York. This I did in order to establish the Free Synagogue, which some months ago celebrated the forty-second anniversary of its founding.

A somewhat amusing postscript remains to be added. Twenty years later, the houses adjacent to the synagogue were occupied by that excellent pioneering, progressive Walden School. The little children were wont to play upon a second-story roof near my study in the adjoining house. One day they were particularly boisterous.

I called down, "Children, would you try to be just a little less noisy? I have a meeting in my study." The noise subsided slightly. A few moments passed, and the children were a little more noisy than before. I went to the window overlooking the playground and called down, not too sternly, "Boys and girls, I beg you to be a little more quiet at your play."

Suddenly a girlish voice cried out, "My grandfather could not muzzle you, and you are not going to muzzle us." I was startled by the reminiscence of an incident of long ago. Sometime later, the child's father, the distinguished lawyer and educator James Marshall, elder son of Louis Marshall, said to me, "The little girl who called out to you, 'You are not going to muzzle us,' was my daughter." Thus again out of the mouths of babes and sucklings!

Thus far I have dealt only with the outward circumstances which marked the founding of the Free Synagogue in 1906– 1907. I had half resolved to found a Free Synagogue even before my series of "trial sermons" before the Temple Emanu-El. The task proved more difficult than I had foreseen. I soon found myself facing a rather wide, if not deep-seated, hostility on the part of temple and synagogue groups within the community. The hostility sometimes verged upon the vulgarity of abuse, as in the case of one of the so-called leading rabbis of New York, who described the Free Synagogue in its earliest days as "a hall, with an orator, an audience, and a pitcher of ice water." Orator was meant to be a contemptuous substitute for preacher. Hall it really was, first in fact the Hudson Theatre by the kindness of its owner, Henry B. Harris, and after that the Universalist Church of our Father on West 81st Street for two years. Thereafter we entered into and for thirty years, 1910–1940, occupied Carnegie Hall in succession to

Felix Adler, who with the Society for Ethical Culture, had been its tenant from its erection in 1892 until 1910.

An unexpectedly hospitable response greeted my first addresses or lectures. Some supporters, I do not doubt after all these years, were attracted by the mere novelty of the undertaking—David, challenging, without wishing to slay, the Goliath (of a synagogue) of the Philistines. Perhaps the daring of a still young Rabbi (of thirty-two years) to found single handed, a synagogue organization awakened some admiration for the proposal and its author.

Among these supporters were such as were appealed to by the vitality and freshness of the venture, seeing that there had been nothing new and vital in American synagogue life for a generation. Many of them wondered at the vigor and directness of my Jewish affirmations and my still more Jewish self-affirmation. I made clear beyond all doubt that the Free Synagogue would never become a retreat or asylum for fainthearted and pusillanimous Jews, that it was to be wholly, unequivocally a Jewish adventure, that it would be deeply, unreservedly, and even rejoicingly Jewish. In my first address delivered in January 1907, I asked the question: What is a Free Synagogue, and answered:

> A Jewish society, for I am a Jew, a Jewish teacher. The Free Synagogue is not to be an indirect or circuitous avenue of approach to Unitarianism; it is not to be a society for the gradual conversion of Jewish men or women to any form of Christianity. We mean to be vitally, intensely, unequivocally Jewish. Jews who would not be Jews, will find no place in the Free Synagogue, for we, its founders, wish to be not less Jewish but more Jewish in the highest and noblest sense of the term.

Underlying, in truth inspiring, the liberalism of the Free Synagogue lay my own deep protest against the lifelessness of what had once been a great and living Jewish movement, the lifeblood of which had been pressed out as witnessed by the smugness characterizing New York temple Judaism. This had ceased to be Reform Judaism without even ever having become liberal. Its strength, such as it was, lay merely in its opposition to equally unvital Jewish Orthodoxy.

It was the pulseless, meagerly attended Sabbath service that moved me to establish within the Free Synagogue in the fall of 1907 a Sunday-morning service. This was not meant to replace the traditional Sabbath service but to supplement it for those who could not take part in the seventh-day Sabbath service. We did not seek to disestablish the Jewish Sabbath, as Emil Hirsch had frankly, even militantly, moved Chicago's Sinai to do. What we sought was to substitute the living voice of the Hebrew Prophets for the little-understood reading of the Hebrew Pentateuchal or Torah Scroll.

Herein we erred, for, as I have long seen, even the form of the Torah, the Scroll of the Law, had become too precious to the tradition of the synagogue to be lightly, indeed on any account, abolished. For years its use has become a part of traditional Sabbath and Holy Day services. I made a further mistake in taking it for granted that my unchanging Zionist position was fully understood by those who flocked to the services, not that I for a single moment concealed or minimized my Zionist loyalty. But I failed to make clear, as I ought to have done, the duality of my faith in liberalism as the (religious) expression of the Jewish spiritual genius and in Zionism as the faith and hope for the future of the Jewish people. I must frankly add that my sabbatical year, which came in 1913, meant my first visit to Palestine and resulted in the final and irrevocable decision that there was no other way than to rebuild the land and the people—land and people, people and land, reacting reciprocally, the land rebuilding the people, the people recreating the land.

To return to the persons and groups warmest and eagerest in welcoming the Free Synagogue, the largest number of its adherents was made up of such as had not only been estranged but actually had come to feel repelled by the unvital character of temple and synagogue institutionalism and were trembling on the edge of come-outism. It was such Jews, quite a few members of the secular, withal spiritual, Society for Ethical Culture, whom the prophetic mood of the Free Synagogue recalled and regained for positive relation once again to the faith of their fathers.

Many of these were not merely flirting with but closely approaching the Ethical Society. This was true because of the great appeal of Felix Adler, who was the one prophetic Jewish voice in the life of the city, though even he seemed to fail to understand that in truth he was in his own generation in the authentic line of the Hebrew Prophets—Emerson in form, but his spirit that of Isaiah.

One further group was halted in its exit, those Jews who felt that the Unitarian Church, too, was monotheistic. That feeling was vastly reinforced by the attractive personality of a group of noted preachers of religion over two generations in the Unitarian pulpit of New York—Collyer, Wright, Williams, Slicer, Chadwick, Savage, Chapin, Hall, and most notably in my own day the second Theodore Parker of his own Communion, bravest of teachers, noblest among men, John Haynes Holmes.

To such as these, my clear and uncompromising Jewishness made appeal, plus the adventurous tale of a young, little-known rabbi out of the West, remembered if at all only as a Zionist protagonist, who had dared to refuse the premier Jewish pulpit of America.

Perhaps I have not thus far made wholly clear the principle on which the Free Synagogue rested or was to rest. It was the principle, as I saw it, of pulpit freedom, which, according to Mr. Marshall, had uniformly been denied to the men who stood in Emanu-El's pulpit. This denial had done most to make the American Jewish pulpit without significance save in the fewest of instances—Hirsch in Chicago—Sinai, and before him the most prophetic figure who has stood in an American Jewish pulpit—David Einhorn. He had been almost alone among American rabbis in braving the wrath of slavery's defenders in an almost wholly Southern community, Baltimore. My first and last words alike in my Portland congregation were the demand that its pulpit must remain free, and in truth its freedom had given me the strength to battle through a number of critical situations that had arisen during my six Oregon years. What I had named as the *sine qua non* of my acceptance of the Emanu-El pulpit was merely a restatement of my experience in the Far West congregation of Beth Israel.

One of the deepest satisfactions of my life has been to see that the Jewish pulpit is become free, that is to say as free as the men who stand in it will it to be, and that many younger men in the Christian ministry have generously acknowledged that they owe the freedom of their pulpits in part to the battle I once waged when I declared that a pulpit that is not free is without moral and spiritual meaning.

My second and not minor plea was that the synagogue must again become democratically managed and that there could be no synagogue democracy as long as the pews and dues system obtained. Both together introduced into what should have been the democratic fellowship of religious communion all the unlovely differentiations of the outer world—pews occupied by and reserved solely for their owners, and definite sums exacted from those who chose to be affiliated with synagogue or temple. Pews in a religious assembly thus became a purchasable and taxable commodity, and the best places—what ought to have been the places of honor—reserved for the possessing, never for those in humbler circumstances. We therefore introduced the system of unassigned pews, to which we added the concept and practice of voluntary and free contributions. Beyond all this, we sought to introduce the mood and manners of democracy into the traditional but almost forgotten democracy of the synagogue.

Not only was the pulpit to be free and unfettered and the pew untaxed and voluntary in its support but something more important than these, the synagogue was to be inwardly free, free in its innermost ideals and aspirations, free to follow the high traditions of its prophetic genius. This was the beginning of my never ending revolt against that reform which had become formal and lifeless, which, after having long fought orthodoxy, had with the years become no less unvital than orthodoxy, without evoking the loyalty that the rich and traditional beauty of the Synagogue at its best was still capable of commanding.

I felt and feel that neither conformity nor reformism is the secret of Synagogue power, but solely its right to develop with such freedom as is the guardian and guarantee of the strength of progress. The synagogue can never forswear or forfeit that free development and unhindered growth that, apart from and above reform and orthodoxy, has been the quintessence of its genius. If I have a regret in relation to the launching of the Free Synagogue, it is that its earliest appeal rested too much on unessential aspects of its program, the Sunday service, the substitution of English and voluntary prayers for the Hebrew liturgy with its undeniable majesty somewhat marred, alas, by repetitiousness.

Yet another aspect of the Free Synagogue movement became of high importance. I had felt from the beginning that a synagogue should be more than a gathering of divine worshipers and that within the synagogue's life worship should be translated into collective and organized human service. I could not abide the reproach that in most synagogues social service is left to the sisterhoods when these do not limit themselves to the meeting of mortgage interest, as if the wise and true care of the needy bore no relation to brotherhood and brotherliness.

I called Rabbi Sidney E. Goldstein, then the assistant superintendent of Mt. Sinai Hospital, to become the head of the Social Service Division of the synagogue. He shared my views and we proceeded to put them into practice, beginning with the service of our volunteer synagogue members among Jewish patients at Bellevue Hospital and later Lebanon. This formula was continued throughout forty fruitful years. Notable among the contributions of the Social Service Division throughout a generation was the service among the tuberculous of Bellevue and later Montefiore, out of which, with our help, there grew the factory for the tuberculous with its opportunity for part-time employment under medical supervision and our very special and socially enlightened service in the field of mental hygiene at Bellevue.

From the beginning, our plans with relation to social service as a part of the synagogue life had met with the approval of the social-service leaders, such as Dr. Lee K. Frankel, Homer Folks, happily still among the living, then and up to recently secretary of the State Charities Aid Association, and later Frankel's successor, Dr. Solomon Loewenstein. The Social Service Division formally began its work and among those to speed it on its way was Jacob Schiff, who said:

> The word of God heard in the Synagogue becomes of value only if it is carried into everyday life. This is so well understood that it sounds like a commonplace to repeat it. And still how few in daily life practice this! How few stop to consider how egotistical are their lives, and that most of their acts, unknown to themselves, are done for their own personal comfort.
>
> There is, perhaps, no more cruel principle, even though it be inexorable, than that upon which, as Herbert Spencer has expressed it, the world rests, "the survival of the fittest." Because of this we should feel that duty calls us to step in and be of help to those who are left behind in the race by reason of this inexorable rule. These we meet everywhere,—in our families, among our acquaintances, in the pursuit of our daily vocations, and we so often pass them without taking notice.
>
> In this large community how many need us, to how many can we be useful! It need not only be the sick and the needy who perhaps more readily excite our compassion, to whom service can be rendered in many forms. To every one of our fellow-citizens, through work for the municipality, to the dependent classes, through cooperation in movements for the benefit of the dwellers in tenements, to the immigrant, to the delinquent, to numberless others who need us and to whom we can become of service.

Social Service is service to the very society of which we form an integral part, to which we owe a constant duty and in rendering service of value to society, we bestow the greatest benefit upon ourselves. It is in this spirit of benefiting all who need you, that I wish you Godspeed in the work of Social Service which you are about to inaugurate. If you achieve success therein, as I doubt not you will, you will only the more largely increase the claim for recognition of the movement which your self-sacrificing leader has taken up with so much inspiring enthusiasm.

But the story of the founding of the Free Synagogue does not tell the whole tale. Within a year thereafter many requests came to me to found a Free Synagogue branch on the East Side. These requests were fortified by a meeting held at the Henry Street Settlement, suggested, if not called, by Lillian Wald, a meeting for the most part of young people under Henry Street Settlement inspiration. That meeting did much to convince me that it was my duty as well as privilege to bring the teaching and influence of the Free Synagogue not only to the favored and possessing groups but to the masses, who had not forsaken their Orthodox Jewish moorings and yet were eager in the midst of their humbler milieu to hear the word and the message of an intensely loyal Jewish liberal. We found a meeting place, namely, Clinton Hall near Grand Street, for Sabbath Eve services, and we conjoined with this a religious school to provide a pleasant and friendly meeting place for young people, who were all but compelled to find their social life amid places unfit for the young intellectuals of the East Side.

Here a difficulty arose that was bound up with the generous spirit and good will of Mr. Schiff. It was he who, soon after I returned to New York from Oregon, made the proposal that instead of founding a synagogue in the center of the city I go to the crowded East Side Jewish district and there establish and conduct a Downtown East Side Free Synagogue. For two reasons I found it necessary to decline the offer, which included a budget large enough to maintain a planned program of such synagogue activities as I visioned, without calling on me to perform the painful task of securing the needed funds.

First, I knew that the East Side Jews had in no wise been taken into the counsel of the New York Jewish community. East Siders were still regarded, a full generation after their fathers' arrival in this country, as beneficiaries, whom "uptown" and its charities had once served and might again be called upon to serve. East Side Jewry was in no real sense consulted with respect to Jewish problems, great or small. Counsel was given, asked or unasked; decisions were taken; consultation there was practically none. I felt at once that I would place myself in an intolerable, indeed inexplicable, situation if I preached and conducted religious services exclusively for the masses, the ill to do. This would be doubly true if it were known, as I would insist that it should be known, that the services were subventioned by the well to do, even though the subsidy should come from one of large substance who was a man of deep, traditional Jewish piety. Mr. Schiff, whose judgment was rarely questioned, whose generosity was still more rarely rejected, agreed with some reluctance.

The East Side services were held regularly on the Sabbath Eve with a crowded attendance, made up for the most part of the sons and daughters of conservative and orthodox families, which probably looked a little askance at a service conducted in English by a rabbi quite frankly liberal, who did not wear the traditional cap. As for that cap, it would have been the part of wisdom and conciliatoriness to have worn it. To have done so would have violated no personal conviction; not to wear it offended many of the older generation, whose children in that case attended the service without the approval of their parents.

No man could have preached to a more finely intelligent group, deeply concerned about Jewish and general problems, religious, racial, political. Some years later it was suggested to me that the Downtown Branch of the work was unnecessary. I frankly placed the question before the Executive Committee of the East Side Free Synagogue. Their response was reassuring and heartwarming not only to me but to my associates ir this pioneer work:

NEW YORK, MARCH 23, 191!

DEAR DR. WISE:

It is our earnest hope and wish that the Free Synagogue wil continue its work on the East Side. A very wide gap would be left here if the Free Synagogue should remove its beauty and inspiration from the life of the Downtown people. More people than we can even imagine have come under the influence of the Free Synagogue, although these people are not consciously aware of it their lives have been filled with beauty and kindliness to ward their fellowmen as a result of this influence. We hope and pray that the Free Synagogue may long continue its beneficent work, doing true Social Service Work, not merely almsgiving. . .

We, who have been interested in the work from the very begin ning, feel that the Free Synagogue is constantly appealing to a larger number of people Downtown day by day. The results of such work as you are doing cannot be felt definitely within a year or two or three, but needs years to build it up and show something really tangible in results obtained. But the influence is constantly at work, and will bring the results aimed for surely

SINCERELY YOURS,

[signed] CELIA HENTEL

To this day, after nearly forty years, I meet in every part of the country with men and women who tell me of regular at- tendance at the Clinton Hall services of the Free Synagogue of long ago. Among these are some of the Jewish leaders and scholars, of our time—to name only one among them, the learned, the brilliant Dr. Solomon Goldman of Chicago.

It might by way of heartening be told for the benefit of younger ministerial pioneers that the Free Synagogue begar with no more than forty or fifty members in April, 1907, and that I accepted no salary for the first year and the sum of three thousand dollars in the second year. Henry Morgenthau, Sr.

Speaking at a Liberty Loan rally at the Sub-Treasury, Wall Street, New York City, in 1918.

With Nathan Straus, Sr., Justice Louis D. Brandeis, and James Waterman Wise after World War I

Abram I. Elkus, Adolph Lewisohn, Oscar S. Straus, Charles E. Bloch, Joseph M. Levine, were among my cofounders, some of them retaining their temple or Ethical Society membership, for I laid down the rule that no one should forsake his religious affiliations in order to join us.

Morgenthau became and for a number of years remained the helpful and generous president of the synagogue. After his return from Turkey, Morgenthau took a strong anti-Zionist position. On this issue he broke with the Free Synagogue after years, I must repeat, of most generous helpfulness. His ill will to Zionism was quickened by his and Louis Marshall's resentment against the advent to the leadership of Zionism, and in a sense of the American Jewish community, of one who had long been alienated and self-exiled from Jewish life. Such Jewish leadership Louis Brandeis never dreamed of claiming, but once he appeared on the Jewish scene Jewry swiftly claimed him as its leader.

I owe it to myself to add that the personal relations of Morgenthau and myself remained unchanged to the end of his many years. Glad and blessed and full of honors in many ways was his life, but above all blessed in the honor and distinction of his son, Henry Morgenthau, Jr., as a servant of the Republic through virtually all the years of the presidency of Roosevelt— and by virtue of his dedicated and untiring leadership of the 1947 and 1948 United Jewish Appeal for the largest sums ever secured by a world Jewish organization.

Of one incident, and more than incident, in the early history of the Free Synagogue I must tell. I had been deeply impressed by what I had read, and above all by what Dr. Theodor Herzl had told me in 1898 of the Czech leader Dr. Thomas G. Masaryk and his magnificently courageous defense of a wretched young Jew of Slovakia, who had violated and slain a non-Jewish girl. Hilsner was his name, and, beyond Polna—the scene of his crime and prosecution—nothing more would have been heard of the case had it not been for the charge that was bruited about, namely, that it was "ritual murder" which Hilsner had committed. That hideous charge sufficed to bring to his defense Dr. Masaryk, professor of the University of Prague and representative of the then Bohemia in the Austrian Reichsrath or Parliament. Masaryk took no issue with the prosecution but insisted solely, as other great teachers and scholars in similar cases have done before him, that there could be no such thing as "ritual murder" by a Jew. But the makers of the hideous charge succeeded in arousing the population against Masaryk. The result was that he was made to forfeit his chair at the University, and his seat in the Austrian Parliament was canceled.

Nearly a decade later, Dr. Masaryk came to America to meet his wife's family, the Garrigues, and to keep alive Czech sentiment for national independence. The first Sunday morning services of the autumn of 1907 I invited him to occupy the pulpit of the Free Synagogue. His German speech was far from clear, and the story of Hilsner, alas, too few had known or after a decade remembered. But he himself left an indelible impression of greatness.

We did not meet again until the World War—I little dreaming that he would become one of the world's great liberators, his country's Washington. The greatest tribute to him was yielded not by his people's love or by the world's admiration, but by Hitler's fear. Though Nazism had no shrine and though Hitler flayed and seared Masaryk's successor, President Benes, Hitler did not dare to lay profaning hand upon Czechoslovakia while Masaryk lived. I saw him often during the period when he was appealing for support of a free and independent Czechoslovakia. He was one of two men who made the deepest appeal to President Wilson, the other being that great artist in the realm of music, Paderewski. Whatever their present or future fate, Poland and Czechoslovakia owe more than they will ever know to these two emissaries, each unique in his way, the one a wizard of the piano, the other a veritable emancipator of long-enslaved people.

My interest in Czechoslovakia was so obvious that it is not unfitting to tell of one other offer or opportunity of political service. Shortly after the war Justice Brandeis received an inquiry from Masaryk to the following effect: "Could and would Rabbi Wise be ready to accept an invitation from the newly established government of Czechoslovakia to serve for a time as administrator of Jewish affairs?" The invitation was most tempting, and I believe that Justice Brandeis would have been pleased by my acceptance.

I declined on several grounds: First, there was my disinclination to render service through the occupancy of a government office. Again, I felt that the Jews of Czechoslovakia, including the very old Jewish community of Moravia, whence my paternal ancestors had come to Hungary two centuries earlier, were entirely able to manage their own affairs without the intervention of an American rabbi even though he was a friend. It might well have been regarded as offensive to the whole Czechoslovakian Jewish community if an American Jew took it upon himself, even though he was known to be an old and helpful friend, to deal with the internal affairs of the Jewish community, with which that community was abundantly able to deal.

The very day that the political independence of Czechoslovakia was recognized, Masaryk turned to one of his adjutants, saying, "Now I am repaid for Polna." Without thought of self he dared all; without thought of self he had won all.

I have only to add that after forty years the Free Synagogue included within its anniversary celebration an address by the son of President Masaryk, acting as his country's representative to the United Nations. The address of Jan Masaryk was a deeply moving ethicopolitical appeal for human liberty which its hearers will never forget.

Czechoslovakia enjoyed years of glorious independence under Masaryk before being doomed to destruction by the Nazis. Poland's years under Paderewski and his successors were less glorious, and the nation was doomed by its own frenzied hyper-nationalism and its psychotic anti-Jewish racism. But these did not evoke the destructive wrath of Hitler as did the truly democratic union and spirit of Czechoslovakia. The land of Huss and Masaryk somehow will not long cease to be free.

VI

Pulpit and Politics

SHALL a minister, ought a minister go into politics? What are the reasons that make it unwise for a minister to go into politics? I have heard them given over and over again: "Politics and religion have nothing to do with each other; for the minister to go into politics leads to divisiveness; religion should deal with general principles and not their daily applications; the minister in politics is apt to go off into partisanship as he did in the work of the Anti-Saloon League and during the days of Prohibition fanaticism." The maxim of Jesus, "Render unto Caesar," was repeated over and over again to enforce this position, and too often it was joined in spirit with the phrase, "The poor ye have always with you."

I felt very early in my ministry the necessity and advantages of the minister going into politics. To me neither religion nor politics was remote or sequestered from life. Religion is a vision or ideal of life. Politics is a method, or *modus vivendi.* To say that the minister should not go into politics is to imply that ideal and reality are twain and alien. Politics is what it is because religion keeps out of it.

I am persuaded that the minister can go into politics without partisanship, without compromise. And most important, he must seek nothing for himself or his church, and accept nothing. Convinced that the ideals of religion, separated from their day-to-day application, were meaningless, I early entered into one area of controversy after another that many might call political, and which I recognized as part of the sociopolitical life of America. There were many state, national, and international issues in which I felt that as a minister of religion I had a place.

Throughout my life it seemed to me that all ministers of religion were for justice in principle, but too ready to be silent about injustice in practice. One of the dangers of all of us is that we are willing to fight for justice for ourselves alone, forgetting that justice will be for all or none. For me the supreme declaration of our Hebrew Bible was and remains: "Justice, Justice shalt thou pursue"—whether it be easy or hard, whether it be justice to white or black, Jew or Christian.

This conviction caused me as a young minister to seek out ways in which I could be of service to those who suffered injustice. In 1904, when I was in Oregon, the Mitchell-Kahn Bill was introduced in Congress by Senator John Hipple Mitchell of Oregon and Representative Julius Kahn of California. It was not an honest measure. Nominally designed to keep Chinese immigration at a minimum, in practice it was to deal with every Chinese as if he were a coolie or a criminal. The law was to be one of many sops to be thrown to the Cerberus of anti-Chinese and anti-Japanese prejudice. I spoke in earnest protest against it in my pulpit, doing this because I felt it my duty to take into the pulpit for consideration every problem of public life that involved a moral question.

As early as 1908, on the request of Harriet Stanton Blatch, I joined with a small group to secure the right to vote for women in the United States; and the battle to secure full citizenship for women was at times as exciting here in the United States as it was in England. Our suffragettes were not always treated with chivalry in the national capital any more than on the streets of New York, and men who supported them were subject to what now sound like rather amusing jibes that questioned our masculinity. I remember speaking to a very charming and wealthy lady in England, who summed up the mood there by saying that she wished Mrs. Pankhurst (leader of the suffrage movement in England) would shoot Lloyd George (too liberal) and then be hung for it! But we went on, and

SOMETHING DOING IN LITTLE OLD NEW YORK

CARTOON FROM DAILY OREGONIAN, 1903

eventually equal suffrage for women became part of our American Constitutional rights.

Again in 1914 the condition of the unemployed and the need for social, legislative, political action caused me to seek support for a commission bill to inquire into old age, sickness, and unemployment insurance—and the slow struggle for these measures became a part of my work as a minister of religion. On April 9, 1917, I saw Colonel House, to urge that our government enact legislation to provide adequate care for our enlisted men in the Army and Navy. The next day I followed it up with a letter in which I wrote:

> If this war is to be fought democratically, if the spirit of the nation is to be kept upon the high level to which President Wilson has summoned it, if there is to be no abatement of our democratic loyalties, then it should be understood at the outset that the care of the families of the enlisted men is not to be made a matter of private charity, but must be taken over by the government and dealt with in a national way.

While study, reading, conferences, and work with committees of citizens and experts were part of my own self-education and the day-to-day work I could do as a minister, I felt there was more that I should try to do in the world of politics. That was to use my voice—and to do so in no uncertain manner—to challenge or stir the conscience of men so as to force those with political power to correct social evils and abuses wherever I saw them. The application of the moral teachings of social justice, taken seriously, led me into many fields—always, however, closely related to the central theme of true religion.

So it was that in 1928 I did not preach in general terms of social justice, but I felt I had to lash out at both political parties in an address, "If I Were Writing the Democratic Platform in 1928":

> Our Party will never be trusted by wealth and privilege as is the Republican Party, which is much safer for power and privi-

lege.... In the matter of reduction and re-distribution of taxes, the representatives of our Party in Congress have vainly and for the most part unworthily sought to compete with the managers of the Republican Party. We have sought to be the deputy-agents of "Prosperity." "Prosperity" accepts no deputies; it insists upon its utterly trustworthy agent, the Republican Party. We are so fearful of annoying the few who will never trust the Democratic Party that we alienate the many who might and ought to trust our Party....

The whole sordid, shameless spectacle [Teapot Dome Scandal] grows out of the theory of Government which the Republican Party embodies, namely that prosperity means "growth in individual fortunes" and not the number of those who share the increase in the National Income. Hence the protection of industry and swollen fortunes and the utter neglect of the basic industry of the Nation, which is farming and not steel or aluminum. ... One may sympathize with the cry against overmuch interference on the part of Government with business. But the control of Government by business, which has come to pass in the current and preceding administrations is the most disheartening spectacle of a generation.

During the presidential campaign of 1928, when Al Smith opposed Herbert Hoover, the politicians did not leave religion in the churches or to the pulpits. Religion became the central issue despite high-sounding denials by some candidates. Instead of discussion of national problems, the forum of the national election became nothing more than a nationwide whispering gallery. The foulest of methods were used by those prepared to do anything short of lawlessness in order to prevent a son of the Roman Catholic Communion from becoming President of the United States. The Klan seemed to be revived in spirit without having been brought back to life in letter.

Here was an issue, both religious and ethical, to challenge every pulpit. Too many church leaders were silent, and some men who deplored the intense bigotry that came to the surface took the position that the Democratic candidate should have been wise enough not to accept the nomination lest the church

issue be injected into the campaign. This position was all but
identical with the counsel too often urged upon Jews, sometimes from without and usually from within the household of
Israel, that they must not do this or that, even though it be
right, lest the Jewish question be dragged into the foreground.
Such counsel I had always spurned for my own people because
it violated the dignity and self-respect of Jews as men and as
citizens of America. It was equally abhorrent to me when applied to Al Smith. Perhaps, because I had experienced the hurt
to my people of such counsel, I felt a special obligation to
speak out when it was addressed to another minority group:

> As for the counsel that no member of the Roman Catholic
> Church permit himself to be a candidate for highest office lest
> he drag the Church into politics, the answer to be made is, that,
> if that danger be ever-present, then the churches are in poli-
> tics, and it is just as well to know that the churches are in poli-
> tics, and that they are prepared to use their power in the most
> un-American of ways.

Some Protestant Christians, as well as some of my fellow
Jews, imagined it was needful to remind me of what my people
had suffered at the hands of the Roman Catholic Church in
other days and centuries. I was not unmindful of that. I could
not be. My answer was that, though I was a Jew, it was for me
to remember that America meant a new start in the life of the
world. If America was to mean to me nothing more than the
perpetuation of the past, then the promise of America would
come to nought.

Just as I fought the injection of religious bigotry and divisiveness into the political life of America—so too I opposed some
years later the all too successful efforts by both churches and
some synagogue groups to inject sectarianism into the public
schools of America. The teaching of sectarian religion in our
public schools or the separation of children by religious de-
nominations during school hours so that they may go to different nearby churches and synagogues not only leads to

divisiveness, but threatens one of the basic assurances of religious freedom in America, the absolute separation of church and state.

Hoover was elected in 1928, and the policy of government aiding the possessing classes with the alleged hope that such aid would trickle down to the masses became almost a state doctrine, while the numbers of unemployed and their suffering mounted. I felt forced to deal with unemployment because to me it was no mere economic problem, either recurrent or unavoidable—but also a moral problem.

Within my own lifetime I had witnessed five sieges of unemployment: 1893–1897, 1907, 1914–1915 (that siege was halted only by our sale of war munitions practically to the whole world), 1921–1922, and 1929 and after. I had seen the effect on men and women of the fear of unemployment, the fear of old age, the fear of poverty. We as a nation had done naught to allay the fear of unemployment, perhaps because of the notion that unemployment was a necessary concomitant, an indispensable item of the capitalistic system. As a teacher of religion and ethics I spoke from my pulpit on February 1, 1931:

> The unemployment disaster is the test of the present social order, of its basic justness, of its capacity to live. Men threaten that the unemployment tragedy, such as is now being enacted, is bound to be followed by Bolshevism. True it is that regularly recurrent unemployment, with all of the hardships and suffering and ultimate moral degradation as well as physical damage which it entails, is only another name for chaos. After chaos anything may happen, as everything happened after the chaos of Czarist dominion. Bolshevism will never be a substitute for orderly, reasonable, worth-while government. It will always be a danger to government that is no government, but rather a planless and chaotic industrial life which guarantees nothing more than rewards to a few and the denial of even the decencies of life to the many.
>
> Unemployment is a social or industrial disease, the gravest disease of our industrial organism. It is not unpreventable. Inso-

far as it is not unpreventable, it is an economic crime. Above all,
unemployment, from the viewpoint of human values, is a tragedy
of gigantic dimensions, comparable to the tragedy of war.

The disease, the crime, the tragedy have come to pass because
of planlessness. Men are planless because they are purposeless,
save for the purposeful, who think unemployment not too great
a price to pay for the social order as it is.

I then proposed certain steps as necessary and urged their
adoption with a minimum of delay if disaster were not to
overwhelm us:

1. Provision of immediate and adequate relief for the unemployed, with full recognition that because relief had not been
   planned in advance, we would now have to pay the price of
   wasteful and overlapping administration.

2. The adoption of unemployment insurance in order to provide
   reserve funds for unemployed wage-earners—recognizing,
   however, that such insurance was no panacea but rather an
   organized and relatively efficient form of relief in the nature
   of a mechanic's lien upon the funds of industry.

3. The development of public employment services, so that the
   scandalous and wasteful abuses of the private employment
   agencies should cease. And the introduction of true vocational
   guidance in industry so that there might be scientific engineer-
   ing of the human intake of industry as well as in the regulation of output.

4. The complete and planned revision of the technological side
   of industry so as to avert unemployment. All changes—including shorter hours of work, fewer days, higher wages—must be
   aimed at serving the greatest possible number of more than
   marginal consumers.

I added:

What is needed today is an expression of the deepest convictions and yearnings on the part of the unemployed, the tragic
army whose plight mocks yesterday's vulgar boast of American
prosperity for all. As long as government, whether of city, state

or country, will not speak and act for the unemployed, then these at last must speak for themselves. And my question today is whether it is not the duty of church and synagogue to speak for the unemployed and, best of all, to move or enable them to speak for themselves.

Soon after my return from Oregon to New York, I joined that fine group of men who founded the National Association for the Advancement of Colored People—so as to cast in my lot with those determined to fight against injustice to Negroes. In those days one found prejudice and sanctimonious justification of injustice to the Negro on all sides. I can still recall the campaign of a Southern "statesman" for the office of United States senator, his platform being the observance of the golden rule and the subjugation of the Negro. Was ever such miscegenation known before as the attempt to unite the observance of the golden rule and the subjugation of the Negro?

The motion-picture industry was employed in 1915 to incite hatred against and fear of the emancipation of the Negro in a vicious picture—*The Birth of a Nation*. At that time I spoke in bitterness and scorn not only against the perpetrators of this picture of hate but against the National Board of Censorship, which passed it for distribution. Here again the pulpit was challenged to speak out against the gravest of moral wrongdoing, the approval of a picture that divided the citizens of America, that evoked the lowest form of race hatred through inspiring fear. The support of censorship to avoid scenes in movies that might be regarded as against the ten commandments should have been vigorously applied to a picture that threatened the hopes of the Negro people for admission to the gate of American brotherhood. Censorship that barred petty wrongdoing from the scene and accepted, even approved, such a picture as *The Birth of a Nation*, seemed but to befog the moral values of the American people.

In those days, unhappily, economic discrimination was practiced by employers and organized labor alike. Despite my ardent support of the organized-labor movement, I felt it necessary to challenge their practices in this area. As a friend, I spoke to organized labor:

> Few tendencies in American life today are more menacing than the shutting out of the Negro toiler from the ranks of organized labor. In his own defense and protection, I would ask the American workingman not to commit the injustice of color discrimination. If the Negroes are to be deliberately and continuously shut out from the ranks of united, self-respecting toilers, the result will be to Cossackize the Negro race. They will be converted into an army of hirelings, bought and bribed from time to time to break down the strength and the dignity and the self-respect of the American toiler.
>
> Make the Negro a Cossack and his end will be tragic, but no less tragic will be the consequences to the American industrial democracy which will have wrought this deadly evil and terrible injustice to two races.

Discrimination of any kind is doubly damning—it damns the man who discriminates, and it damns the man discriminated against. No man can proclaim himself a superior and set out to prove his superiority by degrading the so-called inferior, without making himself a victim of the very degradation that he seeks to impose upon another.

As president of the American Jewish Congress I, therefore, did all that I could to support those gifted younger Jewish men who were eager as Jews and Americans to seek to break down the barriers of discrimination in America so as to deepen the meaning of democracy and extend its application to all Americans. It was a source of great pride to me when I went to Washington in 1944 to support the enactment of a permanent Fair Employment Practice Law, that I went not only as an American citizen, as a minister of religion, but also as the spokesman of the first national Jewish organization to take its stand in this battle for justice.

Then in the halls of Congress I faced some American legislators whose prejudices led them all too successfully to avoid their obligations to end discrimination in employment. I found covert anti-Semitism and overt anti-Negro sentiment.

After presenting the case for a permanent FEPC, I was faced by a barrage of questions, friendly and unfriendly.

> Congressman from Texas: You would take from the employer then the traditional freedom of choice that employers have had in this country for 300 years of selecting their employees, those whom they feel, on the basis of their own business experience, as a result of their business acumen and good judgment, would be more likely to make their investment a success; and you would leave the final determination of whether he denied a particular applicant a job on the ground of discrimination to the FEPC, a bureau sitting in Washington, is that correct?
>
> Congressman from Nebraska: Would not that be fascism?
>
> Congressman from Texas: Would not that be fascism of the first order?
>
> I answered: It would be fascism to place success in industrial investment above life and equality of industrial opportunity for Americans irrespective of race. You will forgive me for saying— one speaks with very great respect to a member of the House of Representatives—but I do not feel that your question is fairly put. You assume that the supremely important thing in America is to give to the employer the right of choice, of discrimination in the matter of choosing employees. My own position as an American, although I am not a member of Congress—is that no fundamental right of that employer is violated because the Government steps in and says, "You shall not deny opportunity of employment to a man because he happens to be of the race of Jesus Christ and Peter and Paul and John and Mary, or because he happens to have a skin the color of which is different from your own." The American democracy, which I take seriously, perhaps because I am not a native American, because I lived the first year of my life in another land—the American democracy is not concerned primarily with the right of a man to exercise an arbitrary and capricious choice among the people whom he seeks to employ, but is concerned with the right of every American to have equality of opportunity in order that he may live and labor, in order that he may labor so that he may live.

Perhaps I am an old-fashioned person, whose concept of ethics belongs in the nineteenth century. I hope not. But I still can find no truer, finer summing up of the role of the minister in politics than in the words of Theodore Parker:

> Men say that religion has nothing to do with politics. They mean that morality has nothing to do with politics; that in making and administering the laws, no consideration is to be had of charity, truth, justice or common honesty.
>
> ... Men in pulpits say that the minister should have nothing to do with politics. They mean that he should never preach in favor of good laws or against wicked ones, never set forth the great principles of morality which underlie the welfare of the States, never point out measures to embody and apply mere principles; and never, never expose the false principles and wicked measures which would lead the community to ruin. ...
>
> A church should be the means of reforming the world. It should therefore bring up the sentiments, the ideas, the actions of the times, and judge them by the universal standard. If there is a public sin in the land, if a lie inside the State, let the Church give the alarm. Here let no false idea or false action of the public go without exposure and rebuke. And let no noble heroism of the times, and no noble man, pass by without due honor. In this way a church shall be a society for the promotion of the public weal.

VII

The Art of Speaking

IN view of my long-time experience in the art of preaching and public speaking, I have often been asked by aspirants in that field to give them some rules or prescriptions. The truth is "there ain't none." Or, if there are, I have not learned or even heard of them. I can do no more than repeat suggestions, rather than rules which, for more than a quarter of a century I have offered to incipient preachers and public speakers—and tried to follow myself; (1) Have something to say. (2) Believe in what you are going to say. (3) Say it clearly and without fear. As to the first, I am not interested in how to say something, but in how to have something to say. Homes and colleges and universities must be the chief helpers, not teachers of elocution or rhetoric. Reading is supremely important. But thinking and knowing are even more important than reading. And the least thing that reading is meant to do is to supply plums for quotation. I attach great importance to reading, as I have said, not for the sake of quotation-mongering or showing off, but for the sake of self-enrichment—I had almost said self-ennoblement. It may be very old-fashioned on my part, but when in my own religious school I have seen students poring over rather ephemeral columnists, I have at times rudely asked them, "When did you last read Plato?" or "When did you last read Bachya?" who is a medieval ethical philosopher.

If a man has something to say, I would add one very prudent word of counsel, which I have repeatedly given to my

own class in preaching. It is not original; it stems from Isaac
M. Wise, the organizer of American Jewry and the founder of
some of its great institutions. "When you start, begin. When you
are finished, stop." Never were two wiser rules for public speaking laid down—to start a-flying when one begins, and not to
linger unduly at the close. I must frankly add that only the
guiltiest of speakers in this respect could speak with as much
feeling as I do.

As to the second, nothing is quite as important in public
speaking as to believe in what you are going to say, assuming
that you are not dealing with trivia. I am not even thinking
of what Emerson wrote—namely, that what you are speaks
more loudly than what you say. Oh, that, for their own sakes,
speakers generally—preachers most especially—would understand that the most likely reaction of their hearers is, "Does he
mean it?" "Does he believe what he is saying?" "Is he sincere?"
And if doubts arise and, above all, persist, the speaker is lost.
Noise and vehemence, far from proving and achieving sincerity,
are ordinarily accepted as disproof thereof.

As to the third, say it clearly and without fear. My father, one
of the best of preachers, often repeated for my benefit a simple,
wholesome rule, particularly as he put it when he felt that,
as a very young man, I was trying to speak with an Episcopalian singsong or twang: *"Sprich wie der Schnabel Dir gewach-
sen ist,"* "Talk the way your beak grows." Be yourself when
you speak; don't imitate anyone else. There are too many
imitators of Fosdick and Holmes among younger men in the
pulpit. Whenever I came upon a youth foolish enough to try
to imitate my manner of public speaking, I would warn him,
"One of me is quite enough, perhaps too many. Be yourself."
I remember having heard that, at the installation of the Reverend Theodore Williams in the Unitarian Church of the great
Dr. Bellows, every speaker, save the last, urged Williams to
follow in the footsteps or to cherish the ideals of his great
predecessor. Robert Collyer spoke more wisely. He said, "Everyone who has spoken has bidden you to be like Dr. Bellows.

You cannot and you will not be like him. Be yourself. Be the best Theodore Williams you know how to be".

Whenever young and would-be preachers have lamented to me, "I have such a poor voice," I have been tempted to answer, "Better a poor voice with something to say than to be possessed, as too many preachers and some so-called orators are, of *vox et praeterea nihil*." Nothing can be more deadly to a public speaker, to say nothing of his audience, than to be endowed—I had almost said cursed—with the oft fatal gift of mellifluousness. A voice of honey is no substitute for the salt of thought. If a man who aspires to be a public speaker, whatever his calling, is handicapped by an unpleasant or ineffective manner of speech, he can if he chooses make that handicap good or even more than neutralize it by wide reading, deep study, clear thinking, brave speaking—that is to say, by speaking with a sense of respect for his subject, his audience, himself. Voice and gesticulation may count but not for too much. Bryan's voice did not make him a great orator, though he had the former and was the latter. He was able among other things to poke fun at himself. I remember hearing him at a Chautauqua tent meeting in 1914 when he said, "Some people object to my being on the Chautauqua platform. I gave the American people three chances to take me off the Chautauqua platform. They preferred to have me remain on it."

Sometimes I have been asked to name the great or greatest speeches I have heard. The thing to be borne in mind is the context—that is, the circumstance—in which a speech is made. In every case, circumstance, the occasion, the setting was at least as important as the character or distinction or power of the utterance. The most thrilling speech I have ever heard, all things considered, was that of former Secretary of War Newton D. Baker, at the Democratic National Convention of July, 1924, at Madison Square Garden. Baker, as chairman of the Resolutions Committee of the convention, had fought long and strenuously to have a pro-League-of-Nations plank adopted as a part of the platform. The delegates were rather wary, be-

cause they remembered their crushing defeat of 1920 under
the banner of Cox and Roosevelt and the banner of the League
of Nations, which these candidates upheld. Baker made an
appeal in its behalf. It was far more than ordinary eloquence
that fell from his lips. Patiently and overwhelmingly he
evoked the memory of his chief, Woodrow Wilson. It was more
than invocation; it was an eerie evocation of the dead, an
unrivaled effort to move the Democratic hosts and their chief-
tains to battle again under his banner. Wilson lived. He rose
before us, but the hearers rose neither to Wilson, living and
standing and battling once again in their presence, nor did
they rise to Baker. It was an unforgettable experience, but
the convention members, dreading defeat beyond all else and
lured by the expediencies of hate, were not equal to the demand laid upon their soul by Wilson's great disciple.

In some ways the most moving speech I ever heard was
that of Henry Wallace at the 1944 Democratic Convention in
Chicago. Wallace had sought to secure a renomination for
the office of vice-president, and a goodly number of delegates
to the Chicago Democratic Convention were pledged to him.
However, it happened that a number of Democratic bosses
made President Roosevelt feel that Wallace would not add
strength to the ticket and that, on the contrary, he might
alienate certain groups whose votes would be needed at the
election. President Roosevelt yielded—how reluctantly we do
not know—and it became clear that Senator Truman would be
the nominee in the place of Wallace. Late in the afternoon on
the eve of the nomination of President Roosevelt, Vice-President Wallace arose and made the speech that has become a
matter of political history. In the first place, it was moving in
its generosity. Wallace knew that he had been turned down,
that he would be denied the renomination, and yet he spoke
of President Roosevelt as if he were certain of his own renomination.

But the most thrilling aspect of the address was not its

generosity, but rather its defiance of the Southern delegates. He pulled them out of their seats, as it were, by the scruff of their necks and shook them until it seemed as if they must cry aloud for mercy. It was the bravest of speeches. Single-handed and on the eve of going down as a defeated would-be nominee, he faced the whole brood and breed of Southern delegates and thundered against them in terms that no one who heard that address will ever forget. The vice-presidency had been lost, but I felt as I listened to him that he had gained his own soul. The Southern delegates looked crestfallen and discomfited. There was some commotion among them, but no one among them dared openly to accept the challenge which the knightly Wallace had flung them.

. One of the most effective speakers I have ever heard on any platform is the first president of the state of Israel. Neither friend nor enemy would accuse Chaim Weizmann of eloquence in the normal sense of that term. His voice is ofttimes hoarse and throaty and even unpleasant to listen to. He has no grace nor manner of speaking. Slowly, awkwardly, he pursues an argument, making his case with almost scientific precision and sequence—always the master of his theme, rarely if ever deflected from moderate and restrained speech by frenzied approval or equally fanatical opposition. I have heard him in Zionist congresses score the most brilliant triumph, supporters, hecklers, opponents joining in tribute to his massive though for the most part unadorned power of public utterance. To sum it up, he knows his case, he makes the best possible use of folk lore and folk manner, with nothing to commend him to his hearers save his own intellectual weight, his salty speech, his command of the cause that for half a century has been his life.

In a very real sense President Woodrow Wilson was no orator, never overwhelming as more or mere silver-tongued speakers sometimes are or imagine themselves to be. Yet I heard him make two addresses, apart from his first inaugural, that stand out in memory after a generation. One was given in the spring of 1912, some months before the Baltimore Convention that nominated him. A group of his friends and supporters, including Henry Morgenthau, Robert Erskine Ely, and myself, had felt that the financial and industrial bigwigs, who were somehow assumed to be "agin him," should have a fair opportunity to hear and appraise him. This was arranged, as I recall, under the auspices of the League for Political Education. He spoke clearly and earnestly with unquailing forthrightness. He knew his audience did not approve the liberalism of his program, knew in a word that he was on trial in the sight and hearing of a group of men whose approval or disapproval might almost be decisive in the weeks prior to the convention. There was not the faintest hint or suggestion of retreat in either the manner or matter of his utterance. He spoke not as a candidate seeking approval, but as an unafraid teacher, as the uncompromising statesman. His hearers sat entranced, and when he had completed the simple outlines of his program, the audience burst into a sustained ovation, which showed that he had held and won an audience, indifferent at best, in sturdy opposition at worst.

If I had to single out a man who represents power, moving and overwhelming, without ever descending to the sensational, I should name the preacher of the Community Church. John Haynes Holmes is so transparently sincere that no one but an illiberal bigot or a bigoted illiberal could think of him or name him as sensational. The stuff in his bosom may be imperiling to certain interests that ought to be imperiled and overwhelmed, but he never stoops to artifice or to sensation. He rouses people with the power of his message.

In writing of John Haynes Holmes I must tell of something seemingly irrelevant. President Taft once asked me whether I knew his "summer Minister at Manchester, Robert Collyer." I answered that I knew and loved him and that when I went to Oregon to serve as rabbi, the only letter I took with me was from Robert Collyer to the spiritual father of Oregon, Thomas Lamb Eliot, cousin of President Eliot of Harvard. Thereupon I asked the President whether he knew the successor of Robert Collyer, my friend John Haynes Holmes.

He did not know Holmes. I ventured to suggest to him that sometime when in New York he go to the Church of the Messiah and hear Mr. Holmes preach. Quite early on a Sunday morning prior to the election of Woodrow Wilson, I had a most excited telephone call from Mr. Holmes in his always stentorian and slightly rasping voice. "Wise, you once asked President Taft to worship in my church. His secretary has just telephoned that the church keep a pew for the President".

I quite understood why Holmes was terribly disturbed, but calmly proceeded to inquire, "What of it?" "But, Wise, I am preaching on Tuesday's election and I shall urge the choice of Theodore Roosevelt." I could only answer, "You will say what you had planned to say, but be as gracious to President Taft as you can be." Mr. Holmes preached his sermon in favor of Roosevelt and certainly, by implication, against Taft and Wilson.

Shortly after the election, I met President Taft. He at once recalled my suggestion, and with one of his most delightful and broad guffaws he said, "I went to hear your friend, Holmes, the Sunday before election," and after another roar of uninhibited laughter he slyly said, "The only thing Holmes did not do for Teddy was to take up the collection!"

I have since been more careful in the matter of recommending preachers to presidents.

I cannot bow out this mighty preacher of righteousness, in whom Theodore Parker lives again, without telling that in the course of World War II, Roosevelt, who knew that Holmes and I were the closest of friends, asked of me, "What is the matter with your friend, Holmes?" Evidently he was referring to his antiwar speeches. "Does he not see that we had no other choice without losing our country and without the world losing human freedom?" I could only answer, "Holmes's conscience is his

highest law. Above all else, he cannot reconcile war with Christianity, that is with the teaching of Jesus. Holmes remains opposed to war." Roosevelt said no more. His only further comment, which was no comment, was a sign of wonderment.

Public speaking is not a trick, though some tricksters succeed
in public speaking. People sometimes ask about F.D.R.—
wherein lay the greatness of his speaking? The answer is simple
enough. His was a matchless combination. He was the hand-
somest of men, had the most mellifluous of voices, and his
speech was simple, unvarnished, and straightforward. And he
always had something to say. *"Mein Liebchen was willst du
noch mehr!"*

VIII

A Rabbinical Seminary Is Born

T HE least eventful and yet perhaps one of the
most significant years in my life was that in which I reached the
decision to found a rabbinical seminary, ultimately named the
Jewish Institute of Religion. I had for some years been speaking and preaching at universities throughout the land, and
from time to time young men had asked me whether they
could prepare themselves for the rabbinate under my guidance.
I had to reply in the negative and I usually proceeded to name
the Reform or Orthodox seminaries to which they could go.
Upon a number of occasions, such young men responded hesitantly, "I am not sure whether I am going to be Orthodox or
Reform. How then can I, who have not yet made my choice,
be expected to attend a seminary avowedly Orthodox or avowedly Reform?" Such response caused me to question the
validity of rigidly patterned seminaries.

Again, in founding branches of the Free Synagogue in a
number of communities, it became necessary to depend largely
upon young graduates of the Hebrew Union College or even
upon its undergraduate students. Among the former were the
present president of the Central Conference of American Rabbis, Reverend Doctor Abraham J. Feldman of Hartford, and
Lewis Browne, who later left what he came to feel was the
narrow path of the rabbinate for the broader highways of literature. My associate in the rabbinate of the Free Synagogue

since its founding, Dr. Sidney E. Goldstein, was a graduate of the Hebrew Union College, and he, too, felt that we should train the future leaders of the Free Synagogue and its branches. He also shared my insistence that in a seminary rabbinical students should be trained in social-service leadership, an aspect of rabbinical training uniformly neglected by the seminaries of a quarter of a century ago.

There were other and larger considerations which, after some years, finally moved me to take the initiative. I found that there were too few American-born young Jews who entered or felt called to the rabbinate. Cincinnati, site of the oldest of the American Jewish seminaries, had somehow ceased to be the large and vital Jewish center it had been in the earliest days of its great founder, Isaac M. Wise. With a Jewish population then, as now, of fewer than twenty thousand, it offered its students an inadequate experimental station. New York had uniquely become such a station, with its great Jewish population, made up of representatives of virtually every Jewish community on earth.

With the passing of Isaac Wise in 1901, Cincinnati's glory had largely departed. Only immovable buildings and local piety or patriotism had kept the college in Cincinnati. Its removal to Chicago and the placing of the college under the leadership of Rabbi Emil G. Hirsch, in connection with the University of Chicago, had been mooted only to be vetoed.

As for the Jewish Theological Seminary of New York, it was, or purported to be, Conservative with a leaning toward orthodoxy. Sabato Morais, who was born in Leghorn, had been its first, though not too active, president. He had been succeeded by the great Schechter, a Rumanian-born Jew, who assembled a faculty of learned and brilliant teachers.

As a result of my talks with young Jewish college graduates and undergraduates, I had come to see that these wished to prepare for the rabbinate under the direction of one active as an American rabbi. I refused to be deterred by reason of the seminaries then extant in the American Jewish community.

That community comprised nearly four million souls, and the German-speaking countries of Europe, including Hungary, with a Jewish population of fewer than two millions had supported five superior seminaries, which, in the order of their establishment, were Breslau, two in Berlin, Budapest, and Vienna.

There were other not wholly minor considerations that led to our decision. Students were admitted to the two chief American seminaries at a tender age—before, in any event, they were old enough or mentally mature enough to make a life commitment to Orthodox or Reform Judaism. As long ago as 1886 I remember a Hungarian compatriot of my father, Samuel Hertz, bringing to our home his two sons, Joseph, who after a generation came to serve as chief rabbi of Anglo-Jewry, and his older brother Emanuel, who later became noted as a Lincoln biographer. He asked my father, who was then a trustee since he was one of the founders of the Jewish Theological Seminary, what course he would recommend for his two young sons whom he could not afford to send even to such a free college as that of the city of New York. My father at once suggested that the lads be enrolled at the seminary, which granted every needy student a monthly subvention, I think, of twelve or fifteen dollars.

Such was the practice of the two seminaries, each accepting youths before entering college and sometimes, in Cincinnati, even in pre-high-school years. I had grown to feel that no man was fit to begin his theological studies until after receiving an adequate college education. Still more important, I felt and insisted that teachers and students alike must remain intellectually and spiritually free, that there should be no shackling of the minds to Orthodox or Reform dogmas. Finally, my plan rested on the premise that the teachers and students would be carefully and discriminately chosen.

I knew the Cincinnati Seminary well enough to understand that under its first two presidents, Wise and Kohler, it had shown a deep-seated intolerance of Zionist advocacy; especially

to Kohler, Zionism seemed an intolerable refutation of Reform
Judaism. But it never seemed to suggest itself to him that anti-
Zionism was a still graver refutation of the fundamentals of
Judaism. This intolerance came to a head in the early years
of the century when Professor Max L. Margolis, my one-time
teacher at Columbia, and other distinguished scholars, including Judah Leon Magnes, later of Hebrew University fame,
found it impossible to remain at Cincinnati.

The attitude of the Jewish Theological Seminary in New
York was likewise not wholly unimpeachable. President
Schechter was not quite an anti-Zionist, but his intimate association with Louis Marshall moved Schechter not so much
to intolerance of Zionism as to intolerance of Zionists—this,
of course, before Marshall's entrance into the Jewish Agency
for Palestine in 1929 and his subsequent complete reconcilia-
tion with all his people.

Basic to the founding of the institute were certain ideas—
in those humble days men held ideas and had barely heard of
ideologies. Those ideas we believed to be true and valid twenty-
five years ago. They remain true and valid today, though not
unaffected by the two and a half historic decades that have
passed. American Jewry had by 1920, when first we dreamed
our dream, become by half a century more tolerant and understanding and catholic than it had been in the seventies and
eighties! Reform Judaism had ceased to be horror to its enemies
and fetish to its followers. Orthodoxy and Conservatism had
become less intolerant and less sure of their uniquely redemp-
tive power. It had come to be recognized—in any event by us,
the founders of the Jewish Institute of Religion—that the old
differences and quarrels and even battles over creed were of
little moment by the side of the consciousness of the deepening
need of Jewishness. For us, Jewishness meant and means a sense
of oneness with our Jewish brothers in all lands and times,
whatever their circumstances, their so-called faith or unfaith.
Jewishness meant loyalty to historic Jewish ideals—spiritual,
moral, social, intellectual. Jewishness could only be perpetuated

through understanding and appreciation of the best that has been thought and said and done throughout thirty centuries and more of Jewish history. This Jewishness of life and loyalty was the bond that linked us alike with the storied centuries of the past and with our people's deathless hopes and dreams for the future.

We could not be unaware of the truth that schools of honorable and distinguished record for service obtained in New York and Cincinnati. Both alike seemed to us committed to an uncatholic sectarianism, which in both cases seemed survival of yesterday rather than prophecy of tomorrow. Wherefore, the founding of the Jewish Institute of Religion, in a community that was itself a Jewish cosmos.

In this spirit, without criticism of, or competition with, the Cincinnati college or the New York seminary, the institute began its work, in September, 1922. It has been blessed, if its president may say so, with a group of eminent teachers and a corps of admirable students and disciples. Over and above and beyond its honored faculty, the institute is proud to recall that it has been instrumental in bringing to its service for a term or terms scholars of such high renown as Israel Abrahams, George Foote Moore, Felix Perles, David Yellin, Ismar Elbogen, and Professors Gressman, Torrey, Sholem, Torczyner, and Diesendruck. These are in addition to its own notable faculty, this great company of scholars illustrating the truth that one of the offices of a rabbinical institution is to help men to pursue the richly rewarding career of learning and research in *Juedische Wissenschaft*.

Chief among the founders of the institute were the first two chairmen of the Board of Trustees: Dr. Lee K. Frankel, chemist by profession, one-time head of the United Hebrew Charities of New York, industrial consultant and ultimately, as an industrial statesman, vice-president of the Metropolitan Life Insurance Company of New York; and Julian W. Mack, United States Circuit Court judge, member of the Board of Overseers for several terms at Harvard University, and valiant proponent of Zionism at the side of Justice Louis D. Brandeis. With these two men, as with the last president of the institute, Judge Joseph M. Levine, it had become a passion to train men for the field of Jewish scholarship.

We were on the eve of beginning the work of the institute. We had succeeded in collecting enough funds to serve as the basis of the first two years of budgeting, thanks to Adolph Lewisohn, donor of the Lewisohn Stadium, Judge Abram I. Elkus, and Mrs. Bertha Guggenheimer, who generously underwrote the initial sums required. We had counted upon the Free Synagogue house, in process of building, as the first habitation of the institute, but its completion was delayed. We turned to Temple Israel—its rabbi, the beloved Dr. Maurice H. Harris, and its president, the Honorable Daniel P. Hays— and were generously granted the use of its rooms throughout the first academic term, by which time the synagogue house was completed and ready for institute occupancy. Provision had been made for joint tenancy by the synagogue and institute, thanks to the never ending generosity and hospitality of the Free Synagogue. There was at once established, with my own personal library and gifts of many books by Dr. Emil Hirsch, a library, which today contains more than sixty thousand books and pamphlets.

The greatest need of the institute remained to be met, securing the academic staff for the first years. In this, mine was the never failing help of an extraordinarily gifted scholar and life-long friend, Dr. George Alexander Kohut, who, because of his love for Jewish learning and his unique filial reverence for our teacher, Dr. Alexander Kohut, who compiled the *Aruch Completum,* became a veritable Maecenas of Jewish scholars the world over. In every way of friendship and counsel he facilitated this most important quest of all, that of securing members of the faculty. Upon reaching Berlin together, we had the interest and the help of one who modestly called himself "the maid of all Jewish work in Germany," the active head of the Berlin Juedische Hochschule, Dr. Ismar Elbogen, famed as

Jewish historian and liturgist. Dr. Elbogen had in advance arranged all necessary introductions. We went to Breslau and met with Dr. Felix Perles, chief rabbi of Koenigsberg. Upon coming to know these two fine scholars, I initiated the practice, continued by the institute for years, of inviting visiting scholars to teach.

These two learned Jews together with two Englishmen constituted the institute faculty for the first year. The latter were Dr. Israel Abrahams and Rabbi Harry Lewis of Toynbee Hall fame, whom Zangwill fitly immortalized in *Children of the Ghetto*. Abrahams was the Cambridge successor of Schechter, co-editor with Claude Montefiore of the first twenty invaluable columns of the *Jewish Quarterly Review*, long-time and foremost teacher in his day of Jews' College, the rabbinical seminary of England. The second Englishman became a resident in America although he remained an Englishman of Englishmen all his days, and as the end of his life drew near, he returned to England in order that he might be buried in English soil. Early in life he had gone from the West End to help and, above all, to serve in the East End at Toynbee Hall, the forerunner of Jane Addams' Hull House. He became the institute's first chaplain and remained at that post until his return to England.

The students of the first fifteen years will never forget the piety, beauty, and variety of the chapel services, always touched by his own devout and whimsical personality. When students would ask him for some help in coaching, he invariably replied, "Come any hour between six and eight in the morning." He actually succeeded in habituating some young men to early rising and study!

Thus the institute began. Recognizing my own obvious limitations, I refused to accept the post of presidency and for years served the institute, by my own choice, as its voluntary acting president. I thought, too, that such an attitude on my part would help to dispose of the ludicrous charge that I had founded the institute in order to be its president. The truth is that I offered the presidency successively to three men, each of whom, for reasons of his own, found it necessary to decline—first to Dr. Emil Hirsch of Chicago's Temple Sinai, whose most scholarly contributions as co-editor of the *Jewish Encyclopedia* have never been adequately appreciated. He could not accept my offer, he said, because of family reasons that weighed too heavily with him to make it possible for him to leave Chicago. He became and remained a staunch friend of the institute and its library, to which at his death a goodly part of his own library was presented by his learned son-in-law, Rabbi Gerson Levi. The library has been given his and his father's name, the Samuel and Emil G. Hirsch Library.

After that my associates and I felt that Israel Abrahams of Cambridge would be ideally suited for president. His ties with his country, however, and with his important work at Cambridge and in London were, as he felt, indissoluble. But for two years he remained an inspiring teacher and, together with Elbogen, Perles, and Kohut, had a large and important part in the shaping of the institute. He was the author of the first publication issued by the Institute, *The Glory of God*, a little volume of mystic beauty.

Twice the presidency was offered to another Jewish scholar and leader, Dr. Mordecai M. Kaplan, one of the finest creative minds of the American Jewish community. The institute had very good reason to feel that the offer would be accepted. But for reasons that have never quite come to light, Professor Kaplan, after a long and trying period, including weeks and even months of indecision, appeared to find it impossible to accept.

It was only some years later that the Board of Trustees insisted that I, its founder, become its president, after the office had thrice and oftener been refused by others.

The institute was enriched in its earlier years by a number of eminent visiting teachers and lecturers, including George Foote Moore of Harvard University, whose omniscience and stature alike had led to the nickname "Jehovah"; Professor Harry A.

Wolfson of Harvard, his younger Harvard student and colleague, a man of massive learning and scholarship, as witnessed by his recent work on Philo; Professor David Yellin, who brought to the student body the beauty and purity of his Palestinian Hebrew speech. Among the eminent men called upon to instruct the institute's students have been Professor Adolph Gressman of Berlin University; Professor Charles Torrey of Yale, Professor Charles Albright of Johns Hopkins University, Professor Gershon Sholem of the Hebrew University of Jerusalem, Rabbi Joshua Loth Liebman of Boston, whose lectures on religion and psychiatry, given by him at my suggestion and upon my urgent invitation, proved to be the forerunner of his extraordinary work, *Peace of Mind;* Reverend Doctor James Parkes, clergyman of the English Church, whose lectures, recently published by the Chicago University Press, are sure to prove of great value to students truly concerned with historical Christian-Jewish relationships.

Two men became the giants of the faculty. Of both I must make grateful and more than passing mention. One, Professor Chaim Tchernowitz, of widest European fame, was a member of the noted Odessa group of Jewish writers and scholars, which included Bialik, the poet, and Ahad Haam, already become Hebrew classics, and described by Tchernowitz in his recent autobiography. He brought to the institute the prestige of a great and beloved name, and his students, especially those well prepared, have come to cherish the teacher and the man.

Another great figure of the institute, almost from the beginning, was and is its long-time and beloved dean, Professor Henry Slonimsky. He is a truly great and inspiring teacher, beloved by faculty, trustees, and students alike. With all of them, including its president, he has been most closely and helpfully associated in shaping institute policies.

I must not fail to speak of the distinguished Jewish scholars whom the institute has from time to time invited to America and in turn prepared for other schools of learning: Professor Salo Baron of the Vienna Rabbinical Seminary, now professor at Columbia University; Julian Oberman of Hamburg University, now professor of Semitics at Yale; Sholom Spiegel, successor to Davidson in the Seminary; Zevi Diesendruck, eminent in philosophy and translator into matchless Hebrew of the Greek philosophical classics; Professor Ralph Marcus, now of Chicago University; and his father, Moses Marcus, a pious lay Jewish scholar of an earlier day.

Animated by the purpose to welcome within its walls teachers and students, who should alike be free, in teaching and learning, the Institute required no commitment of teacher or disciple save to communicate and master the fundamental and historic truths of Jewish life and letters. It welcomed students from all groups within Jewish life and trained rabbis for service in Reform, Orthodox, and Conservative congregations.

It may seem bizarre to mention that the Hebrew Union College leadership, through some of its local saints, lay and academic, vigorously attacked the institute upon the mere mention of its coming into existence. The then chairman of its Board of Governors wagered a hat that it would never open its doors! An appeal, which I initiated, that representatives of the institute and college meet to discuss methods of cooperation, short of absorption, was rejected. What lay back of the unwillingness to enter into anything savoring of negotiations was largely the unreadiness to parley with those known in Jewish life, as were Judge Mack and I, as active in the Zionist movement.

More than fifteen years later, Ralph Mack, chairman of the Hebrew Union College Board of Governors, acting largely under the inspiration of Rabbi James G. Heller of Cincinnati, proposed that the institute and the college meet to discuss questions of cooperation and even coordination. A series of meetings were held in a friendly spirit, but still to no avail. Two things then clearly stood in the way: (1) the unreadiness of the Hebrew Union College to accept liberalism in the place of too largely standardized Reform Judaism. From the institute's point of view Reform had had its day and at its worst had become so illiberal and static that it ceased utterly to accord with the dynamic spirit of the founders of Reform Judaism. (2) There was the threat of Zionism, which, though not part of the explicit program of the Jewish Institute of Religion, had become part of the thinking of ninety-five per cent and more of the nearly two hundred graduates of the Institute.

As I began to write this chapter, negotiations were under way for the third time looking to coordination, not merely cooperation, even to union, of the two schools, college and institute. I felt at once that such union could be effected at last, because the college had come under the leadership of the youthful and dynamic personality of its newly elected president, Dr. Nelson Glueck, who had served for many years in Palestine as gifted and creative head of the American School of Archaeology.

Some of the difficulties had finally been overcome. The college, in the utterance of its president at the Central Conference of American Rabbis' session at Montreal in 1946, virtually renounced anti-Zionism as a part of its program. I do not mean that in the curriculum of the college or in the union of the schools it should be declared that Judaism and Zionism are interchangeable terms, although for me they are, but rather that the anti-Zionist improvisations of Isaac Wise and the persistent anti-Zionist hostility of his successor, Kohler, will no longer be regarded as an article of faith by the conjoint school.

One thing more, perhaps most important of all. In the course of the earliest negotiations Dr. James Heller and, in more recent years, Dr. Maurice Eisendrath pointed out that, zealous reformer though he was, Isaac Wise had from the earliest days of the college insisted that it was to serve all American Jewry. not merely one wing or faction thereof. In effect, although Wise did not make use of the later Schechterism concerning "Catholic Israel," he was indeed broadly and definitely catholic as a Jew and, if one may make use of an inept term, a wholly nonsectarian Jew. He willed to unite as well as organize American Jewry.

Needless to make clear, the Jewish Institute of Religion, founded in a sense in protest against a non-Jewishly rampant sectarianism, could never be brought to part from its fundamental principle—that rabbinical seminaries must prepare men for service in the rabbinate, for contributing to Jewish learning, and for community service, leaving the faculty and student body free, not merely in the matter of ritual observance, but intellectually and spiritually free in accordance with undogmatic liberalism, which is at the heart of the genius of Judaism.

As I journey throughout the nation, I have found that the institute alumni individually and collectively are faithful and dedicated servants within the Jewish fellowship and the community at large. The knowledge of their service gladdens my heart and richly rewards us who dared to pioneer.

I cannot forbear to mention one further achievement. When World War II began, the number of graduates was about one hundred and fifty. Of this number, before the war ended, fifty enrolled in the chaplain's service of our nation's armed forces, and not a few obtained high distinction—a record that fills my heart with pride and gratitude.

At the last commencement exercises of the institute in 1948, I summed up my concept of the spirit that should inform its graduates in my charge to the students:

> Laugh at those who speak of dual loyalties and divided allegiance. We have an allegiance to the spiritual heritage of a great and imperishable people. We have another allegiance to the people of our great country, of whom we are a part. There is no divided allegiance. There is a transcending allegiance crowning and glorifying both.
>
> If men say to you, ask of you, "Are you a citizen of the State of Israel?" or "Are you a citizen of the American Republic and teacher of its people?" answer them, "The memories, the traditions, the hopes, the dreams, the sufferings, the sorrows of four thousand years have not sundered me from the blood and the race of the people of Israel. I am one of them. As a citizen I

belong wholly to America. America is my country and I have none other. To it I give the utmost of my loyalty, the deepest of my love, the truest of my service."

I have been thinking of a new way of translating that phrase I love, the word of the second chapter of the Prophet Ezekiel: "Son of man, stand upon thine own feet and I will speak not with thee, *but through thee.*" Remember, you must strengthen the infirm, you must reassure the timid, you must rebuke the cowardly. Remember you are teachers in Israel; you have not only the right to speak frankly, simply, sincerely to those who hear you in your congregations, but you must speak as men to your fellow-Americans of Christian faith. When they deserve your praise, praise them, but when you must speak harshly and bitterly, be not afraid. Sometimes it is more important to utter the clearest dispraise of that which is wrong than to speak in terms of praise, even when that praise is deserved.

This be my last word to you if we never meet again. God speak not to you chiefly or alone, but through you to your congregation, to your people, to American Israel. I part with you in sorrow but with limitless hope and with a deep affection for you, my dear boys. And I pray that the God of our fathers may bless you, bless you now and always.

As I close this chapter, the union of college and institute has come to pass. The differences were not so deep and basic as to make union impossible. Liberalism as a mood had come to take the place of Reform as an end. The plans of union are such as to satisfy the friends of both institutions. The union means the creation of a great teaching institution of liberal and progressive Judaism, minimizing the things that seem to divide, magnifying the things that unite. The college-institute is to continue to teach alike in Cincinnati and New York. Cincinnati is the center of a long-time liberal tradition. New York is the center of the largest Jewish population in history, containing one half of the American-Jewish population and between one fourth and one fifth of the entire world Jewish community. None of the major articles in the creed of the founders of the Jewish Institute of Religion has been abandoned or waived. That is equally true of the college, as brought out by the address of President Glueck when recently I installed him as president of Hebrew Union College–Jewish Institute of Religion.

IX

A Figure of Light

WHAT could a rabbi have in common with one of the great jurists of American history? How and when did their paths cross? It was my privilege to meet Benjamin N. Cardozo at the home of my future wife in 1899. At that time his family name was still under a cloud.

The story of Cardozo's father is all too familiar. He had been elected judge of the New York State Supreme Court in 1870, serving together with Chief Justice Barnard. They became involved in the Boss Tweed Ring, both having been placed in office by Tweed. In order to escape impeachment, they were ultimately compelled to resign. As I heard the tale in my youth —it may be a mistaken version—Cardozo was not accused or even suspected of venality. His crime was that he obeyed the orders of a truly venal and corrupt boss.

When I met Cardozo, the son, he was about thirty-five. It was difficult to associate the exquisite eighteenth-century gentleman either with his father, of then lamentable fame, or with his private tutor, a favorite childhood author of my day, Horatio Alger, Jr. He looked as if he had just stepped out of the pages of a Thackeray novel. His English speech, rich with the overtones of Spain, Holland, the British West Indies—the well-known route followed by his ancestors to the shores of America —was perfect in form and music to the ears. If he had a fault— and I never heard one attributed to him—it was that his speech

143

was too precise, too bookish, almost too classical. I believe it was generally felt that no member in the history of the court commanded a more beautiful, simple, fluent English style than Cardozo. I heard one of his associates of the Supreme Court say of him with respect to his opinions, "Their form was equal to that of Holmes; their content to that of Brandeis."

After my family and I returned from Oregon, Benjamin Cardozo and I saw more of each other. He came to think of me as his rabbi—"Dr. Angelicus" was the playfully affectionate way he addressed me. He was, actually, a member of the Spanish and Portuguese Synagogue, the oldest in America. An uncle of his by marriage had long been the honored minister cantor of Shearith Israel, in New York City, and there were bonds of friendship between him and Rabbi H. P. Mendes, to whom he paid eloquent tribute upon the occasion of the latter's seventieth birthday. Yet when his twin sister Emily died, I served as minister, and when he was utterly broken by the great sorrow of his life, the death of his sister Nellie, I rode alone with him as she was taken to rest by the side of her parents.

If the letters of Cardozo to his sister could be published (some of them were in my wife's possession), it would be found that they equal in loving tenderness and beauty the famous letters of Ernest Renan to his sister Henriette. I once asked him, with such delicacy as I could muster, why he had never married, and he answered quietly and sadly, "I never could give Nellie the second place in my life." After her death he was a lonely figure. He retained a certain elasticity and never lost the extraordinary charm and grace that made him a coveted dinner guest in the friendliest of Washington circles. But he was lonely without Nellie. While he was a member of New York's Court of Appeals in Albany, he wrote a daily letter to the beloved invalid. Loneliness, indeed, was part of his life. In Washington he missed his cherished colleagues of the New York Court of Appeals; their friendship and daily association meant as much to him, the most humble of men, as to them.

And I like to feel that our own friendship had for him, as for me, a more than ordinary significance.

I am proud to tell of my own small part in helping Cardozo to rise to his ultimate place. It began in the fall of 1911 when I spent a day with President Taft at the White House. I had gone to urge him to nominate for the Federal District Court a friend of mine and an eminent lawyer, Abram I. Elkus, who later became American ambassador to Turkey and a member of the New York State Court of Appeals. As soon as I arrived, the President, amidst the genial chuckles for which he was noted, launched forth into a story. This was about a Jewish delegation that had recently visited the White House, the members of which he rather curiously described to me as "Ike" (Isaac Ullman, one of the Republican political bosses of Connecticut), "Jake Schiff," and "Judge Wurzburger." When I interposed that I could not place the last-named, he described him as "the Philadelphia judge with the handsome head of a Roman senator" to whom he had offered the post of minister to Turkey. And he added, with another chuckle, "Jews seem to like Turkey." I suggested that he meant Judge Meyer Sulzberger. There was another chuckle as he commented, "Down where the Sulzberger flows."

The story of this delegation leads directly into that of Cardozo, so I shall tell it briefly. The men had come to Taft to urge him to name Louis Marshall for appointment to the United States Supreme Court. Schiff acted as spokesman, commending Marshall most warmly. The President told me that he listened patiently while Sulzberger added his own words of praise; then he turned to them all, especially to Schiff, and said, "Schiff, if you were President, would you name Sam Untermeyer's partner to the Supreme Court?" Though ordinarily a strong and self-contained man, utterly different from the sycophantic portrait painted by his biographer, which I have always thought made him resemble a bridegroom on a wedding cake, Schiff, according to Taft, lost his temper, and when Taft repeated his question, arose and left with the delegation.

Then, finishing the tale with a resounding roar of laughter, Taft said to me, "Of course they did not know that while I was talking to them, I had in my pocket the acceptance of the appointment I had already offered to Governor Charles E. Hughes. He has agreed to resign his office in New York State to begin work at the fall session of the court." Without criticizing President Taft, for whom I had much personal affection—though I never voted for him—I cannot help observing that it would have been rather more generous of him confidentially to have told the facts to the delegation at once, without subjecting Marshall's name to the needless indignity of rejection. But perhaps it can be explained by the strong, even bitter, animus of Taft, as lawyer and former Circuit Court judge, against Untermeyer, about whom later, while he was chief justice of the Supreme Court, he wrote a blistering opinion with unanimous concurrence.

But to get back to the Cardozo story, after I had brought up the name of Elkus for the District Court, the President spoke of naming to the vacancy instead a certain politician lawyer of New York. When I ventured to suggest that this man was rather a lightweight as a jurist, Taft replied in his jolly way, "Yes, but the court is made up of heavyweights, and it is just as well to balance them with one lightweight." It was all spoken, of course, in good fun. Suddenly he said, "My brother, Harry [Henry W. Taft], has been telling me of a brilliant young lawyer in New York, Carduza [sic] by name." For a moment I did not realize whom he meant. Then I launched into a eulogy of Cardozo, saying to the President, "What your brother says of Cardozo is the opinion generally of the bar of New York." Either the President did not know the story of his father, or else had failed to associate their names. I assured President Taft that I knew Cardozo well enough to feel that the deepest hope of his soul was to serve on the bench and create a record of such high and impeccable service as to blot out the earlier record. The President said, "Offer the post in my name to Cardozo and let me know the result."

I telegraphed to Cardozo and saw him in New York the same evening. He expressed great satisfaction as I told him the entire story. But he said at once, "I am not free to accept. I am under a heavy burden of which few know, that of maintaining a home for our sister, Elizabeth. As you know, she is sick and requires a place of her own in the country." This sister was, like their cousin Emma Lazarus, a gifted poet, "a failure half divine," in the words of one of her own beautiful sonnets. "Much as I appreciate the honor President Taft does me," Cardozo said, "much as I should wish to serve on the bench instead of practicing law, I must decline. I am not free to accept."

He continued in the practice of the law, adding to his reputation from day to day as a jurist of great learning and of highest ethical standards. He became known, too, as a lawyer's lawyer, serving as counsel in many cases of importance.

It is well known that he was nominated to the New York Supreme Court in 1913 on a Civic Reform ticket and elected. Almost immediately he was promoted to the Appellate Division and soon appointed by Governor Smith to the highest court of the state, then unanimously elected as a member of it. There he achieved a most eminent position.

Some years later, after Cardozo had become the pride and ornament of the court, Chief Justice Hotchkiss retired because of age. I had been abroad for the summer. Upon my return early in September, I read with great surprise that Governor Smith had spoken in favor of nonpartisan nomination of another member of the court, Judge Cuthbert W. Pound, this in spite of the fact that Cardozo was senior to his colleague by some days or weeks.

I read the news at the pier as we landed. Before unpacking my bags, I dictated a long letter to Governor Smith, expressing my incredulity over the announcement in the press that Cardozo, with his incomparable record on the bench, should be bypassed in favor of a junior associate, however slight the margin of time between them. I received no immediate reply.

Some weeks later, early in the evening after the Atonement Day, the maid brought me this telephone message: "Al wants to speak to you." I was not as quick to get the point as on a previous occasion when the same maid had announced, "Pontius Pilate desires to speak with the High Priest Caiaphas," and I hurried to the phone to greet the one-time governor of Jerusalem, Sir Ronald Storrs. This time Al proved to be Governor Smith, who asked to see me at the earliest possible moment.

After a hurried post–Atonement Day dinner, I joined him in his rooms at the Biltmore. He at once began to discuss the chief justiceship, the nomination to which, in the circumstances, meant unanimous election. He spoke at length in terms of the deepest regret that he could not comply with my request and the wishes of others. Nevertheless, I urged the cause of Justice Cardozo, than which no task could have been dearer to my heart. I pointed out that not only was he slightly the senior member of the court, but also that he was considered by the citizens of New York, irrespective of party, an extraordinarily able and upright judge. Al Smith interrupted to inquire whether the same was not true of Judge Pound. I assented. "But it is uniquely true of Cardozo," I added. "Besides, the lawyers of the country will remember your tribute to Cardozo when first you named him to the Court of Appeals and will not be able to understand why you should forfeit the good will of the bar throughout the country in the present situation." I had in mind the presidential election campaign to come, in which Smith hoped to be the candidate of his party.

Finally, he admitted that he was no longer free; he had promised Jim Wadsworth—and he mentioned also the name of Wadsworth's lieutenant—that he would comply with Wadsworth's request to appoint Pound. "And I cannot break my word to them," he said. Quietly, but firmly, I told him that he had made a rash promise which he actually had not been free to make; it was up to him to explain everything to Wadsworth and insist that he be released from his promise. He hesitated a long time.

Finally, after some difficult hours during which I, as an old friend, hammered away—knowing well I was serving in the interests not of Cardozo alone but of Al Smith as well—he consented to talk to Wadsworth and nominate Cardozo. Shortly thereafter, Cardozo was nominated by both parties and elected unanimously, serving on the highest bench of the state with such distinction as made inevitable the urging of his name on every hand when the vacancy arose in the Supreme Court through the resignation of Justice Oliver Wendell Holmes.

It might be appropriate to mention at this point Cardozo's nomination to the Board of Trustees of Columbia University, of which he was an alumnus in the class of 1888. It was a tradition of Columbia, my own alma mater, that Cardozo had all but equaled the brilliant record of Alexander Hamilton, a student more than a century earlier. No Jew had served as trustee since the American Revolution, and that Jew was Benjamin Mendes Seixas, of whom I believe Cardozo was a descendant on his mother's side. Apparently it was necessary for Cardozo to become chief justice of the Court of Appeals before he could be considered for membership in the august body of trustees, under its charter largely of Anglican Episcopalian membership. I sometimes wonder that Cardozo accepted the post. He had been a great and most eminent judge for years before his election to the board. He of all men could, and I think should, have said to Columbia, "I am no longer young and strong. When young, I might have served Columbia as a trustee. Now the honor comes too late." But he accepted. His successor remains the "sample Jew" of that board; though of course it is not explicitly written, "No other Jew need apply. We have one."

There was still a third time when I found myself, as Cardozo's revering friend, profoundly involved in the furtherance of his judicial career. I happened to be in Washington the day of Justice Holmes's resignation. The story goes—though it may be apocryphal—that, as Justice Holmes passed through his doorway after resigning, he said to his secretary, "I hope my successor may be Chief Justice Cardozo." It occurred to me as soon as I heard of Holmes's resignation to go to the office of Senator Borah and mention Cardozo's name. I found him most responsive, and even enthusiastic, about the suggestion. "I know well what a great and learned judge he is," he said, adding, "I will speak to the President and do what I can."

In New York the following day, I sought out the head of the Columbia University Law School, Dean Smith, and Cardozo's friend and former associate at the bar, Walter Pollak. They got to work at once, easily securing the warm support, I believe, of nearly all the law schools and faculties of the country. I saw Borah again, who, in the meanwhile, had put the name of Cardozo before President Hoover. He promised to keep me posted. The following night, after preaching in a Christian church in Bridgeport, I returned to my home to learn that Senator Borah had been trying to reach me by telephone.

This is the story in Borah's own words:

"I saw the President today. As I began to speak of appointing Cardozo, he seemed disinclined, and mentioned three or four others, including Senator Joe Robinson of Arkansas. I said none of these men would be confirmed by the Senate, not even Robinson. As I stressed the name of Cardozo, Hoover commented, 'You know, Senator Borah, there is a great deal of anti-Semitism in this country.' I said to the President that might be all the more reason for scotching it by appointing Cardozo, who alone was qualified to succeed Holmes. Thereupon the President added, less firmly, 'New York already has two justices on the Supreme Court.' 'But Justice Cardozo is not a New Yorker,' I said. 'He is a great American jurist and judge. He is the only man to succeed Holmes.' I then proceeded to deliver my parting shot. 'Just as President John Adams is remembered for his appointment of John Marshall as Chief Justice, your administration will be remembered for your appointment of Cardozo to the Supreme Court.' Hoover finally said, 'I will send in Cardozo's name to the Senate tomorrow morning.' And he added, 'You may tell Judge Cardozo that he will be appointed tomorrow.'"

I confess that at this news, my wife and I were tempted to go to Judge Cardozo. But we resisted, for two reasons: one, we felt he should hear this directly from the President and not from me; two, the President might change his mind if some senator, like Jim Watson of Indiana, should warn him in the morning not to do this. In the morning, as is well known, Cardozo, upon reaching Albany, was told by his secretary that the President desired to talk with him over the telephone. Hoover made the tender graciously, and Cardozo accepted. He had not lifted a finger in his own behalf, but, I later learned, had recommended another lawyer.

Books have been written, more will be written, about Justice Cardozo and his opinions in two great courts. I speak of the man himself. When I begged him to give the commencement address at the ordination exercises of the Jewish Institute of Religion in 1931, he hesitated to accept, aware as he was of his own attitude toward religious doctrine. For he was, to paraphrase Thomas Huxley, a "most hopeful and ethical agnostic." But at last he overcame his scruples and delivered an extraordinarily fine—yes, a noble—address on "Values," which the institute and other organizations have been requested over and over again to reprint. Those who heard him can never forget the impression he made. It was an unashamed pouring forth of his own idealism for the benefit of young men about to enter a sacred profession. It is amply worth including here:

> Defying an ancient canon of the rhetoricians, I begin with an apology. I do not know whether I have the right to talk to you today. I have felt that to earn that right I should be able to say to you that your beliefs are wholly mine, that the devastating years have not obliterated youthful faiths, and that in the darkness of the universe I can see with clearness and certainty a consoling shaft of light. Unable to say this, I have wondered whether

my message could be of worth to you—to you who are going forth to spread the teachings of religion—wondered whether with good cause you might not even resent it as an impertinence; at the very least whether fitness and good taste might not exact another spokesman for the lesson of the hour.

The great spiritual leader who has given to this Institute the dignity and glory of his leadership has talked with me about these things, and has brought me to believe that my troubles are unreal. Dr. Stephen Wise has said that a message would be welcome from any one who has been able, however black the depths of nescience, to hold fast to certain values transcending the physical and temporal. He has assured me that what such a one would say would be listened to without resentment, and even indeed with gladness by those of greater faith, with the gladness born of the perception that what is noble and high and sacred reveals itself in many forms and is discerned in many aspects by the faltering sons of men. Sixty years and more ago Huxley published to the world a memorable volume which is known by the title "Lay Sermons and Addresses." A lay sermon by one whose beliefs are not so very far removed from Huxley's is what you will hear from me today. And to hold fast to what your leader said to me, to shelter myself squarely behind the shield of his authority, I am going to talk to you of "values."

A theme is here, not for a brief fragment of an hour, but for a lecture, a series of lectures, a volume, almost one might say, a library. What values shall we choose—those of today, or of tomorrow, or of a future that is close at hand, or of the unplumbed future, trackless as the sea? Every one of them is a good. Let us not make the blunder of decrying any of them. Asceticism has made that blunder at times, and has suffered for its partial view of the shifting aspects of reality. The values of today are good, and those of tomorrow are good and those of a future that is not remote, and those of an unplumbed future, trackless as the sea. If we could have them all, it would be well, but seldom can we have them all. There is need to make a choice. How shall it be guided? Not all of us will make the same choice, not all of us ought to make the same. What choice is it worth while to make if one feels the mystery of the universe more deeply than one's fellows? What choice will be made by you? Before that question is answered, let me tell you an anecdote. Let me tell you of the choice that about four centuries ago was made by some one else. Let me tell you of the choice that was made by Tycho Brahe.

Tycho Brahe was born in Denmark of goodly lineage, and educated in youth at the University of Copenhagen. He thought in his boyhood that he would like to study law, but he became diverted from law to the study of astronomy. While yet a young man he discovered a new star, and the discovery brought him fame at home and in many distant lands. Denmark had a king then who was a patron of learning, and the king built an observatory for Tycho at the center of a little island, and Tycho called the place Uraniborg, the City of the Heavens. Here for years and years Tycho worked by day and night, watching the heavens by night, and figuring his observations by day, till star after star with exquisite precision had been set down upon his chart. But Frederick, the King, died, and young Prince Christian came upon the throne with a host of flippant courtiers, who grudged the treasure that had been lavished upon the upkeep of the observatory and this feckless charting of the stars. They could not see the value of it all, and so at last messengers went forward in the name of the new king, who were to visit Tycho Brahe, to learn, if they could, the use of all his labor, to quiz him about it, and to pit their values against him.

You will find the tale set forth with moving eloquence and beauty in a poem by Alfred Noyes, the noble and inspiring poem which he calls the "Watchers of the Skies." The messengers asked what Tycho had been doing these five and twenty years. He showed them tables of the stars, seven hundred set down, each in its proper place, "And is this all?" they said. "Not all, I hope," said Tycho, "for I think before I die I shall have marked a thousand." You can almost hear their laughter, can you not? All the prophets and the seers have listened to the like. Einstein has heard it in our day, and every lover of truth and beauty, every man who has seen visions and tried to live them in his life, has heard the same sardonic mirth. To what end, said the messengers, to what end the travail and the waste? Show its uses to us now, show them now before we go. Resounding through the centuries I hear familiar echoes. Never a philosopher has lived, nor a saint nor a scientist nor an artist, but has been summoned to a like proof—to show the value for today—not the value for the unplumbed future, but the value for today. I will read you Tycho Brahe's answer as I find it in the poem:

" 'In the time to come,'
"Said Tycho Brahe, 'perhaps a hundred years,
" 'Perhaps a thousand, when our own poor names
" 'Are quite forgotten, and our Kingdom's dust,
" 'On one sure certain day, the torchbearers
" 'Will, at some point of contact, see a light
" 'Moving upon this chaos. Though our eyes
" 'Be shut forever in an iron sleep,
" 'Their eyes shall see the Kingdom of the law,
" 'Our undiscovered cosmos. They shall see it—
" 'A new creation rising from the deep,
" 'Beautiful, whole.
" 'We are like men that hear
" 'Disjointed notes of some supernal choir.
" 'Year after year we patiently record
" 'All we can gather. In that far off time
" 'A people that we have not known shall hear them
" 'Moving like music to a single end.' "

They could not understand—the messengers who had come to appraise the values and report. They went back to the king, their master, and they said that Tycho Brahe's dreams were fruitless, and worse than fruitless, perilous, since "any fruit they bore would fall in distant years to alien hands." Tycho went forth to exile, and Uraniborg, City of the Heavens, went down into the dust.

" 'Yes, I still hope,' he said,
" 'Yes, I still hope in some more generous land
" 'To make my thousand up before I die.
" 'Little enough, I know—a midget's work.
" 'The men that follow me with more delicate art
" 'May add their tens of thousands; yet my sum
" 'Will save them just that five and twenty years
" 'Of patience, bring them sooner to their goal,

" 'That Kingdom of the law I shall not see.
" 'We are on the verge of great discoveries.
" 'I feel them as a dreamer feels the dawn
" 'Before his eyes are opened. Many of you
" 'Will see them. In that day you will recall
" 'This, our last meeting at Uraniborg,
" 'And how I told you that this work of ours
" 'Would lead to victories for the coming age.
" 'The victors may forget us. What of that?
" 'Theirs be the palms, the shouting and the praise,
" 'Ours be the fathers' glory in the sons.' "

That, gentlemen of the Institute, was Tycho Brahe's choice of values. If you are true to your mission as sons of this Institute of Religion, summoned from this day forth to live its deepest verities, your choice will be the same. The submergence of self in the pursuit of an ideal, the readiness to spend oneself without measure, prodigally, almost ecstatically, for something intuitively apprehended as great and noble, spend oneself one knows not why—some of us like to believe that this is what religion means. True, I am sure, it is that values such as these will be found to have survived when creeds are shattered and schisms healed and sects forgotten and the things of brass and stone are one with Nineveh and Tyre.

I have spoken of a man who was one of the famous of the earth, whose name has re-echoed through the corridors of time. Let us not make the blunder of supposing that to live in communion with these ineffable values of the spirit, to spend oneself utterly in sacrifice and devotion, is a lot reserved for a chosen few, for an aristocracy of genius, for those that will be ranked in history among the mighty or the great. Not so, friends and brothers. To the glory of our humanity, the lowly equally with the mighty may be partakers in this bliss. I have seen it in my own life, and so I am sure have many within the compass of my voice. Along the common ways I have walked with men and women—you would not know them from the crowd—I have walked with men and women who had made the choice of Tycho Brahe. They had made it in humbler forms, by love, by gentleness, by sweetness, by devotion, by sacrifice of self within the narrow circle of the home; but, be it said to their undying glory, they had made it, none the less. We know it when death takes them if in hours of pride and darkness we have been blind to it before. The life seemed simple while it lasted. We may not always have been conscious of its beauty. The end comes, and behold it is illuminated with the white and piercing light of the divinity within it. We have walked with angels unawares.

This is the summons that I give to you today. These are the values—the values of the spirit—that by your witness shall prevail. I have been reminded by Felix Frankfurter of the noble words of Huxley in celebrating the opening of Johns Hopkins University. "I cannot say" (said Huxley) "that I am in the slightest degree impressed by your bigness (i.e., the bigness of America), or your material resources as such. Size is not grandeur, and territory does not make a nation. The great issue about which hangs a truè sublimity, and the terror of overhanging fate, is what are you going to do with all these things? What is to be the end to which these are to be the means?" So it is, my friends, with all the teachings of universities and schools. The learning and the wisdom stored in many books have been taught to the youth, the rabbis of the future, who have come together in these halls. All the study has been wasted except in proportion as it strengthens them to make a choice hereafter between competing and conflicting values. It is wasted unless it strengthens them to the choice of Tycho Brahe.

One life I have singled out as the subject of my parable. I could have chosen many others, the lives of men and women of our race, the lives of prophets and saints and heroes and martyrs, who were kinsmen in spirit of that watcher of the skies. In persecution and contumely they knew that there were values of the spirit greater than any others, values for whose fruits they would have to wait, "perhaps a hundred years, perhaps a thousand," values whose fruits might elude them altogether, yet values to be chosen, unfalteringly, uncomplainingly, with cheer and even joy. What does a ministry of religion mean if it does not mean the preaching and living of that truth? For what have we come together this morning, in the springtime of the year, unless to say to this little band of eager men, still in the springtime of their lives: You are going forth today as preachers of the eternal values. You will find mockery and temptation on the highways, and for the values that you hold to be eternal many a tinsel token will be offered in exchange. Sycophants and time—servers and courtiers and all the lovers of the flesh pots will assail you with warnings that you are squandering the happy days under the sun, and will ask you to tell them to what use, just as in the Danish city of Uraniborg, City of the Heavens, the messengers of the Danish king taunted and challenged and drove at last unto exile, that other watcher of the skies. Then will be the time when you will need to gird yourselves with the strength that this Institute of Religion, this Institute of the better life, has striven with all her might to bestow upon her sons. Then will be the time when you will need to bethink yourselves of the values that were chosen by the prophets and saints of Israel, and by the goodly and noble of every race and clime. You will remember in that hour the choice of Tycho Brahe.

When the course is finished, when the task is ended, when the books are closed, may the last appraisal of all values reveal his choice as yours.

I must tell about one other episode, not generally known, in the life of Cardozo, which reveals something of the character and quality of the man. In the post-Balfour Declaration days of 1918, those of us who were active in the leadership of the Zionist movement were anxious to secure to the adherence of the movement such Jews as had distinguished themselves in the life of America. On September 4, 1918, Judge Mack and I talked about the problem and we found Cardozo more sympathetic than we had anticipated. The next day, I wrote him a note expressing my joy over his words. I added, "I am going to enclose an application for membership. I want to have the joy of receiving it and forwarding it to our Chief, Justice Brandeis." A few days later, Cardozo replied in a letter that bespeaks both his modesty and character.

You do me too much honor. I have signed the application with some misgiving, for I have confessed to you that I am not yet an enthusiast. But to-day, the line seems to be forming between those who are for the cause and those who are against it, with little room for a third camp. I am not willing to join those who are against, so I go over to the others. If I am charged with inconsistency, I shall say that a great spiritual leader sustained me in my choice.

In reply, I wrote him of the great pleasure his letter had given me and, I added "You think you are not yet an enthusiast but you will be, I am certain, in good time." Judge Mack and my colleagues were delighted with Cardozo's action and were anxious to quote publicly from his letter. I had in the meantime written Justice Brandeis that Cardozo was considering the possibility of joining the Zionist organization but might find it somewhat difficult at the time. Brandeis wrote in comment, "I think Cardozo should be pressed to sign now. If it is unpleasant for him, he deserves it for his procrastination." When I sent Brandeis a copy of Cardozo's letter, his further comment was, "The letter is right in a way. Jews should understand that those who are not with us are against us and act accordingly, whatever their doubts. 'Under which flag, Bensonian?' " I wrote Cardozo again, telling him of Brandeis' comments and of our eagerness to quote his letter, particularly the passage about the lines forming as between those who were for and against, with no room for a third group. He replied by return mail.

Sometimes I suspect that he was wearying of my persistence which, I have been told, brought more converts to Zionism than my persuasiveness or my logic. But Cardozo, as those who knew him will testify, was the last man to permit his name to be used in association with any cause or movement in which he did not fully and firmly believe.

I cannot leave this—one of my favorite themes—without adding one last observation about Cardozo. His life began under a cloud that darkened its way. No one could know him without feeling what he must have suffered in his youth because of his father. How he must have winced when, in connection with attempts to elect an unworthy or corrupt judicial

Allenhurst, N.J.
Sept. 19, 1918

Dear Dr. Wise,

Do what you please with my name and my letter.

The sentence which you quote does not sound to me like a bugle-call, but perhaps it will fit the mood of some other laggards like myself.

Faithfully Yours,
Benjamin N. Cardozo

candidate, some such phrase was used as, "Shall we have another Barnard or Cardozo?" Yet from the earliest moment of his own practice at the bar he came to be known as a man of finest rectitude and loftiest motives. Without the faintest self-seeking, which would have been unimaginably alien to his exquisite spirit, he early gained a rare reputation among his colleagues, and throughout the last twenty years of his life filled with distinction one high judicial place after another.

Happily for him, because of his great learning and even greater character, the shadows lifted. The handicap was canceled out. The name was restored to honor. If anyone today were to make a disparaging reference to the name of Cardozo, he would no longer be understood. Henceforth it will rank high in the judicial process of our country.

As James Russell Lowell, while ambassador to England, said beside the grave of Coleridge:

> It sounds like stories from the land of spirits,
> If any man obtain that which he merit
> Or any merit that which he obtains.

And he added,

> Both conditions are fulfilled today.

So it was with him who began life under the shadows and who, before life ended, stood as a figure of light—Benjamin Nathan Cardozo.

X

Woodrow Wilson: Leader and Friend

Woodrow Wilson believed in himself, clearly perceived the star of his own high destiny. I recall once having asked Wilson, "When did you first think or dream of the Presidency?" His answer was startlingly simple. "There never was a time after my graduation from Davidson College in South Carolina when I did not expect to become President of the United States." I could not help almost impertinently inquiring, "Even when you were a teacher in a girls' college?" He repeated, "There was never a time when I did not expect and did not prepare myself to become President." This remark by a good Presbyterian helped me to understand Calvinistic pre-ordination.

I shared his faith even before its partial fulfillment. On a Sunday before his election as governor of New Jersey, in 1910, I made a nonpolitical address before the Trenton Y.M.C.A. To these fellow Jerseymen of Woodrow Wilson I said, "On Tuesday the President of Princeton University will be elected governor of your state. He will not complete his term of office as governor. In November, 1912, he will be elected President of the United States. In March, 1917, he will be inaugurated for the second time as President. He will be one of the great Presidents of American history." Very different this from another prediction, that of Adolph S. Ochs, publisher of the *New York Times*, who at a luncheon meeting in early June, 1912, commented sharply on my prediction in the presence of our host, the late Henry Morgenthau, "Woodrow Wilson will not be reelected; he will not be elected; he will not be nominated by the Baltimore Convention." What a troubling gift prophecy must be when it runs counter to the interests of the mighty and wealthy, who, too often even for their own sakes, surround themselves with sycophants.

On February 10, 1911, I heard Woodrow Wilson speak for the first time. He was clear minded, thoughtful, incisive. He put so much of himself into his thinking that his utterance sounded entirely representative of the man. I saw him for a moment, and he asked me to call on him the next Monday morning at his hotel. The next day I went to call on him with Henry Morgenthau, then president of the Free Synagogue, to invite him to speak at its annual dinner. The Governor knew of the work of the synagogue and received our invitation cordially and then urged us to stay so that we might discuss the political situation. Mrs. Wilson, who was present, added that she had been following my work and writings and that she wished to thank me for what I had been saying about Mr. Wilson.

We quickly drifted into a discussion of the power of the press, and Governor Wilson told us this most interesting and significant fact—before he led the fight against Senator Smith, word had gone throughout the country, "Feature Wilson." Since he had led the fight, the interests caused word to go out that the least possible attention be paid Wilson. Mr. Morgenthau later confirmed this by telling me that Wall Street had chosen Harmon of Ohio as its candidate for the presidency.

People were beginning to think about and see Woodrow Wilson as a national figure. I remember my first meeting with George Foster Peabody in the early spring of 1912 after I had spoken on "Religion and Industrial Justice" in the Baptist Church at Glens Falls. He called for me and took me by sleigh to his home where we talked until morning. He seemed a rarely beautiful soul, without any affectation. He said he had become overburdened with possessions, that he had not started out to be as rich as he had become, and that he had succeeded in almost divesting himself of the whole of his fortune as a result of his philanthropies—though he did not use that term. He said, after realizing that he had to give away his possessions in order to feel in touch with the multitudes, "Society has permitted me to do this—to name my own wage for my own service—and that is wrong." We talked of many problems, including the national political scene. I was happy to hear such a man as this say he felt Woodrow Wilson was the only hope of those of us who were convinced that, unless he was nominated, we must have a third party.

During the next few months I heard and saw the Governor on many occasions. His stature grew steadily. As the guests of the Economic Club we sat together, and I heard him speak for over an hour, simply and forcefully. He made a deep impression, which was really a victory, because he spoke to men whose minds were not open. And at the Free Synagogue dinner, addressed by Senator Borah, Judge Julian W. Mack, John Haynes Holmes, and others, Governor Wilson made *the* address of the evening. He was simple, quiet, and precise in his mode of utterance, but the man—real, genuine, single-minded—shone through every luminous word. Mr. Morgenthau that evening offered his help in the matter of the presidential fight, and Governor Wilson seemed very grateful. It was evident that he would shortly announce himself as a candidate.

Long before that evening when Colonel Roosevelt, with what I believed to have been perfect sincerity, announced that he would not again be a candidate for the presidency. I felt that, save for the nomination of Justice Hughes, which I knew the latter would himself forbid, the best course to pursue would be to help secure the nomination of the ablest man in the Democratic party. I felt, as did Colonel Roosevelt, that President Taft was not entitled to a renomination, but I knew what

Colonel Roosevelt apparently did not, that by fair means or foul, "proprietors" of the Republican party would renominate the President.

Knowing that President Taft's renomination was inevitable, I did what I could to bring about the nomination of Woodrow Wilson. I felt that the Republican party, to which I had always belonged, had become hopeless and irredeemable, that it was owned body and soul, insofar as it still had a soul, by the bosses of the Aldrich-Cannon regime, which Colonel Roosevelt had failed to overthrow. It was my hope that something might be done to make the Democratic party a serviceable agency of our political life. It appeared to me that if Wilson with his antiboss record could be nominated, such nomination would mean either that the bosses were actually vanquished or else that they, unlike the overlords of the Republican party, had read the handwriting on the wall before it was too late.

Indeed, I felt at the time that the Republican party was so irreclaimably dominated by corrupt and unscrupulous bosses, that Roosevelt should not have offered himself for its nomination, and I urged his friend Amos Pinchot to beg Roosevelt not to become a candidate, but, win or lose, to found a new party. Roosevelt chose to do otherwise, and his friends regarded his defeat for the nomination at the Chicago Convention as a theft. Even if this had not been true at Chicago, the character of the Republican party would have been little changed, for under the mastery of the Barnes-Penrose gang, it would not have been anything more than the sad survival of a one-time noble company.

In the meantime, while the Republican party eagerly went the way of destruction, the Democratic party nominated Woodrow Wilson, whom I then described as "one of the finest figures in our political life for a generation." The good news came on July 2 while I was vacationing in Lake Placid, and I shouted for joy. My son Jim, then ten, was in the woodshed, and I told him first. Tears began to trickle down his cheeks and he said, "That settles Roosevelt, and I prayed for Clark." The little rascal had been praying for Clark because I had told him that, if Clark were nominated, Roosevelt would be elected. He called me a turncoat because I had long been a Republican, and now was about to vote for the Democratic party. That same night he threatened to pray for Roosevelt, and I said to him, "Don't do that, Jim; instead of that, do as I will do—pray that God may give us the best man, the man best fitted to lead this great nation to honor." Whereupon he added, "That's Teddy all right."

On July 22 I wrote to Wilson in such terms as would perhaps help him to see that personally I was prepared to support him, not because I cared a halfpenny for the Democratic party, but because I believed that his own election might be the ending of both parties in their old estate:

LAKE PLACID, N. Y.
JULY 22, 1912

MY DEAR GOVERNOR WILSON:

My message of congratulation will have conveyed to you my sense of rejoicing in the outcome of the Baltimore Convention. This line is added in order that you may know of my determination to support your candidacy in every possible way.

Member and supporter of the Republican Party though I long have been, I am deeply persuaded that your nomination and election may, by reason of the power of your leadership and the character of service by you to be rendered, bring to pass the re-birth of the Party you represent. The fate of the long-time Democratic Party, either in feeble opposition to, or in covert alliance with the Republican Party at its worst, concerns me in no wise. But I am of the faith that the Democratic Party, by virtue of your nomination, has given token to the Nation that it is ready once again to square itself and its great name. Truly do I rejoice in your nomination which I ventured throughout the land to urge and to predict at a time when the bosses yet hoped to avert it. But, as your well-wisher, I am happiest of all in the thought that it is to be given to you to make the Democratic Party what both Parties alike have ceased to be—a Party scrupulous to safeguard the interests of all the people, inflexibly opposed to every bestowal of privilege even though less obvious than the abhorrent bounty-system of the Protective Tariff, and zealous to maintain its principles of Democracy which alone can keep, as they have made, this Nation great and free.

I feel that these ideals of Democracy, to their faith in which many of us have held fast in the despite of every discouragement, are safe in your hands. Matching your conduct as the administrator of a Commonwealth to your political creed you have shown in clearest fashion that neither corrupted political leaders nor corrupting financial interests shall separately or together deny to the people the substance of self-government. You will pardon my saying that many men who like myself have turned to the Democratic Party at this time because of your leadership thereof look forward to the notification exercises, which will afford you opportunity to make vigorous and unmistakable re-affirmation of your own faith touching the fundaments of political and industrial Democracy.

That the Nation will give you its mandate of leadership for the next Presidential term in November is humanly speaking certain; not less certain I believe it to be that you will meet the duties of that honoring mandate with deep wisdom, with high courage, with noble purpose.

FAITHFULLY YOURS,
[signed] STEPHEN S. WISE

Just before Wilson's election in 1912, I was to address a great meeting with him in Philadelphia and before doing so went to his room with Peabody. We had just discussed our government's failure to recognize the Chinese Republic, and so, as we entered the room, I said, "Governor, we have saved you the trouble of thinking about your foreign policies. Mr. Peabody and I have settled that trifle for you." He laughed and said, "Just a little beforehand, I should say." I told him we both felt it was an outrage that the United States government at the dictation of the Wall Street interests operating through the Assistant Secretary of State, had failed to recognize the republic of China. I saw that he made a mental note of it, and later he spoke of the duty of our republic, the oldest of the republics, to recognize the integrity of the newest of them.

I asked the Governor whether he felt confident of the outcome, and he said he feared nothing, but at the same time he did not permit himself to think about the outcome at all. "If I do," he said, "the matter would become purely personal, and I want to think of the contest and the issues at stake." At the meeting he spoke for an hour, and in the most simple, clear, and earnest manner. He had a fine reception, though one missed the roar one was accustomed to hear at the Roosevelt meetings. He might not command the frenzy of the zealous, but he did command the respect of the thoughtful.

When the election was over, I received a gracious letter from President Wilson, which I offered my children that they might keep it for future generations. My son, not quite eleven, would have nothing to do with it because of his ardent devotion to T.R.—but my daughter, aged nine, and not yet so politically independent, gladly claimed it:

> BERMUDA
> Nov. 20, 1912
>
> MY DEAR FRIEND:
> Your generous note of November 6th gave me a great deal of pleasure. I am sure you know how proud I have been to be supported by you, and this little message completes my happiness.
>
> CORDIALLY AND SINCERELY YOURS,
> [signed] WOODROW WILSON

Soon after his election I visited President-elect Wilson at Trenton, and we had a lengthy session together. As we sat down to luncheon, I insisted that he be seated first, saying, "You will have to learn to be seated first at the White House."

He answered, "Won't you let me be a gentleman a little longer?"

I told the President that he ought to feel relieved to think that one man had come to see him who was not an office seeker. He said, "Are you sure?" And I replied, "Absolutely sure." Whereupon he said, "Well, Rabbi, let's shake hands again." Years later, Joseph P. Tumulty, long-time personal secretary of President Wilson, rejoiced my heart by telling me that on the morning of President Wilson's departure from the White House, the President sat ruminating while awaiting the car that was to take him to the inaugural of President-elect Harding. He thought aloud in these terms, "Some friends, a very few, have never asked anything for themselves and given me every service." The name of Cleveland Dodge was first; the writer's was mentioned third.

Many interesting matters came up in the course of the luncheon. I brought up the subject of the Industrial Commission, because all of us, who had long been working for such a commission, had been so deeply disappointed by the nominations of Taft that we hoped they would not be confirmed by the Senate before the end of his term. The lack of confirmation would give Wilson a chance to appoint his own commission. I had been told by Senator Borah that this could only be achieved if the labor people received assurance from Wilson that they would be well treated as far as their representatives were concerned—and were therefore willing not to press for immediate confirmation. Wilson told me that I might say to Gompers that labor might count upon his treating them fairly in the matter of the appointment of the commission if it should be left to him.

We discussed Russian affairs with special reference to the treatment of Jews, and I suggested an early conference of persons familiar with the problem so that the attitude of the government might be carefully mapped out, adding that, of course, his own attitude was known. Referring to his Carnegie

With Rev. Dr. John Haynes Holmes at Carnegie Hall on the twenty-fifth anniversary of the Free Synagogue in 1932.

Leaving the White House after a conference on refugees from nazism, April 13, 1938. Left to right: Professor J. M. Chamberlain of New York, Assistant Secretary of State George S. Messersmith, Rabbi Wise, Henry Morgenthau, Sr., Rev. Michael J. Ready, Secretary of Labor Frances

Hall address of December, 1911, he said, "Everyone knows my attitude." His address, "The Rights of the Jews," had been given at a meeting calling for the abrogation of the eighty-year-old treaty of commerce and navigation between Russia and the United States, which guaranteed that the inhabitants of the two nations should have the liberty of entering any part of the territory of either that is open to foreign commerce, and which had been violated by Russia in its treatment of Jewish citizens of the United States. He had then spoken out in unmistakable terms:

> For some forty years the obligations of this treaty have been disregarded by Russia in respect of our fellow-citizens. Our government has protested, but has never gone beyond protest. After forty years of mere correspondence, the Russian govern-ment naturally does not expect the matter to be carried beyond protest to action, and so continues to act as it pleases in this matter, in the confidence that our government does not seriously mean to include our Jewish fellow-citizens among those upon whose rights it will insist.... Only once or twice, it would seem, has she ever thought our government in earnest. Should she ever deem it in earnest, respect would take the place of covert indifference, and the treaty would be lived up to.
>
> But there lies a principle back of our life. America is not a mere body of traders; it is a body of fine men. Our greatness is built upon our freedom—is moral, not material. We have a great ardour for gain, but we have a deep passion for the rights of man. Principles lie back of our action. America would be inconceivable without them. Our principles are not incompatible with great material prosperity. On the contrary, unless we are deeply mis-taken, they are indispensable to it. We are not willing to have prosperity, however, if our fellow-citizens must suffer contempt for it, or lose the rights that belong to every American in order that we may enjoy it. The price is too great.
>
> Here is a great body of our Jewish fellow-citizens, from whom have sprung men of genius in every walk of our varied life, men who have become part of the stuff of America, who have con-ceived its ideals with singular clearness and led its enterprises

with spirit and sagacity. . . . They are not Jews in America; they are American citizens. . . .

I am glad this question has thus been brought into the open. There is here a greater stake than any other upon which we could set our hearts. Here is the final test of our ability to square our policies with our principles. We may now enjoy the exhilaration of matching our profession with handsome performance. We are not here to express our sympathy with our Jewish fellow-citizens, but to make evident our sense of identity with them. This is not their cause; it is America's. It is the cause of all who love justice and do right.

The President-elect added he could have no conference of the kind I proposed until his secretary of state was appointed. Since this was late January, I could not help saying, "I suppose you are giving the men, whom you are appointing, a month or more notice," to which he replied that he thought men should have sufficient patriotism to serve their country upon short notice. I agreed, but said a man might still need a little time to arrange his affairs. He turned and said, "I think a few hundred trunks are packed already."

We discussed the possibility of having a group of men and women unofficially appointed by him to act as a sort of committee to take counsel with him on problems of social welfare. I said I thought it was a pity that the Progressive party's social program should be appropriated and made a partisan affair. He seemed to like the idea and said that soon after the election he would be glad if I would get to work and bring such a group together. He saw no reason why some of the most imperative items of the Progressive social program could not be adopted by him but showed the deepest distrust of the Progressive leaders.

In the course of our discussion of men who might be considered for public office, Wilson asked, "What do you think of Brandeis?" I answered that the important question was not what I thought but what he thought of Brandeis. He said, quick as a flash, "He is a great personality and has a great

mind." He then proceeded to tell me a stirring and, in the light
of what has happened since, an all but incredible story. "As
soon as the press carried rumors with respect to Cabinet ap-
pointments mentioning the name of Brandeis, I received a
series of letters from Massachusetts in bitterest denunciation
of him. You know that I respect him as one of the finest servants
of the Republic. I thereupon dispatched Norman Hapgood to
Boston to ascertain what these charges really meant. Norman
went to Boston and returned with a most startling report, seeing that he is the warmest of the friends of Brandeis. His investigation showed that the largest number of those interrogated
spoke of Brandeis as though he were a shyster and charlatan.
Hapgood was told by leaders of State Street [financial center
of Boston] that Brandeis' appointment as attorney general
would be followed by a financial panic." Wilson concluded,
"If I don't appoint him to my Cabinet, it won't be because I
have accepted their stories as true."

These malignly unjust charges against Brandeis did not deter
the President from nominating him as associate justice of the
Supreme Court about three years later. As one of the friends
and associates of Brandeis in the Zionist movement, I had come
to know the lofty quality of the man. As soon as I learned that
there was wide criticism of the appointment, particularly
among Republican senators, I went to Washington to see Senator Borah of Idaho, my friend since the years I lived in
Oregon. He spoke highly of Brandeis, placing no credence in
the charges inspired if not actually leveled by the Boston
bankers and the "New York, New Haven crowd." In view of
his outspoken admiration for Brandeis, I assumed that he would
vote to ratify the latter's nomination. Believer that I was in
Borah's independence and integrity, I was shocked to hear him
say that he had to be careful about his voting "for Idaho is a
lumber state and you know what Brandeis and his client
Gifford Pinchot have done to our timber industry." Had he
been frank, he would have used another term, namely, timber
thieves.

Weeks passed and President Lowell of Harvard, to his discredit be it recalled, had virtually assumed the leadership of the anti-Brandeis forces. I say discredit, for not long before I had asked him to give his support to Heney, who, after a brilliant record as district attorney, was then a candidate for the governorship of California. He purported to regret that he could not, saying, "I must not drag the name of Harvard into political quarrels." So overwhelming was his hatred of Brandeis, however, that he overcame his political detachment in order to cabal against the latter's confirmation.

The last word to me of Senator Borah had been that he would investigate further and see whether he could not vote for confirmation. He spoke sharply, even bitterly, against Wilson, making the grave charge that President Wilson had not really cared about Brandeis' confirmation and that he had nominated Brandeis solely to get the benefit of the support of the radicals at the presidential election of the following year. He added, "You may tell that to the President."

Through Henry Morgenthau I repeated to the President what Borah had directed me to say. Within a few days there appeared a decisive letter of the President to Senator Culberson of Texas, member, as I recall, of the Judiciary Committee of the Senate. The warmth of the President's communication was little more honoring to Louis D. Brandeis than an almost simultaneously issued letter of former President Eliot of Harvard, which tribute was invaluable because of its author. The vote was taken, Senator Borah being among those who vainly voted against confirmation.

On another occasion I took up with President Wilson the question of the tensions among Negroes, due to a sense of being driven back to further segregation under a Democratic administration. He answered, "We have merely continued the policy of the former administration, but the mere fact that it is the Democratic party causes all this vociferous protest." He spoke as a true Southerner when he added, "White people do not wish to work in too close proximity to the Negro." I still persisted, asking, "Are you not paying too great a price for a little comfort in doing a thing which seems to segregate the Negro?" He replied, "Yes, I am afraid we are, and I have given orders that the thing is to be changed." Then he told me that he had the thing on his heart and would do what he could, adding, "I must first gain the leadership of my party and then I can do a great deal more." He went on to speak of the great pressure from the West as well as the South not to give the Negro any place in the government. I found him weaker on this subject than on any other.

Before leaving, in referring to a certain man, who was under consideration as our representative to St. Petersburg, the President said one very amusing thing: "It is true he is not distinguished as an office holder. No Democrats are. We poor fellows have been out in the cold so long that we have to learn how to hold office all over again."

This half-humorous remark revealed one of the difficulties of the Wilson administration, which led to disappointment and disillusionment on the part of men who had believed that Woodrow Wilson would effectively replace the boss-ridden appointees of the Democratic party. A letter from one such young Wilsonian Democrat, addressed to me after I had spoken on "Civic Religion" in North Carolina, was so deeply disturbing that after rereading it I felt it was my unpleasant duty to bring it to the attention of the President.

MAY 31, 1914

MY DEAR DR. WISE:

I have spent the better part of the morning thinking over your address on "Civic Religion." It was an inspiration to those of us who believe that idealism will work as well in politics as religion.

But what would you say if I were to tell you that it has proven a failure here, at least for the present, if we are to use the pragmatic test—that an idealist, President Wilson, has contributed more to set us back than all other forces combined? . . .

The politicians were not then, are not now, and never will be, Wilson men, for they are by nature opposed to the things that the President stands for.

But to change now! Those who were most vehement in the pre-Convention days in their denunciation of Wilson as a school teacher are loudest in their acclaim of him now as a wise man and patriot. And why? Loaves and fishes, my dear Sir. Excepting Mr. Daniels, every presidential appointment in our state, save two, has gone to a reactionary and machine politician. . . .

What is the result? A ten year set-back has been given to the Progressive movement, its very heart taken out of it for the moment. . . .

Today in our state the loudest advocates of progressive politics are the machine politicians who can be relied upon to cut the heart out of all progressive measures. . . .

Take the political result of it. I heard the charge made upon the floor of the Senate that Senator Overman's first election had been bought and paid for with thirty thousand dollars by the American Tobacco Company. The reply of the Senator from Overman's home country was that if this were true, Overman knew nothing of it. Incidentally, this gentleman holds a five thousand dollar sinecure under the President.

Anybody knowing anything about North Carolina politics will tell you that Overman's going to the Senate was as bold and bald as Lorimer's. . . .

The thing that Progressive Democrats cannot understand is why a presidential policy, that works in New York and New Jersey, won't work in North Carolina. . . .

My heart is sad over it. Understand, I am not an office-seeker. I want no office other than the one I have held for some years as Trustee of the State University. So I can without partisanship see the pity of it, the awful pity of it.

SINCERELY YOURS,
D.—— S.——

Within a few days I received what to me was a deeply moving answer and one which gives insight into a man who could accept criticism when offered in good faith:

JUNE 4, 1914

MY DEAR FRIEND:

I thank you for your letter of June second and for the enclosure from D.S., which I herewith return.

I am very much distressed that the friends in North Carolina with whom you spoke, should have got the impression they have got. I do not blame them in the least, but there are many circumstances upon which I do not think they reflect. In the first place, I am bound by the old practice and expectation of everybody, as opinion is organized here in Washington, to respect and accept the recommendations of Congressmen and Senators, if they recommend men unexceptional in character and ability. I have again and again turned away from recommendations made me because I wished to recognize the men closely associated with what I had striven for, but I have had no means of getting advice on that head except from individuals, and very often individuals who offered advice were interested parties. It is a thorny and difficult matter altogether in which I have not satisfied myself and in which I am grieved to learn I have not satisfied my friends.

CORDIALLY AND SINCERELY YOURS,
[signed] WOODROW WILSON

Again, when I found it necessary to write the President that I deplored his advocacy of a preparedness program in 1915 and that I felt in conscience bound to dissent in the pulpit and on the platform from his position, I received the most generous of letters, which satisfied me that the myth about Woodrow Wilson's being unable to endure disagreement was just another myth.

By February, 1917, I had become convinced that President Wilson had kept the United States out of the war as a result

November 18, 1915

My dear Rabbi Wise:

I have your letter of November twelfth and I need not say that it distresses me very deeply. I always mistrust my own judgment when I find myself disagreeing with you, but in this case I fear the disagreement is inevitable. I want you to know, nevertheless, that it does not affect in the least my estimate of you or my personal feeling. It is painful to go different ways but we can thoroughly respect one another in doing so.

Cordially and sincerely yours,

Woodrow Wilson

Rabbi Stephen S. Wise,
23 West Ninetieth Street,
New York City.

of high statesmanship and infinite patience, but that the time had come for the American people to understand that it might be our destiny to have part in the struggle to avert the enthronement of the law of might over the nations. As we entered the war, I noted with deep concern the element of discord among the American people arising from the explicable attitude of those who could not reconcile the British championship of democracy with the facts that obtained touching the denial of self-government to the Irish people. I therefore wrote to the President on April 11, 1917:

> I venture to ask the question whether this were not an opportune time, in such a way as may commend itself to you, to appeal to the British Government to do that which the best thought of the British people has long been prepared to do—namely, to accord *home rule to the Irish people*. Such an act at this time on the part of Great Britain would not merely answer the question touching Britain's right to stand out as the champion of smaller and oppressed nationalities; would not only end disaffection among the Irish people and the unrest which obtains among the Irish elements of the American people, but would, like the self-liberation of Russia, support the position taken by you on behalf of the nation in eloquent terms—that we are battling for the freedom and democracy of the peoples of earth. . . .
>
> I belong to a people who have known for centuries the meaning and burden of the struggle. Every liberty-loving and liberty-seeking people has a peculiar place in the sympathy of my own people, which hails with unique joy your message to the Congress of the United States, destined to become a Magna Charta for all the peoples and places of earth.

Within two days I received the warm though cryptic response:

> You may be sure, though I have only time for a line in reply to it, I deeply appreciate your letter of April eleventh and that I share the thought that you express in it. It may be that I can find some diplomatic and suggestive way of putting the idea into the minds of those across the water.

I shall leave to another chapter the story of Wilson's historic service to the re-establishment of the Jewish National Home in Palestine and his role in the issuance of the Balfour Declaration.

I would close these paragraphs in lighter mood. I once ventured to say to the President, when he was speaking sharply of the British government and particularly of the then Minister of Transport, Lord Robert Cecil, "Mr. President, you have not a drop of non-British blood in your veins, for you are English, Scotch, Irish, but you do not seem to trust England. I, on the other hand, son of Abraham, have only Jewish blood in my veins and not one drop of British blood, but I trust and revere England." His whimsical reply was, "I know my family better than you do."

I was in Paris throughout January, 1919. Among several meetings with Wilson, two stand out. One of the editors of *Le Matin* had begged me for an interview on President Wilson. I gave it and told some characteristic tales about the American President. The next day to my consternation I came upon the headline: *"Mon Ami Wilson."* I saw at once how unfitting it was for an American citizen to speak in such terms of the President of the United States, visiting and negotiating a peace treaty in Paris. I went to him at once, eager to explain that I bore no responsibility for this flippant reference to himself, without even his title. He smiled his most gracious smile and, brushing away any attempt at an apology, asked me almost impishly, "But are you not my friend?"

One final memory of those days: Before the Paris Peace Conference I suggested to President Wilson that he include Justice Brandeis among the American delegation. He answered: "I named Brandeis to the Bench and you remember how difficult it was to get him confirmed. He has not been on the Bench long enough to make himself felt, as he is bound to do in time. If he comes here he will have to resign from the Bench. It would not be easy for me to secure Senatorial confirmation of another great liberal, even if I could find him." Finally, as if summing up the entire case, he said, "Dr. Wise, I need Brandeis everywhere, but I must leave him somewhere."

Wilson and Brandeis had much in common, which constituted an irrefragable bond between them. Each was a democrat in the truest sense of the term, not a democrat on parade or out of expediency but because of inmost faith in the people. Each had a touch of the quality of Lincoln, whom Brandeis physically resembled. Wilson had come to lean heavily on Brandeis, on the latter's profound understanding of the economic aspects of democratic government and administration.

In May, 1919, former President Taft advised Joseph Tumulty, a secretary to the President, that he was much troubled that the conference at Paris was unable to adopt a provision in favor of religious freedom throughout the world. He expressed the opinion that there was an acute necessity for it with respect to Poland, Rumania, and those other new states carved out of Russia, Austria, and Germany. He therefore requested Mr. Tumulty to transmit the following cable message to President Wilson:

> The Jews of the United States are greatly disturbed over reliable reports coming to them of continued abuses of their coreligionists in Poland, Roumania and in the new Slav States created under the auspices of the conference. Is it not possible to impose on these States, as a condition of their recognition and membership in the League, the maintenance of religious freedom under their respective governments? What was done in the Berlin Conference of 1879 ought to be possible in the more favorable atmosphere of this conference, with the additional securities of performance that the League will give.

The message was transmitted, and Mr. Taft received within a few days a cabled response from President Wilson that he was endeavoring to take substantially the action suggested. I had been working closely with Mr. Taft and he kept me informed of his efforts and the responses he received.

The atrocities against Jews in Poland continued and so I sent a further cable to President Wilson on May 16, 1919:

> Am joining Taft, Lowell and Party in League of Nations State Conventions trip through country to prepare way for acceptance of League Covenant. Find grave uneasiness over omission in published abstracts of anti-religious discrimination clause. Though mindful of difficulties, explained by you, I still believe it would be immensely valuable to have some message from you making clear that in every separate convention of the Allies with countries such as Poland and Roumania, religious and other rights of minorities will be scrupulously safeguarded. Taft desires me to say that he shares my feeling and urges the above course.

I got an encouraging message from the President through Mr. Tumulty:

> Please thank Rabbi Stephen S. Wise for his cable and tell him that he may rest assured that the safeguards against religious discrimination which we have all so much at heart will be embodied in the arrangements by which the new States are to be set up.
>
> WOODROW WILSON

Tragically for the Jews the end of the war brought no peace in Eastern Europe. Despite the efforts made to protect minorities by men such as Wilson, who regarded this as essential to peace and civilization, persecution continued and mounted. As I received reports I forwarded them to President Wilson for his information and so that whenever possible he might be helpful, as I knew he would want to be. Again and again he responded. One letter that reflected his mind and heart dated September 10, 1920, was characteristic of him as a great democrat and great American:

SEPTEMBER 10, 1920

MY DEAR RABBI WISE:

I am deeply moved by the reports which you send me of the trials and suffering endured by your fellow-Jews throughout

Eastern Europe. No American, whatever his racial origin or religious creed, can fail to feel the deepest sympathy with the Jews of Eastern Europe, who continue to bear not only the burden of war but also the sufferings incident to unenlightened and unjust treatment at the hands of governments and peoples.

I am of the hope that those nations with which our own land holds political commerce may do everything in their power to end not only the legal disabilities of their Jewish population as provided for by Minority Peoples Clauses of the Peace Treaty, but all the injustices and wrongs which are laid upon them.

We know in this country wherein Jews of right enjoy entire equality how loyally they serve and how faithfully they support the purposes and ideals of our own nation.

I should greatly rejoice to learn through you that there has come about an amelioration of the status of the Jews in Eastern European lands. This government most earnestly desires that Jewish persecution be ended in all lands and for all time.

CORDIALLY AND SINCERELY
WOODROW WILSON

XI

The Brandeis Epoch

FROM the very outset of World War I, American
Zionists were faced with the serious problem of what should
be our attitude toward Germany and toward the Turkish government, still sovereign over Palestine. The President's counsel
respecting neutrality seemed to be doubly binding in the case
of Turkey, which was not involved in the hostilities at the
beginning. Parenthetically, I may point out that we never
declared war on Turkey. I recall having asked President Wilson
in 1918 why we had not done so. His clear answer was that he
had been urged not to do so by Cleveland Dodge, distinguished
civic leader and philanthropist, who had interested himself
deeply in the Christian colleges in the Near East. Dodge,
according to Wilson, had said that, if we declared war on the
Turks, they might or even probably would destroy the American colleges throughout Turkey beginning with Beirut, at
which Dodge's son was a teacher and, later, its president. I
do not question, of course, that the decision was reached after
fullest consultation with political and military authorities.

Whatever our attitude toward Turkey might otherwise have
been, some of us, notably Professor Gottheil and myself, were
moved by the Armenian atrocities to take our stand against
the hideously criminal government of Turkey. We were accused
of taking a terrible risk in thus giving affront to the Suzerain of
Palestine, seeing that it held our people and our hopes as

182

hostage. Against us were ranged the inflexibly neutral, some who truly dreaded the possible consequences to the Jewish settlement in Palestine of a violation of neutrality on our part as a Jewish organization. There were others, explicably tepid toward the Allied Powers, which included the unspeakable Russian government. I venture to believe that we wisely dared, as did that heroic band of young Jewish men and women in Palestine who, to the horror of the prudent, risked nearly half a century of toil and sacrifice by openly espousing the cause of Britain and dying therefor.

One incident will help to illustrate the delicate nature of the Turkish problem. During 1913 and early 1914, I had set myself the task of organizing an investigation commission to survey all the needs of the Jews of Palestine. I secured the help of a small but distinguished group, including the late Henry Morgenthau, Sr. The outbreak of the war, however, ended all possibilities of the commission. Morgenthau in the meantime had gone to Turkey as American ambassador, in part as a result of my plea to him in Dijon in August, 1913, that his going to Constantinople might serve America by improving Armenian conditions and bettering the situation for the Jews in Palestine. He cabled his alarm in August, 1914, over the irritation of the Turkish government in finding the Ambassador's name coupled with an investigation commission to be dispatched to the Ottoman province of Palestine. I hastened to Washington to forestall any criticism of Mr. Morgenthau that might have reached the State Department from the Sublime Porte. I found Secretary of State William Jennings Bryan superbly impervious to the possible difficulty. But other State Department officials understood at once and declared that my announcement of Mr. Morgenthau's withdrawal from the commission would suffice to avert any misunderstanding. Having failed, because of the war, to organize American succor for Palestine, it fell to my lot a year later, in the fall of 1915, to secure for the Palestinians the then unprecedentedly large sum of $55,000 in Los Angeles,

San Francisco, Seattle, and Portland as a loan for the orange growers who were threatened with ruination.

The second major problem we faced was that of our attitude toward Germany. There were those who felt that, to use a vulgarism, "all our Zionist eggs should not be placed in one basket," and that we must not ignore the possibility of Germany becoming the victor and having Palestine in its custody. Dr. Judah L. Magnes, later chancellor of the Hebrew University in Jerusalem and life-long pacifist—that is, until the Nazi assault on human freedom—was clearly inclined to go along with the German Empire before our declaration of war. Some of us were adamant in our rejection of the proposal to deal gently with Germany, though the proposal had the strong support of such men as Dr. Schmaryahu Levin. A prominent Eastern European Zionist and member of the first Russian Duma, Levin had actually been aboard ship returning to Europe when war was declared and was forced to turn back to the United States. Levin, whose university education had been obtained in Germany, felt that inasmuch as Turkey, sovereign over Palestine, stood by the side of Germany, it was inexpedient for Zionist leadership in a then neutral land to commit itself too vigorously in support of the Allies.

Against this counsel of expediency, I scornfully said to my fellow Zionists in executive session and subsequently at public meetings: "We do not want Palestine to come to us from the bloodstained hands of the Turkish assassinocracy." We prevailed in the end, and the American authorities came to know that we no longer pretended to be neutral in spirit as between Britain and Germany.

Immediately after the war's beginning, an assembly was convened in New York to consider the new orientation likely to arise out of the war. From that meeting there emerged the American Provisional Committee for Zionist Affairs as *ad hoc* successor to the Federation of American Zionists. The first task of our committee was to save as much as possible of what had been planted in the twenty or more colonies in Palestine, the

work of the *chalutzim*—the pioneers—reinforced by the boundless generosity of Baron Edmond de Rothschild.

Nathan Straus made the first large gift for the saving of
the Palestinian settlements, a gift which other and much richer
Jews affected to admire but never undertook to improve upon
or even to duplicate. Our government, thanks to the President
and Secretary of the Navy Josephus Daniels, a never failing
friend of the oppressed, made it possible to assure money and
food to the Palestine dwellers, even permitting the use of battle-
ships and colliers for this purpose. This precedent later resulted
in other humanitarian services by our country.

The real achievement, however, of the assembly from which
the Provisional Committee emerged was to bring actively into
the Zionist movement Mr., later Justice, Louis D. Brandeis,
who in September, 1914, was moved to accept the chairmanship
of the committee.

While Brandeis had long been out of touch with Jewish life,
he was in San Francisco in August, 1897. On the day after
the first Zionist Congress in Basle, he read in the *San Francisco
Chronicle* a report of the session, especially the address of
Herzl. He remarked to Mrs. Brandeis, after reading the speech
aloud, "There is a cause to which I could give my life." That
was prophecy, for he came, after a number of intervening years,
to give a goodly part of his life, almost the best part, to the
Zionist cause, as if in reparation for years of neglect of the
Jewish problem and the terrible needs it involved.

Only Brandeis could have testified to the influences that
shaped his later decision. I believe it fair to say that the Palestinian Aaron Aronson and Jacob deHaas were important factors, the one unconsciously by virtue of his arresting and
passionate devotion to the new Palestine, the other by reason
of his conscious and persistent effort to win the enormous
help of such advocacy as it lay in Brandeis to give to any cause
that commanded his allegiance. Brandeis himself bore testimony to a third and perhaps decisive factor, the impression
made upon him by the social idealism of the Eastern European

workers in the needle industries, with whom he came into contact in connection with some arbitration problems. In any event, Brandeis accepted the burden of leadership with that real humility which his comrades came to know as one of the marks of that uniquely spiritual personality.

Brandeis' public leadership of the Zionist cause lasted for only two years, up to the time of his accession to the Supreme Court. But what enriching years they were and how inspiring to his colleagues! After 1916 he did not cease to stand out as leader, but his leadership took the form of invaluable counsel to a small number of associates. These kept in close touch with him, as he kept in closest touch with the minutest details of the Palestinian settlement. He knew, he read, he remembered everything with respect to figures, acreage, livestock in the colonies and settlements of Palestine. His own financial contributions were the greatest of any Zionist of his lifetime. Nothing escaped his watchful eye or ever was lost to the memory of this most practical idealist, who expected, though he was bound to fail, to find equally comprehensive and accurate knowledge on the part of all those who worked at his side. His leadership in the early years of the war made possible the fulfillment of our major task—the political one.

I had taken occasion to give to President Wilson, even before his inauguration, a rather full outline of Zionism. From the very beginning of his administration, Brandeis and I knew that in Wilson we had and would always have understanding sympathy with the Zionist program and purpose. I have always felt that his sympathetic attitude grew in large part out of filial reverence for his parson father, the Reverend Thomas Wilson, in the manse of whose Staunton, Virginia, pastorate, Woodrow was born. I recall a word of his which made clear that he felt and acted herein at times as his father's son. As I urged him one day to cooperate with the British government re the hope of the Balfour Declaration, he was touched, and soliloquized aloud, "To think that I, a son of the manse, should be able to help restore the Holy Land to its people!" It was then that I reminded him that King Cyrus, whatever else he was, had become a figure of history chiefly because his memory was enshrined in the pages of the Bible as the Persian King who had enabled the exiled Jews of his land to return to Jerusalem and rebuild their land and temple.

From time to time, it fell to Wilson to reach decisions on Jewish matters of gravest import. In reaching these decisions he never took counsel of expediency or self-seeking. He neither yielded to pressure nor consulted the hope of advantage. In all the discussions of Jewish problems covering nearly a decade, Wilson never in the faintest way indicated that he wished merely to please his Jewish fellow citizens, though I believe he rejoiced to be able to serve them and to have a part in the working out of Jewish destiny. A true Christian in the Lincolnian sense, he respected self-respecting Jews, and I noted with unconcealed delight his scant patience with such Jews as imagined that they were "forced to frame excuses for their birth." It became rather amusing to see that lukewarm and less than tepid Jews found themselves under the necessity, as they met with Wilson, of feigning a loyalty they were not big enough to share. Wilson, of course, was most fortunate in leaning heavily, as I well know he chose to do, on Brandeis. The latter, particularly after his assumption of the leadership of the Zionist Provisional Committee, together with myself and others, continued to discuss Zionism and its problems with the President. Throughout, it must be added, we received warm and heartening help from Colonel House, close friend of the President and his unofficial secretary of state. House not only made our cause the object of his very special concern but served as liaison officer between the Wilson administration and the Zionist movement. This was particularly true after it grew to strength, beginning in 1914, through increasing support of Zionism by the Jewish masses throughout the world and the changing world situation, which forecast the historical necessity for a Jewish homeland.

The Balfour Declaration of November, 1917, in which Wilson was to play so vital a role, had a long history. The process of securing the declaration ran through two years and more, beginning with a suggestion of Dr. Gaster, gifted and learned chief rabbi of the Spanish-Portuguese Synagogue of London, to Herbert—now Viscount—Samuel. A small group of English Zionists was called together from time to time for consultation. They included that man of destiny, lately become the first president of Israel, Dr. Chaim Weizmann, who enjoyed the friendship of Balfour and the privilege of making a contribution of great importance to the war in the field of chemistry. The English group had begun discussion of Palestine with members of the earlier War Cabinet under Asquith, and we were kept fairly well informed of these discussions. When Mr. Balfour visited Washington in 1916, Justice Brandeis discussed the Zionist program with him on at least two occasions.

The events in England leading up to the adoption of the Balfour Declaration by the British government have been told at length and in detail by several of the central figures in that historic episode, and are matters of common knowledge. What is less well known, however, is the significant part played by the American government, and particularly by President Wilson.

In the summer of 1917, there came to us, at first through Jewish sources and, only in the early fall, through our own governmental sources, several drafts of what has become historic as the Balfour Declaration. As early as April 9, 1917, I had discussed developments in Britain with Colonel House. I wrote to deHaas at the time:

> I have just had a good long talk with Colonel House and I cannot tell you how pleased I am. He understands the situation and what is better yet, not only is it in his mind and not only did he realize the imminence of the British possibilities but he said he is keeping the papers before him in order to move at the right moment. Of course, we must trust him in the matter and we do.

He is enlisted in our cause. There is no question about it whatever. The thing will go through Washington, I think, without
delay.

Toward the end of June, 1917, when I went to see the
President concerning plans to convene the first session of the
American Jewish Congress, we again discussed Zionism. He
said at that time, "You know of my deep interest in Zionism."
I told him that I did, that I had been in conference with Colonel House who had on several occasions spoken of the President's sympathetic interest, and that Justice Brandeis and I
were greatly heartened by it. He then said, "Whenever the
time comes, and you and Justice Brandeis feel that the time
is ripe for me to speak and act, I shall be ready".

At last, in mid-October, 1917, the Balfour Declaration came
to President Wilson for his final approval. While our government could not publicly announce a policy or make a commitment on the ground that we were not at war with the Turkish
Empire, the British government had stipulated for President
Wilson's assent to any declaration that might be issued. If
the President had not been ready to give explicit assent to
the terms of the Balfour Declaration, it would not have been
made.

Wilson sent the document to Justice Brandeis, and the latter
forwarded it to me to be handed to Colonel House for trans-
mission to the British Cabinet. DeHaas and I were disturbed,
as was Judge Julian W. Mack, upon whose wise and judicial
counsel we often leaned, by the term in the document "national
home for Jews." DeHaas and I bore the draft to Colonel House
and suggested the change from "national home for *Jews*" to
"national home for *the Jewish People*." House agreed at once
to change the phrase and meaning, after discussing it once
more with the President, which he did in our presence over a
private wire to the White House. Some weeks passed, and
at last, to the limitless joy of the Jewish people, the Balfour
Declaration was issued in the form of a letter addressed to

Lord Rothschild from Balfour, then head of the British Foreign
Office.

It should never be forgotten that though the name of Balfour
is most closely associated with the declaration, it was the
Prime Minister, David Lloyd George who, as his memoirs
attest, was most continuously eager to bring about the fulfillment of the Zionist hope. Thus, later at Paris, while boundaries
were under discussion, he would repeatedly use the Biblical
phrase, "You shall have Palestine from Dan to Beersheba,"
which was historically thrilling but not practically helpful in
defining frontiers.

Sir Charles Henry told me, in December, 1918, the story
of Lloyd George's bidding Lady Henry, "Julia, get together
at breakfast the Jewish members of both Houses of Parliament
who are opposed to my Zionist position that I may convince
them of the rightfulness of it and the wrong of their own." She
did just that. A *minyan* (Jewish religious quorum of ten) was
assembled at breakfast to meet the Prime Minister. After bidding Julia, "Bring me a Bible," which happily was to be found,
he thumbed its pages, reading passage after passage from the
Hebrew Prophets, prophesying the restoration of Zion to the
Jewish people and of the Jewish people to Zion. Triumphantly,
he closed with these words to the Jewish members of Parliament, "Now, gentlemen, you know what your Bible says. That
closes the matter." As far as I recall the story, no further discussion took place at breakfast, but not a few of the gentlemen
continued their opposition.

The issuance of the Balfour Declaration in November brought
boundless joy to Jews throughout the world. We in New York
were so jubilant that our joy expressed itself in the form of a
parade—good old Nathan Straus and myself at its head. At a
meeting of celebration, I said by way of challenge to Germany's Bethman Hollweg and his reference to a "scrap of
paper," "The Balfour Declaration is not and never will be
regarded as a scrap of paper. It is written not in German but

in English, the language of freedom and of freemen. It will always be honored in the observance, not the breach."

I was wrong, and I quote that sentence all the more readily because of the bitter tension today between the British government and the Jewish people. Whatever may happen today, the fact uncancelable remains that it was England which, in the Cromwellian tradition and by the Balfour Declaration, was the first nation after more than eighteen hundred years, since the year 70 A.D., to recognize "the Jewish people" and to undertake "to use their best endeavors to facilitate the establishment of a national home for the Jewish people." What the British government failed to do in 1947 must dishonor all those who have shared in the betrayal of the Balfour Declaration, but it does not diminish or detract from the grandeur of British action in 1917.

Soon after the declaration appeared and in the midst of almost universal Jewish rejoicing and gratitude, mutterings of dissent began to be heard. Justice Brandeis asked me to come to Washington and allay the possible misgivings and resolve the doubts of Wilson. Together we decided on what should be said if he were unduly troubled. I sought to indicate to the President that he might hear murmurs of disapproval from a number of quarters, even mentioning the names of the chief among the dissenters—Max Senior of Cincinnati, A. Leo Weil of Pittsburgh, most regrettably Rabbi Henry Berkowitz of Philadelphia, gallant old Simon Wolf of Washington, and Rabbi Shulman of New York. Fortunately I asked the question, "If these gentlemen have not yet protested against your support of the Balfour Declaration, what will you do when their protests reach you?" For one moment only he was silent. Then he pointed to a large wastepaper basket at his desk. "Is not that basket capacious enough for all their protests?"

Late in the summer of 1918, I wrote to the President to say that there were several matters of public importance I wished to bring to his attention and was promptly invited to visit him

on August 27. It seemed that the time was at hand to urge
him to speak out concerning Zionism and that we needed something more than his word-of-mouth approval of the Balfour
Declaration. I was especially moved to do this because it was
rumored that Henry Morgenthau and some laymen in New
York and Rabbi Philipson and other rabbis were preparing an
anti-Zionist conference. It seemed well to say a word to the
President so as to avert the possibility of his taking seriously
the opposition of a handful of men who were not representative of any considerable number of Jews and who, it is not
too much to say, were without imagination to envision the
meaning of the Zionist movement. With this thought in mind,
I prepared a memorandum, first submitting it to Justice Brandeis, who made one change—the insertion of a reference to the
Hebrew University, a very wise insertion, as later developed.

The President was most hearty, if possible heartier than ever
before, when he greeted us, his first words being, "Well, you
have the grip of a shipyard laborer!" I told the President just
what had been in my mind when I undertook that job. I said
I had asked my sixteen-year-old son to do some productive
work during his summer vacation before entering Princeton
and that I thought it would be well for the boy to feel that I
would do any work that he could. Then I added that it seemed
to me important to know just what the men in the shipyards
were thinking and feeling about the war. I told the President
that I was persuaded that the most precious asset of the Allied
cause in America was the unlimited confidence of the American
masses in the President of the United States. The President
turned to me and said, "You are a good friend, but what are
the reasons that moved you to say that?"

I told him I had taken pains to talk to man after man and
group after group in many sections of the shipyard, and I had
come to see three things: First, that the men felt that the
President did not wish to go to war. Again, the President interrupted and said, "Do the men really understand that?" I answered that there was a definite conviction among all

Americans, which is of invaluable help now, that the President would not have gone to war if he could have avoided it, but that he went for no lesser reason than that he had to go, that Germany made it impossible for him and us decently to stay out.

Then I said that the American workingman fully understood that, as long as Woodrow Wilson was in the White House, they could trust him and know that no demand would be made upon them as workers that was not compatible with the ideals of our democracy. I added, "Mr. President, if one of our good old reactionary friends were president now and were making the demands upon the workers that you are making, there would be a great deal of trouble—but they trust you. It isn't Schwab or Hurley that they trust; they trust you." And I added that the years of democratic leadership prior to the war and the great democratic program the President had espoused and executed, had made it possible for the workers to pin their faith in him.

In the third place, I explained to the President that he held the men's faith because they knew that he meant what he said, that he did not go into this struggle in order merely to win the war, but in the hope of ending war itself.

The President took the points one by one, saying, "They are right; I did not wish to go into the war. It is good to know that America understands that." As for the second point, he spoke at some length. We happened to mention President Nicholas Murray Butler's speech of a few days earlier at the Commonwealth Club of San Francisco, and I said that I thought it amusing to think of Butler saying, "There are two kinds of Prussianism that must be combatted. One is Prussianism of Germany, and the other the menace of socialism in America." I said, "Isn't it funny for Butler to try to put that across to an American audience?" The President's answer was, "Do you really think it is funny for Butler to try to put anything across to an audience that gathers to hear him?" Then in more serious vein he added, "Men come to me [and the reference was unmistakably to men like Schwab], and I try to make clear to them what is coming after the war. I explain that we can never go back to the old order. But they don't understand. They cannot believe that we are in earnest. They listen to me but only with the outer tympanum of their ears." And again he used the phrase, "The trouble is we do not speak the same language."

We then discussed the memorandum I had prepared on Zionism, in which the President again expressed his interest, adding that he would be happy to express his views in a letter to me for publication within the near future. Within a few days, practically on the eve of the Jewish New Year, I received the letter from President Wilson reaffirming his support of the Zionist movement and expressing satisfaction in its progress:

AUGUST 31, 1918

MY DEAR RABBI WISE:

I have watched with deep and sincere interest the reconstruction work which the Weizmann Commission has done in Palestine at the instance of the British Government and I welcome an opportunity to express the satisfaction I have felt in the progress of the Zionist movement in the United States and in the Allied countries since the declaration of Mr. Balfour on behalf of the British Government, of Great Britain's approval of the establishment in Palestine of a national home for the Jewish people, and his promise that the British Government would use its best endeavors to facilitate the achievement of that object, with the understanding that nothing would be done to prejudice the civil and religious rights of non-Jewish people in Palestine or the rights and political status enjoyed by Jews in other countries. I think that all America will be deeply moved by the report that even in this time of stress the Weizmann Commission has been able to lay the foundation of the Hebrew University of Jerusalem with the promise that that bears of spiritual rebirth.

CORDIALLY AND SINCERELY,
[signed] WOODROW WILSON

No more joyous greeting for the New Year could have come to American Jewry and the Jews of the world than the utterance of the President. I wrote to Dr. Weizmann at the time: "The general American opinion, I am happy to say, is that the morale of the Central Powers received a damaging blow through the Presidential utterance on Zionism."

In December, 1918, I went to London together with Jacob deHaas, Louis Robison, and Mrs. Mary Fels, by the direction of Justice Brandeis and the Provisional Committee for Zionist Affairs. Arriving a few days after President Wilson, mine was the joy of witnessing the extraordinary demonstration which greeted the first of American presidents to visit London. At the Lord Mayor's luncheon at Mansion House, in honor of the President, the latter introduced me to Mr. Balfour and to the famous editor of the *Manchester Guardian*, C. P. Scott. A day or two thereafter I had tea with Mr. Balfour at the Foreign Office. It fell to me to carry out the mandate of the American Jewish Congress, then in its first session in Philadelphia, to inform the Foreign Secretary of the resolution adopted by the Congress the previous day. That resolution urged the British government to act as trustee over the Jewish Commonwealth of Palestine.

Mr. Balfour, most equable of men and serenest of philosophers, seemed touched by the tidings I brought him, which he had not seen in the daily press, admittedly and traditionally left unread by him. He inquired whether many of the delegates to the American Jewish Congress had lived in England. My reply was to the effect that probably not more than 1 per cent of the delegates had ever lived or been in England. Thereupon he gravely said, "American Jews have honored my country and its government by this request." Before I left, I asked Mr. Balfour for a further definition of the term in the declaration, "a national home for the Jewish people." His reply was prompt withal considered: "This means that Jews who either wish or require, now or in the future, to go to Palestine shall have the right to do so."

We met again at the dinner tendered by Lord Rothschild to King Feisal and the world-famed Colonel T. E. Lawrence.

Feisal looked every inch an Eastern potentate and spoke in Arabic. Lawrence translated the speech in simple, musical English, an easy enough task, seeing that he had probably written the Arabic version for His Majesty.

I then went to Paris, charged by the American Jewish Congress as well as the Zionist movement, to arrange a meeting of Dr. Weizmann with President Wilson. On Tuesday, January 14, after a series of conferences with Nahum Sokolow, Dr. Weizmann, and others, and after meetings with representatives of the French government, I took Dr. Weizmann to see the President in the late afternoon. I first spent nearly three quarters of an hour with the President and then told him that, as he had agreed the previous day, I had brought Dr. Weizmann to see him. Weizmann entered and was greeted most cordially. As Weizmann had indicated that he preferred that I should not be present during the interview, I withdrew. Weizmann's interview was highly satisfactory, and I think he came to feel that the President was not uninformed and that we had prepared the way as far as things could be done in America. When next I saw the President he spoke of Weizmann with such enthusiasm as came to mind after a quarter of a century when President Roosevelt and I discussed Weizmann, whom both great American presidents had come to hold in highest regard.

During the Paris Peace Conference, Wilson's influence for Zion's good made itself felt in the conduct of Secretary of State Lansing. When Dr. Weizmann appeared before the delegates to the Peace Conference to make his classic presentation of the Zionist case, neither Wilson nor House was present. But an incident grew out of a statement, offending and gratuitous, made by a distinguished Jewish Sanskrit scholar of France, Professor Sylvain Levy, who sought to minimize Jewish concern with Palestine and Zionism. Lansing, tested friend of the Zionist cause, was presiding officer of the session. In reply to Professor Levy, he proceeded to invite a statement by Dr. Weizmann. When he asked Weizmann, "How Jewish do you expect Palestine to become?" the latter made the daring, by this time historic, reply, "As Jewish as England is English." That word of Weizmann's, which was imperative as well as predictive, was to be triumphantly fulfilled.

When I saw Wilson in Paris, he promised that he would receive a delegation of the American Jewish Congress during his brief stay in Washington between his two Paris trips. We were concerned both with the fulfillment of the Balfour Declaration and the assurance of minority rights for Jews in East European lands. A delegation including Judge Mack, Louis Marshall, Bernard G. Richards, and myself met with the President at the White House. We presented our case and the President made a vigorous affirmation both on behalf of a Jewish Palestine and minority Jewish rights in Central and Eastern Europe. I stayed behind for a moment, after the others had left, in order to tell the President of some of the difficulties we had begun to face in Paris. "Mr. President," I said, "World Jewry counts upon you in its hour of need and hope." Placing his hand on my shoulder, he quietly and firmly said, "Have no fear, Palestine will be yours."

Our battle did not end with the ceremonial of Versailles. The struggle between the President and the Senate, resulting in our nonparticipation as a nation in the work of ratification, made vigilance trebly needful. But every moral gain achieved at Paris was scrupulously safeguarded at all subsequent meetings of the powers. We Zionists found in Lansing's successor, Bainbridge Colby, an equally sympathetic furtherer of the cause supported by his chief. At San Remo, America was represented only by an observer, but the promises made to us were kept and the British mandate over Palestine affirmed.

As soon as the San Remo Conference had awarded the Palestine mandate to Britain, I wrote to President Wilson:

My dear Mr. President:

My first impulse upon learning of the consummation of our hopes is to write to you and to express to you the deep and abiding gratitude of the Jewish people, for whom I speak, for all you have done to make this great consummation possible.

Jewish history, which is the history not of a day but of centuries, will never fail to make mention of the great and generous service which you were ever ready to render to the cause of a national homeland for the Jewish people.

The cabled reports indicate that the Mandate has gone to Great Britain, and we are of the hope that ultimately things will be so adjusted as to give to Jews the best possible opportunity for realizing their hopes in the noblest way—in a way that shall be in accord with your ideals of the new freedom of peoples.

Once again, dear Mr. President, the deepfelt thanks of all the Jewish people, who will hold you in honor and in gratitude for all generations as one of the great, wise and helpful friends of Israel.

FAITHFULLY YOURS,
[signed] STEPHEN S. WISE

I cannot close this chapter without reverting for a moment to the man who, through these years, was indisputably our leader and inspiration, Justice Brandeis. I have already indicated that after his elevation to the Supreme Court, his public activity on behalf of Zionism had to come to an end. But he remained until his death, for many of us, our guiding spirit and our constant and unfailing counselor. I recall that before I met him nearly forty years ago someone said to me, "I find that every meeting with Brandeis is a spiritual experience." I quickly came to see the accuracy of that observation. One felt as one sat with him in his modest, little study, unadorned save by the radiance of his personality, that one had drawn a little nearer to the sources of truth and justice. Sometimes, as I listened to him at his finest and truest, I felt as if I were at the side of one who, without being oracular or dogmatic, had gained for himself the treasure of truth and was sharing it with those who listened.

He was our leader in the most critical years of American

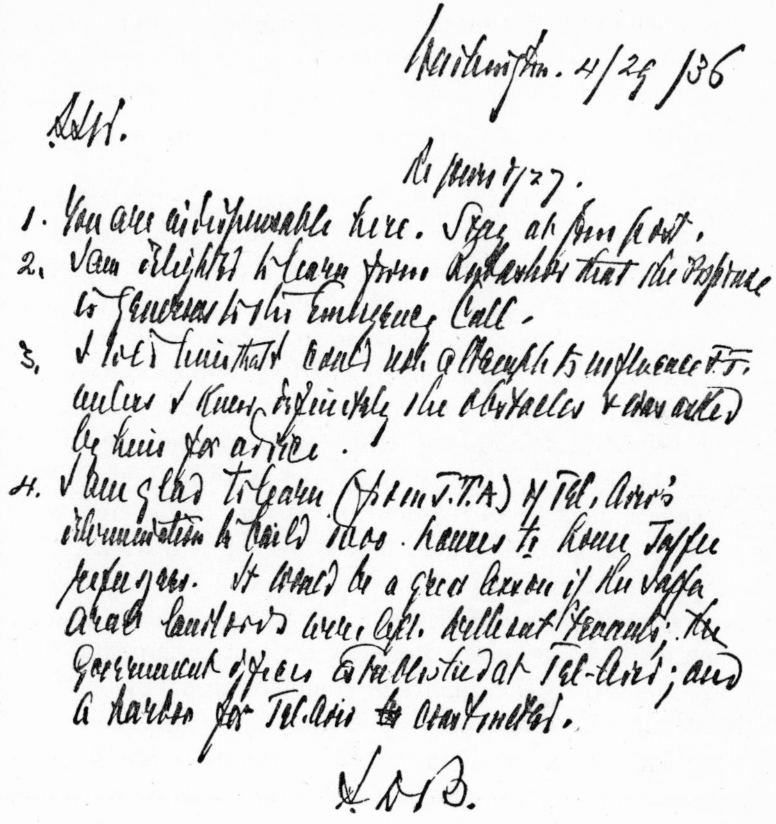
Washington. 4/29/36

S.S.W.

Re yours 4/27.

1. You are indispensable here. Stay at your post.
2. I am delighted to learn from Rubashov that the response is generous to the Emergency Call.
3. I told him that I could not attempt to influence F.F. unless I knew definitely the obstacles & was asked by him for advice.
4. I am glad to learn (from J.T.A.) of Tel Aviv's determination to build 1000 homes to house Jaffa refugees. It would be a great lesson if the Jaffa Arab landlords were left without tenants; the Government offices established at Tel-Aviv; and a harbor for Tel-Aviv constructed.

L.D.B.

Washington 4/29/36

S.S.W.

1. You are indispensable here. Stay at your post.
2. I am delighted to learn from Rubashov that the response is generous to the Emergency Call.
3. I told him that I could not attempt to influence F. F. [Felix Frankfurter] unless I knew definitely the obstacles and was asked by him for advice.
4. I am glad to learn [from J.T.A.,the Jewish Telegraphic Agency] of Tel-Aviv's determination to build 1000 homes to house Jaffa refugees. It would be a great lesson if the Jaffa Arab landlords were left without tenants; the Government offices established at Tel-Aviv; and a harbor for Tel-Aviv constructed.

L.D.B.

Jewish history, when the lofty quality of his ethical idealism meant much to the fortunes of Israel. It was a providential conjuncture that matched the man and the need, that made his the decisive contribution in the working out of Jewish destiny at a time when America had become supremely important in the leadership of world affairs.

Brandeis was one of the commanding figures in the realm of democracy. As much as any man of his generation, he was a leader of the forces of liberalism, not spasmodically or melodramatically but consistently and selflessly. Throughout a generation, he made the imperiled interests of the people his own.

He was an American prophet, but the prophet within his being was enriched and ennobled in the last decades of his life by his self-identification with the Jewish people. The term prophet should not be lightly used, least of all by Jews. When it is used, it must be in relation to one who is dowered with that insight into truth which inevitably translates itself into foresight with respect to the future, with that moral grandeur which compels men to undertake and achieve the impossible. No one could have known Brandeis without recognizing that he was touched by the quality or genius of prophecy.

Hardly less historic than his contribution to the redemption of Zion was his role as founder of the American Jewish Congress. Passionately unyielding democrat that he was all his life, he found to his amazement and regret that little had been done by the beginning of the first war democratically to organize American Jews. He deplored and resented the failure of the wealthy philanthropists in control of Jewish affairs to invite the judgment and participation of those whom, he rightly assumed, were no less qualified than the wealthy to conduct their affairs as Jews in American life. True it was that he saw that to organize American Jews democratically was to insure their effective support of Zionism. But he also felt that only through such instrumentality as the American Jewish Congress would Jews of America be free to use their own voice rather than be the echo of voices which spoke for them, free to reach their own

With Albert Einstein and Thomas Mann at the preview of Hendrik van Loon's film, The Fight for Peace.

ACME PHOTO

With Mayor Fiorello La Guardia at a Madison Square Garden meeting against totalitarianism in 1939.

ALEXANDER ARCHER

At the C.I.O. Convention in Atlantic City, New Jersey, in 1946, with Philip Murray and Jacob Potofsky.

decisions, to speak and act for themselves as Jews in the working out of their Jewish problems. Back of this understanding lay his recognition on the one hand of the contribution every racial and religious group could make to the democratic totality of American life, as well as his deep and unshakable faith in the worth and dignity of Jews as a people. He labored to the end that American Jews might share such dignity and pride, and he knew that they could not be expected to do this as long as they as a body were treated as if they were incompetent to deal with, and however blundering at times, to reach decisions with respect to their own affairs.

He quickly won the honor of being vigorously opposed by those incurably distrustful of the democratic way of life. But Brandeis sounded the watchword of democracy with all the authority of a great personality and with the fearless vigor of one to whom democracy was not a party label but the one and only way of life. Once he had stood upon the American Jewish platform, the prestige of the antidemocratic groups was lowered and their power of control limited.

Others will assess the measure of Brandeis' contribution to American life as lawyer, as jurist, as social thinker. I can affirm however that since the day of Herzl, Brandeis was indisputably and incomparably our greatest Jew. I think not of his gifts as an economist, or even his genius as a statesman, least of all, of his boundless personal generosity. Rather do I think of the spirit he brought to our cause that I can best describe by using the Hebrew term *kedushah*—holiness. I thank God for the fullness of his years and the richness of his days, for what he wrought, and, above all, for what he was.

XII

Battling for Jewish Democracy

THROUGHOUT most of the life of the American Jewish Congress, it has been my privilege to serve as its president; and I find deep satisfaction in the great contributions the Congress has made to the security of Jewish life both here and abroad, to the struggle for the establishment of a Jewish national home, and to the realization of American democracy. Above all, the Congress finally and effectively shattered the dominance of paternalism and benevolent despotism in the internal affairs of the American Jewish community.

It should cause no surprise that so continuous and stern a battle has had to be waged within the Jewish community for democracy in the management of Jewish affairs. It is little more than a century, in many instances less, since Jews, like most other human beings, dwelt in lands untouched by the spirit and methods of democracy. One of the results of the persecution of the Jews was the inevitable rise of a succession of individuals in all lands and ages who stood out as the intermediaries between their people and the sovereigns or authorities of one country or another, by whose grace and favor it alone was possible for Jews to live. Feuchtwanger's *Power* tells something of the series of Jewish ambassadors to whom the Germans gave the name, half-contemptuous and half-flattering, of *Hof-Jude*, paraphrased in Yiddish as *shtadlan*. Their function was to mediate between the non-Jewish oppressors and the Jewish oppressed—hardly conducive to a democratic attitude on the part of either the mediator above or the oppressed below.

The tradition was carried over to this country. Jews from Germany comprised the bulk of the American Jewish settlers during most of the nineteenth century. A number of wealthy and influential individuals occupied themselves with problems of philanthropy and relief and constituted themselves the spokesmen and representatives of the Jewish community whenever occasion required. The masses of Jews, their number growing as a result of the later Eastern European migration, had virtually no voice in the determination of the issues by which they were vitally affected.

But rumblings of discontent were being heard within the American Jewish community, which by 1900 had grown to two million and by 1910 to three million. The outbreak of the First World War lent impetus to the democratic stirrings of the Jewish masses. It was sensed at once that great things were at stake. American Jews had to face the problems of their fellow Jews which arose out of the war: (1) the desperate need in the war countries; (2) the grave threat to the populous Jewish belt in Eastern and Central Europe; (3) the hope that Palestine would somehow emerge as a Jewish land, an aspiration almost unanimously rejected by the men of wealth and influence who dominated the Jewish community. The masses of American Jews correctly felt that there could be no hope for the Jewish restoration of Palestine unless American Jewry was organized and united. To many of us it was clear that the demands of the Jewish people had to be formulated for the peace conferences that would follow the war. And we felt deeply that no persons or groups had a right to speak *for* American Jews unless they were prepared to speak *with* American Jews. In a word, the Jews of America had to take into their own hands the management of their own internal affairs. Needless to say, such views met with bitter opposition on the part of the highly benevolent "managers," who had come to believe that their dynasty was flawless and unchangeable.

The idea of an American Jewish Congress, uniting within a democratic framework all Jewish groups for common action on Jewish affairs, began to gather momentum. The concept, put forth by such persons as Nachman Syrkin, Gedaliah Bublick, and Baruch Zuckerman, was given its clearest formulation by Justice Brandeis. More than any other person, Brandeis recognized the inexorable necessity of ending the reign of the *Hof-Juden* in America and of substituting for it a democratic organization of Jewish life in a democratic land. He fully understood the part played by the "big business" of philanthropy in the management of Jewish affairs, but he deplored and resented the failure of those in control to invite the judgment and participation of those who were no less qualified to direct and control —namely the Jewish masses themselves. He developed the idea in a series of memorable addresses in the early years of the war. And the founding of the Congress was the result of the faith of a group of men led by Brandeis and Julian Mack, Felix Frankfurter and Pinchas Rutenberg, Louis Lipsky and Bernard Richards, Nathan Straus and myself, that American Jews, citizens of a great democracy, could be trusted, understandingly and with dignity, to make use of the normal instrumentalities of democratic life.

After a series of premeetings, the preliminary conference was held in Philadelphia on March 26, 1916. Mine was the historic privilege of delivering the keynote address. Brandeis, who had meanwhile been nominated by President Wilson for the Supreme Court, was not present at the conference. In my address I said:

> This day is destined to be memorable in the annals of Israel —the more because we are thinking not of ourselves alone, nor for ourselves, but after the Jewish manner, of and for all Israel . . .
>
> We again solemnly aver that a people is not worthy of respect which does not insist on the right to be heard touching its own affairs, but surrenders the right of judgment and decision to a company of men, however wise and benevolent, who substitute their own opinions and wishes for the convictions and determina-

tions of the whole people. It were little less than a tragedy if
the Jewish people, first among the peoples in democratic aim
in this land, should succumb to the pressure exerted by those
who for one reason or another are distrustful of the capacity of
the many to manage their own affairs ...

The world cannot be expected to assent to any program touching Israel's future as long as Israel does not unitedly deliberate
and speak. Secrecy, always futile as a curative method, has
proven disastrous in prolonging and intensifying Jewish woes.
We now freely discuss our will where aforetime we furtively
listened to the edict of others. A Congress means deliberation not
agitation, discussion not division, enlightenment not secrecy ...

We reject no leadership for we have known no leadership.
Policies of inaction and aimlessness and timidity have presumed
to erect themselves into leadership, tempered always by the
grace of beneficence. With the substitution of inchoate purpose-
lessness for the conscious direction of our affairs, we have been
patient much too long. Accidentally and whimsically adopted
policies have been set to do the work of undeviating principle.
Such direction as has been has even lacked the merit of wise
opportunism. We have had caution in the place of wisdom. We
have had inaction erected into a program.

The only program acceptable to the men in control of our
affairs has been a program of palliation, as if nothing more than
temporary relief could be hoped for Israel, wounded and oppressed. Relief, alas, is at times sorely needed, was never more
needed than today. But relief is not to be exalted as the policy
or program of a people unless these be hopeless beggars and
that people adopt a program of relief as the only way out. Not
relief but redress, not palliation but prevention, not charity but
justice ... is the only program worthy of a great and proud
people.

The preliminary conference adopted the outlines of a program for the proposed American Jewish Congress, made provision for nationwide elections to the new body, and elected
an Executive Committee whose duty was to push ahead with
the plans. Discussions were carried on with other national organizations and, when the new Executive Committee met for

its first session, virtually all national Jewish bodies were included. After extensive deliberation, an election system was evolved and elections held in the Jewish communities throughout the country on June 10, 1917. On that day, for the first time in modern Jewish history, 335,000 Jewish men and women went to the polls to choose their representatives to the first American Jewish Congress.

Originally, we had hoped to convene the Congress in the fall of 1917, but our entry into the war created new problems, and many counseled postponement. I put the matter squarely before President Wilson in a conference with him on June 29, 1917. He advised postponement, and we accepted his counsel. The President authorized me to say in a statement:

> While it may seem necessary to the gentlemen who have called the Congress to postpone it for some little time from the date fixed because of the urgency of public business, the President is persuaded that the American Jewish Congress will wisely and prudently serve Jewish interests, and that its deliberations and policies will be in accord with and helpful to the aims and policies of the American government.

Meanwhile, negotiations had been continuing between the Congress advocates and those who bitterly opposed the movement. Ultimately, the latter agreed to participate in the Congress provided it was to be regarded purely as a temporary, wartime body to be dissolved as soon as its function with regard to the peace conferences had been discharged. Because we felt the need of unity to be so urgent, we reluctantly accepted that condition.

The first session of the American Jewish Congress was finally convened in Philadelphia on December 15–18, 1918. More than four hundred delegates were present, three hundred having been chosen in the nationwide elections and a hundred designated by national organizations. The participants included the most distinguished figures in American Jewish life and, to this day, I meet persons in all parts of the country whose proudest boast to me is that they were delegates to the founding session of the American Jewish Congress. The session adopted a program for submission to the Peace Conference which included the demand for full and equal civil, political, religious, and national rights for all citizens of any territory without distinction as to race or creed, autonomy in the management of their communal institutions by members of the various national and religious bodies, and recognition of the historic claim of the Jewish people to Palestine. The Congress program was thus a decisive victory for those of us who insisted that the rights of the Jews as a people and a nationality, no less than as individuals, had to be assured. It was no less a triumph for the Zionist cause. It was significant, even prophetic, I may add, that the Congress session adopted a resolution directing the American Jewish Congress "to take necessary and effective steps in cooperation with representative Jewish bodies in other countries for the convening of a World Jewish Congress."

The Congress elected a delegation to represent American Jewry at the Versailles Peace Conference consisting of Judge Julian Mack, as chairman, Louis Marshall, Colonel Harry Cutler, Jacob deHaas, Rabbi B. L. Levinthal, Joseph Barondess, Nachman Syrkin, Leopold Benedict, Bernard Richards, and myself.

I was already abroad, having left for London and Paris as soon as the war ended in order to begin discussions with Jewish and governmental leaders. Thus I was able to present to Mr. Balfour, as I have related elsewhere, the resolution of the Congress, the day after its adoption, calling on Britain to assume a trusteeship over Palestine. In Paris, the Congress delegation joined forces with and became part of the *Comité des Délégations Juives* which was made up, as far as war exigencies permitted, of democratically elected representatives of the Jewish populations of Europe.

When the delegation returned from Versailles it reported to a second session of the American Jewish Congress in Philadelphia on May 30 and 31, 1919. In the meantime, the struggle had been renewed between those who demanded the strict enforcement of the agreement that the Congress should terminate with the signing of the Peace Treaty and the many who recognized that the gains won by the *Comité des Délégations Juives* at the Peace Conference would hardly be permanent unless safeguarded through the unceasing vigilance of some democratically constituted body such as the Congress.

The Congress, adhering strictly to the original agreement, adjourned sine die. But a large body of delegates, myself among them, immediately reconvened in a "conference for the formation of an American Jewish Congress," determined that the gains we had made in bringing democracy into Jewish life should not be lost. Again, it was my privilege to sound the keynote. I warned that it was too late to return to "the undemocratic, un-American, un-Jewish method of dictation from above, however well-meaning in intent, however soft-spoken in manner."

The Conference elected an Executive Committee which was directed to convene a permanent Congress. Elections took place in May, 1922, and the first session of the permanent American Jewish Congress was held in Philadelphia in June.

The groups that had always opposed a democratic Jewish body withdrew from the Congress at the 1919 session. Since that time, they have for the most part continued resolutely to oppose and sabotage every effort to establish a representative Jewish body for the democratic management of the internal affairs of the Jewish community. Fortunately, as I see it, they have failed in these attempts.

During the 1920's, the Congress stood guard over situations affecting Jews in all parts of the world. It lent maximum support to the Zionist movement in the rebuilding of Palestine. It intervened promptly and energetically whenever the safety or security of Jews was threatened in any part of the world. It continually sought to widen the area of cooperation among Jews of all lands on their common problems. It gave fullest support to, and almost invariably took the initiative in, every effort to organize the American Jewish community on the broadest possible basis, efforts which in every instance were brought to naught by the opposition of the die-hard opponents of democratic organization. Above all, the Congress insisted at all times on full and frank public discussion of issues directly affecting the Jewish community, an insistence which, I am not unhappy to say, continued to earn for us the hostility of those who clung to the discredited belief in the efficacy of silence and secrecy touching grave issues in Jewish life.

I have dealt elsewhere in this volume with what I regard as the most historic achievements of the American Jewish Congress: the manner in which, for a decade, we rallied both Jews and non-Jews to an understanding of the menace of Hitler and fascism, and our leading role in the creation of the World Jewish Congress. There are two other equally historic contributions of which I would speak.

Early in the war, the leaders of the American and the World Jewish Congresses recognized the vast problems with which the Jewish people would be confronted at the end of the war. We were keenly aware of the fact that extensive research and preparation would be required in order intelligently to formulate the postwar demands and needs of the Jewish people. Accordingly, the American and World Jewish Congresses created the Institute of Jewish Affairs, headed by the distinguished international jurist, Dr. Jacob Robinson, and staffed by some of the most outstanding scholars in the Jewish world, many of whom had come from Europe at the outbreak of the war. During the war years, the Institute gathered a vast amount of data on every phase of the Jewish catastrophe and its implications. It devoted intensive study to all the problems likely to emerge at the end of the war—problems of relief and reparations, of indemnification and restitution, of the punishment of war criminals, of migration and the resettlement of refugees, of human rights and the international protection of minority groups. The researches of the Institute were published in a series of significant volumes and incorporated in memoranda and documents submitted to the Allied authorities, to various governments and international agencies, and, later, to the United Nations.

These materials provided the basis on which Jewish postwar claims were formulated. It is not too much to assert that concepts first formulated by the Institute have had a significant impact on the development of international policy on such fundamental problems as restitution, reparations, relief, the treatment of displaced persons, human rights, and the trials of war criminals. The formulation of these concepts was given great impetus by the War Emergency Conference of the World Jewish Congress held in Atlantic City on November 26–30, 1944. Despite the extraordinary difficulties created by the war, some 270 delegates representing the Jewish communities of forty countries were present. In welcoming the delegates, I stated:

> This is not a relief conference. This is not a charity conference
> ... Even as we desire that the fullest justice shall be done to
> every people on earth, we shall be satisfied with nothing less
> than the fullest measure of justice to the people of Israel.

The resolutions adopted by the Emergency Conference, the most significant Jewish gathering held during the war, were soon recognized and accepted by Jews everywhere as the basic program for Jewish survival in the postwar world.

There is yet another major contribution of the American Jewish Congress which, I venture to predict, will prove to be a historic and enduring one, not only for American Jewry but for American democracy. Many of us in the Congress movement had long recognized that more than a decade of intensive worldwide fascist and anti-Semitic propaganda would leave a legacy of prejudice which it would prove extremely difficult to eradicate. Concepts of racism, already deeply imbedded in the thinking and practice of so many countries, including, un-happily, our own, had been strengthened and reinforced. It was clear that one of our major postwar responsibilities would be to do whatever we could to counter this threat not only to the security of the Jewish people but to the very fabric of the democratic system.

Throughout its history, the American Jewish Congress had always been actively concerned with anti-Semitism. But our concern was primarily with specific anti-Semitic incidents, movements, and outbreaks. Through various committees, we had continuously dealt with economic discrimination against Jews, particularly in the field of employment, and we had al-ways been active with regard to any legislation that bore on Jewish interests, such as immigration. But it was obvious to us that the postwar situation would require a much more comprehensive and dynamic program, based on intensive scien-tific research and analysis.

My own interest and activity in the field of civil rights had gone back to the beginning of my participation in public af-fairs. But the American Jewish Congress—deeply involved in other issues—had never undertaken a large-scale program on behalf of civil and group rights as an integral part of its work.

As we began to devote ourselves intensively to these prob-lems, we quickly realized that it would be futile to adopt the kinds of programs that had been generally employed to foster better intergroup understanding. Those programs, usually con-sisting of the widespread dissemination of literature and propa-ganda preaching good will, and the sponsoring of interfaith meetings and projects had proved almost wholly futile. What was required was a much more fundamental attack on the problem, based on modern concepts of social science and rooted in the recognition that the security of no group could be assured unless the full rights of all groups were safeguarded and ex-tended. Accordingly, we set ourselves to devise a comprehen-sive program that would not be an anonymous and self-abasing plea for tolerance but a self-respecting and vigorous campaign for the equal rights of all people. In furthering this program we were extremely fortunate in enlisting the active and devoted services of two men of genius, brilliant and dedicated sons of the Jewish people, both of whom, alas, were far too soon to be taken from our midst—Professors Kurt Lewin and Alexander Pekelis.

Lewin, referred to by his professional colleagues as the "Einstein of modern psychology," had come to this country from Nazi Germany in 1933 to teach in American universities. Generally regarded as the foremost student of group psychology in the world, he had founded a research center for group dynamics at the Massachusetts Institute of Technology to train students in the new methods he had developed. He had written extensively on problems of Jewish education and published his now classic analysis of the phenomenon of self-hatred among minority groups. His increasing concern with the problem of Jewish survival brought him to the American Jewish Congress, for which he organized the Commission on Community Interrelations in 1944. Staffed by a group of highly skilled social psychologists and sociologists, the Commission began what is probably the most ambitious and what is likely to prove the most fruitful study of group tensions and group adjustment undertaken in this country. Lewin continued to serve the Commission actively as its chief consultant until his untimely and sudden death early in 1947, in the prime of his intellectual powers.

Alexander Pekelis was, beyond question, one of the most brilliant and creative men I have met in my lifetime. Russian born, German and Italian educated, he had been a distinguished professor of law in Italian universities until he was forced to flee in 1939. Arriving in this country in 1940, he soon embarked on what was to prove a meteoric career as a student at Columbia Law School and editor-in-chief of its Law Review, while at the same time serving as professor at the New School for Social Research. Within a short time, he had mastered the entire range of American history and law, and his papers and writings began to attract wide attention. Legal scholars have told me that they regarded him as the most creative and original legal mind in America. An ardent Zionist, and passionately dedicated to Jewish survival, Pekelis was deeply concerned with every phase of Jewish life. When the American Jewish Congress organized its Commission on Law and Social Action in 1945, Pekelis accepted our invitation to become its active head. From his fertile brain there flowed the ideas and concepts that, applied by his colleagues, have won for the Commission acclaim as the most significant and productive body in its field in the United States. The Commission set for itself the task of surveying such major problem areas as discrimination in employment, education, and housing; racial segregation; and dissemination of racial propaganda through media of public communication. It then formulated in all of these fields comprehensive programs involving the promotion of legislation, test cases before the courts and administrative agencies, and social-action campaigns designed to transform public policy in these areas so as to protect the democratic and equal rights of all groups.

Pekelis's briefs written for the American Jewish Congress in many of these cases are regarded as masterpieces, his brief in a California case involving the segregation of Mexican-American children having been described as "the most important contribution to the socio-legal attack on segregation made in this country in twenty-five years." His briefs in the successful challenge of the American Jewish Congress to the *New York Daily New's* application for an FM radio license, on the grounds of its anti-Jewish and anti-Negro propaganda, resulted in wholly new concepts with regard to the public responsibilities of media of communication.

Pekelis, an inspiration to all of us, was killed in an air crash, returning from the World Zionist Congress in Switzerland in December, 1946. I shall always remember the day on board ship when I learned of his death as one of the saddest of my life. In his early forties at the time of his death, Pekelis was only at the beginning of what would have been a career of historic service to the Jewish people and democratic thought.

Fortunately, he had trained and taught his associates well, and they have continued his creative and pioneering work. From the Commission on Law and Social Action there have come campaigns such as that which led to the enactment in New York State of the first legislative measure in this country effectively to ban racial and religious discrimination in institutions of higher learning, and a long series of notable—and generally successful—interventions in the courts and administrative agencies in major test cases involving the rights not only of Jews, but of Negroes, Japanese, and other minority groups.

It was such pioneering activity by the American Jewish Congress which, I believe, was responsible for my appointment by President Truman to the President's Commission on Higher Education, established in 1946 to survey the entire problem of higher education in the United States. I deem it a unique privilege to have served as a member of that body of distinguished public citizens and educators who produced so significant a report, later published under the title, "Higher Education for American Democracy." My interest, I need hardly state, embraced all phases of the Commission's work. But I must confess that I was particularly concerned with the activity of the subcommittee, dealing with the problem of equalizing and expanding educational opportunity on which I served. This committee investigated the barriers to higher education imposed by financial circumstances, limitations of facilities, and discrimination because of race, color, or creed. I was able, as a result of the work of the American Jewish Congress, to bring to the attention of the Commission a large body of data and suggestions relating to the problem. It was extremely gratifying to me that the final report of the Commission spoke so forthrightly about the problem of discrimination and included many specific suggestions for its abolition, among them the passage of state legislation banning discriminatory admissions practices.

Though the enlarged work of the American Jewish Congress

in this field is comparatively recent in origin, it has already had
a very considerable impact on the programs of other bodies—
both Jewish and non-Jewish—actively engaged in expanding
the frontiers of democracy. Through the Commission on Law
and Social Action, the Congress has greatly influenced American thinking on the approach to, and strategy in, the struggle
for full equality. This, again, has been an outstanding example
of the manner in which, as citizens and builders of American
democracy, we Jews have taken our full part in shaping its
affairs and in taking risks in the battle against privilege and
inequality, not for ourselves chiefly or alone, but for all peoples
and races in the land.

XIII

I Remember Roosevelt

O N September 8, 1914, I first wrote to Franklin
D. Roosevelt offering him my support when I had heard that
he had decided to present his name in connection with the
United States senatorship. I did so because, as I then wrote to
him, I felt that "the Democratic Party in the entire State of
New York became your debtor when you made so fine and gallant a fight against the attempted corruption of the Party
during the last Senatorial campaign."

In 1928, when I toured the country on behalf of Alfred Smith
for President—speaking out everywhere against the flagrant
and covert attack on religious grounds—I had full opportunity
to support Franklin D. Roosevelt for governor and did so whole-
heartedly. His triumph in the face of a Republican landslide
seemed one of the few consolations of that election.

In supporting Roosevelt I opposed Ottinger, to the horror of
a few of my Jewish friends who could never understand that I
never voted as a Jew but always as an American. My support
of Roosevelt and opposition to Ottinger on the basis of what
was best for New York State was credited with having clarified
issues for many of my fellow Jews, and caused bitter resentment
among the followers of Ottinger. My feeling at the time, set
down half humorously in a note of congratulations to Governor-
elect Roosevelt on November 13, has through the years been
confirmed again and again:

I thought you might care to know the troubles of one of the few supporters of the Democratic Party at the recent election. Note the enclosure—one of the Vice-Presidents of the American Jewish Congress resigns because I opposed Ottinger and supported you. And now comes this letter from a very able young Jewish friend, who seems to imply that I released, as he puts it, an avalanche of Roosevelt sentiment. I hope I did. May this one merit plead for me on the Day of Judgment!

In 1929 and 1930 I had reason to work with the Governor as a member of the National Committee on Child Labor and as a member of the small group who first brought to him the request for an old-age pension law in New York, as well as on other matters. I felt, because of his able leadership of the state and his deep concern with enlarging the concept of social justice in our democracy, that he should be re-elected in 1930. By then he had also begun to loom large as the Democratic candidate for the presidency in 1932.

Soon after Roosevelt's election to the presidency, John Haynes Holmes and I, who had felt unable to support him in the light of real doubts that had developed during our fight to cleanse New York City of the Tammany regime, wrote to him on November 17, 1932:

DEAR GOVERNOR ROOSEVELT:

We feel that we wish to tender you our congratulations and good wishes upon your triumphant election to the Presidency. We hope that the years will abundantly vindicate the judgment of the American electorate and that you may rise to the unique opportunity of service which that election affords you. We trust that, whatever have been the differences between us with regard to civic affairs, you may feel free to call upon us for whatever service it lies within the power of American citizens to render their government and President.

The answer, dated December 16th, was frank and friendly:

MY DEAR DR. HOLMES AND DR. WISE:

That is a mighty nice letter of yours and I honestly appreciate the spirit in which it was written. Some day I should much like

to talk with both of you because I am confident that your ultimate objectives and mine in the cause of better government are
the same. I have never differed with you in that objective,
though, as you know, I felt very strongly that you were using
methods last year which would hurt rather than help the objective. If you will let me, I will gladly talk over with you my
reasons for feeling this.

As soon as Franklin D. Roosevelt took office and faced the
emergencies and human tragedies that dominated American
life in 1933, he rewon my unstinted admiration, and I spoke of
him everywhere I went with boundless enthusiasm. In April,
1934, I wrote to an old friend in Cincinnati:

> You are no stronger a supporter of Roosevelt than I. . . . If ever
> a man deserved to be loved for the enemies he has made, it is
> F.D.R. I am looking forward to the fight in 1936, for if Roosevelt
> remain equal to the Roosevelt of his first year, we will have the
> prettiest fight of a century, for all the forces of "grab and hold"
> and bitter and violent reaction will be arrayed against him.

Despite our old friendship and the President's gracious message to Dr. Holmes and myself following his election, he first
asked me to come to the White House in late 1935 or early
1936. I felt at the time that this delay may well have been due
to Louis H. Howe's unforgiving enmity, which he treasured because I had not supported the President for nomination or
election in 1932. I went and had a good talk with him. It was
not easy to go, for no man of importance in public life had ever
attacked Holmes and myself as he had. Still, I could not permit
personal rancor or resentment to stand in the way of giving my
support to him, who, after all, had dared to do that which the
Liberty League folks so savagely resented. I felt it was my duty
to support Roosevelt against the "Al" Smiths (1935–1936 version), the Raskobs, and the Du Ponts. There was no reference
to the past in our conversation. We resumed where we had
left off before the break.

It was natural that in this, our first conversation in over

three years, we should discuss the Nazi situation. Knowing that, except for Justice Brandeis and Felix Frankfurter, the Jews who had been seeing the President were timorous, I broached the German situation and suggested his saying a word in personal approval of James McDonald's recent report. His reply, "But Max Warburg wrote to me that the situation in Germany is so hopeless that nothing can be done." I confess I went away cussing Max Warburg's head off, for he had no right so to dispirit the President, and I knew from Sir Herbert Samuel that Max Warburg was still naïve enough to be trying to work things out with Dr. Schacht. In any case from then on I felt free to take to the President my knowledge and views on the Nazi situation—and from then on I found the President sympathetic and eager to be of help.

On my return from Europe in August, 1936, I wrote to President Roosevelt of the faith in his leadership that I found among European peoples everywhere. I also offered my services in the forthcoming campaign, and on September 24 issued the following statement to the press:

> I am not a life-long Democrat. I became a Democrat in order to help elect Woodrow Wilson President. I call myself a Wilson-Roosevelt Democrat because Wilson and Roosevelt in our own day together represent the ideal of democracy. Franklin Delano Roosevelt became President after four tragically inept years of administration which, up to the day of Roosevelt's inauguration, had brought our country to the brink of economic and moral disaster. Some opponents of President Roosevelt do not hesitate in their folly to impugn the integrity of our savings banks and insurance companies, though they know that these banks, and companies are absolutely sound today and that on March 4, 1933, the nation's financial institutions were on the verge of absolute bankruptcy. President Roosevelt might, like his predecessor, have permitted things to continue to slide and thus have acted as the receiver of a bankrupt nation. Instead, he applied himself with the vigor of youth, the wisdom of maturity and the daring of a pioneer to the task of setting the American house in order. In doing this, he has lifted the whole nation from the lowest

economic level to which it has ever sunk, to its present vast improvement and resistless progress to prosperity.

The Liberty-Leaguers would have wished to see recovery achieved with a magnificent disregard of the needs of forty million men, women and children, who, at the close of the Hoover administration, were through no fault of their own without food and other necessities of life. President Roosevelt on the one hand made business recovery possible by averting the supreme disaster of human destruction and degradation and by affording relief and work-relief to millions whose place in the life of the nation President Roosevelt would not permit to be blotted out because of their unemployment. The greatest service that President Roosevelt performed was to avert that human deterioration and that social degradation which would have come about if the nation had continued under a Hoover-like administration. President Roosevelt thus did no more than serve the whole American people by daring to use America's resources for all its people. The Roosevelt way was frankly the way of experimentation, but that experimentation was necessary and resulted in immeasurable benefits to the American people.

Roosevelt already belongs to the tradition of our great American Presidents. It is impossible to over-estimate the service that he has rendered the ideal of democracy. It was Roosevelt who saved the American democracy at a time when its ideals were in greatest peril. It was Roosevelt who saved the American people from the undemocratic ways of acquiescent despair or violent revolt. It was Roosevelt who saved the American democracy for the well-being of all mankind. . . .

No one who has experienced the clash of forces on the Continent or has mingled with the leaders and peoples of the Western democracies can be unaware that Roosevelt is the most potent force in the world today for human peace and understanding. . . . Himself a devout member of one of the great Christian churches, he is the good neighbor to all Americans, irrespective of race or creed or color. He is a good neighbor to all mankind, which has come to know him as the leader, striving diligently, wisely, forcefully to maintain the United States as a symbol and hope of democracy for all the world.

In a talk with President Roosevelt early in October we discussed the election and he showed me a confidential report saying that he could count at that time on no more than 277 electoral votes—too narrow a margin for victory. I told him of the reasons for my confidence, told him that many people would quietly vote for him who were not saying anything about it, because if they said much for Roosevelt, they might be suspected of having been among the beneficiaries of relief—or because they were fearful that, should there be a change of the political parties in power, they might be dropped from relief or work-relief rolls. That seemed a new consideration to him— and appeared to hearten him not a little. I gave F.D.R. my own estimate, which was 347 electoral votes, including New York and Pennsylvania. He seemed sure of Pennsylvania, but not quite so sure of New York.

On January 15, 1937, just before F.D.R.'s second inauguration, I wrote him at length about Colonel Beck's extraordinary and, for the Jewish people, catastrophic declaration that of the three and a half million Jews in Poland three million were superfluous and must emigrate. In that letter I said:

As a result of your great leadership, our country did not forget those whom economic breakdown left without means—twenty to forty million people whom you refused to permit America to forget and to forsake. Oh! that you might say one word, dear Chief, on Wednesday to the effect that, wide as are the boundaries of our land, there is no room for forgotten men. Every American citizen is the subject of his country's interest and concern. Nor will the American Democracy ever hold any faithful and lawabiding group within its border to be superfluous.

That, after all, is your conviction, and you have lived and led by virtue of that faith. I beg this of you because your word next Wednesday will, of course, be listened to by the whole world and will serve as the inaugural of what I know will be an administration of worldwide influence for justice and for peace throughout the world.

The answer, already sent throughout the world, came January 23.

This was only one of many occasions when the word of Franklin D. Roosevelt gave courage if not hope to the victims of Nazism throughout the world.

Within a few weeks of the second inaugural, the President presented the Judiciary Proposal as well as the Sharecropper's Program and the Crop Insurance Plan, thus showing that he meant to act on the platform on which he had been elected. The resurrected federalists of our day, treasonable to every ideal of democracy and every vision of the people, rose as one man to pillory the President for the Court Plan.

America had twice chosen Franklin D. Roosevelt for the Presidency, the second time by an overwhelming vote in support of a program as well as a person. That program, which was clearly announced in Madison Square Garden on October 31, 1936, became impossible of attainment because of the composition of the Supreme Court. The Supreme Court was not contemporaneous with the America of that day. Save for a few exceptions, it represented the America of Harding, Coolidge, and Taft, who had named its majority.

When President Roosevelt came to grips with that issue, the real regret of his opponents was not over the "presidential usurpation," but over the failure of the President to resort to usurpation. Extraconstitutional action on the part of the President had been confidentially predicted. Presidential usurpation would have been damned with partisan delight and profit. But the proposal of the President contained every element of unforgivable surprise.

Among those who decried the presidential proposal there were none who had opposed the nomination of Justice Parker by President Hoover, which had been prevented by a handful of liberals in and out of the Senate. President Lowell of Harvard uttered his pious soul against the Roosevelt proposal, but he fought with equal vehemence against the confirmation of Jus-

THE WHITE HOUSE
WASHINGTON

January 23, 1937.

Dear Stephen Wise:-

Yours of January fifteenth came just in the nick of time -- i.e., when I was going over the final draft of the Inaugural speech. Your sentence, as you will have noticed, was included verbatim!

As ever yours,

Franklin D. Roosevelt

Reverend Stephen S. Wise,
40 West 68th Street,
New York City,
New York.

tice Brandeis. Among those who purported to be shocked by the President's proposal I found no one who had ever expressed one word of surprise or regret over the basically unconstitutional usurpation of legislative function by the Supreme Court in the preceding years—which had in fact negated the will of the people and the decisions of the Congress to correct through the New Deal the evils of the great depression.

Because the real basis of the proposal and its vehement opposition were not in my eyes a legal or constitutional question, but rather a conflict of forces for and against the program of social justice as presented by Roosevelt, I supported the President, and took issue with the Bar Associations, local and national, who led the opposition.

> The Bar Associations, local and national, have no special status in the real referendum which the President has invoked. Verily they are *amici curiae*, friends of the court, rather than the people. These are for the most part fearful lest the social dreams and hopes of liberals such as is the President receive the legal warrant of that court, which, in its steadfast and unbending defiance of the nation's will, does most to halt the march of American democracy to the goal of social and economic justice.

Throughout this period I kept the President informed of the facts concerning Zionism and Palestine. This I have described elsewhere—but it is important to record here that, despite the indifference if not hostility of certain gentlemen in the State Department and the continuing timidity of certain Jews, who failed to recognize the true significance of Hitler's program against Jews and kept referring to "atrocity" stories in the first year of Hitler, the President grasped what was occurring with more feeling and understanding than these so-called "friends" of the administration. I sometimes felt that not a few of the Jews who had access to the President at this time did us a great disservice. They were so eager not to seem to plead the Jewish cause that they failed accurately to interpret either the true mood or determination of Jews in Palestine or the tragic plight of their brother Jews in Hitler Europe. Therefore, in writing to the President on May 22, 1939, I not only thanked him for his efforts to avert the disaster which, through the White Paper, threatened the Jewish National Home, but also wrote:

> Please understand that we are not lamenting nor acknowledging defeat, for the Jews in Palestine mean to go forward in unshattered ranks and to continue building the Jewish National Home.

This determination and courage of Jews to live with dignity and as free men, whether displayed in the Warsaw Ghetto or Palestine or New York, happily shone through, and was of far more significance to the President than was the extreme caution of the handful of Jews who never caught the gleam, but sought to minimize the role of the Jewish people as they did their own Jewishness.

The tragic plight of the Jews in Nazi lands and the threat to the entire community of Jews in Palestine caused me to seek help from the President when such help seemed the last possible hope of the beleaguered Jewish people. Time and again Franklin Roosevelt responded.

On May 13, 1941, I found it necessary to send the President first-hand reports from Palestine and write about the imperiled state of the unarmed Jews who asked only for the right to defend themselves against a Nazi invasion:

> Thanks to the interest you have already shown, the British have taken some action to make better provision for the defense of the country and its population, but not enough in view of the greatly increased gravity of the situation. There is imminent danger of mass destruction of the Jews, without adequate means of fighting and going down fighting if need be.
>
> The British government ought to be made to understand how enormous would be the shock and how damaging its effect upon the democratic cause, if there should be a general slaughter because of failure adequately to arm the Jews as well as to

strengthen the defenses of Palestine with guns, tanks and planes. Only your immediate intervention in London may avert a tragedy the horror of which is too awful to contemplate. Upon occasions not a few you have intervened as a friend of the Jewish people. We rely upon you as upon no one else to lend us your saving help in this time of crisis.

On June 9, 1941 the President answered:

In this particular matter [the Near East campaign] therefore, I can merely call to the attention of the British our deep interest in the defense of Palestine and our concern for the defense of the Jewish population there; and, as best I can, supply the British forces with the material means by which the maximum of protection to Palestine will be afforded.

The next day I left for Washington, and after conferences with high government officers felt more confident that the British would be made to understand that there must be adequate equipment—guns, tanks, and planes—for our people in Palestine. Excepting for one member of the Cabinet—who wrote off the whole Mediterranean, Suez, Egypt, and Palestine—I found the deepest confidence on the part of others that England would stand at Haifa and through the Emek, that she was tremendously armed. And probably thanks to the intervention of F.D.R., the business of parity—enlisting only the same number of Jews and Arabs, though the Jews wanted to enlist and the Arabs did not—had been dropped to a large extent.

However, the situation seemed so desperate in the light of Nazi military successes that the suggestion was made at this time (not by our government) that we attempt to evacuate our people in Palestine. I was among those who vetoed that proposal, however unhappy I was over the possible fate of individuals. Five hundred thousand people could not be evacuated save by a nation with abundant resources, and also the Jews faced the fact that there was no other place to go.

In May, 1942, the President wrote to extend his sincere

greetings to the American Jewish Congress meeting in war-emergency session, and on July 17, 1942, sent a message to the mass meeting held under its auspices at Madison Square Garden:

DEAR DR. WISE:

Americans who love justice and hate oppression will hail the solemn commemoration in Madison Square Garden as an expression of the determination of the Jewish people to make every sacrifice for victory over the Axis powers. Citizens, regardless of religious allegiance, will share in the sorrow of our Jewish fellow citizens over the savagery of the Nazis against their helpless victims. The Nazis will not succeed in exterminating their victims any more than they will succeed in enslaving mankind. The American people not only sympathize with all victims of Nazi crimes but will hold the perpetrators of these crimes to strict accountability in a day of reckoning which will surely come.

I express the confident hope that the Atlantic Charter and the just world order to be made possible by the triumph of the United Nations will bring the Jews and oppressed peoples in all lands the four freedoms which Christian and Jewish teachings have largely inspired.

VERY SINCERELY YOURS,
[signed] FRANKLIN D. ROOSEVELT

Anti-Semitism in America was as abhorrent to President Roosevelt's concept of America as Hitlerism abroad, and he made that clear in a letter I shall always cherish:

FEBRUARY 9, 1944
DEAR DR. WISE:

The attempt by Adolf Hitler and the Nazi party to rule Germany, to rule Europe and then to rule the Western World, was based on two brutal devices: organized terror and organized anti-semitism. Terror put Hitler in power and kept him there. Anti-semitism was the terror's counterpart in propaganda. In the name of the self-styled Master race, Hitler robbed, first his own people, then the peoples of Europe, and tomorrow, by his own boast, would have robbed the world. In the past months we have defeated Hitler's plan for world conquest. We have recovered some of his stolen gains and in the months to come, we shall recover more, and we shall meet and defeat Hitler on his own ground.

Some of the sources of anti-semitism in this country were created to serve Hitler's purpose. Let every American look to his own mind and actions so that while we defeat Hitler's armies we also defeat his poisonous propaganda. Whoever condones or participates in anti-semitism plays Hitler's game. There is no place in the lives or thoughts of true Americans for anti-semitism.

VERY SINCERELY YOURS,
[signed] FRANKLIN D. ROOSEVELT

In 1940, the world situation and the problems of America at home called for the re-election of Roosevelt. While supporters of Wendell Willkie stated that he agreed with F.D.R. on international policies but not on his national policies, I did not agree that they could be separated. I felt and said then that anti-New Dealers would undo every plan and method of national self-defense. The talk about Rooseveltian dictatorship and the third term or bureaucratic despotism surely gave infinite comfort to the enemy—and the enemy was then Hitler-Mussolini totalitarianism.

It became necessary to deal with the third-term abstraction and remind those who sought to make this the issue that, after all, the Founding Fathers fully debated the third term possibility and omitted any rule on this point in our Constitution. With full consciousness of the problem and after full debate they did so for a good reason, as put by Washington in a letter to Lafayette in 1788, "that the nation should not thus deny itself of a particular resource if circumstances required."

The Hitler-Mussolini totalitarian Axis with its assault on civilization and all that America held dear, surely provided the circumstance which demanded that America should not deny itself the greatest of human resources in 1940—Franklin D. Roosevelt. The third-term tradition seemed almost trivial compared with the imperative necessity of keeping in office the man who had been first to realize the significance of the aggressor nations and, in the next place, had done most to fortify the nation against successful aggression.

Again an attack was made on the so-called pro-Roosevelt Jewish vote. I was questioned as to whether it was not unwise to support Roosevelt because people would say that this was because "he had been friendly to Jews." Again self-appointed "Jewish leaders" failed to see that such inverted thinking involved an acceptance of second-class citizenship. They failed to recognize that the first and only duty of every American citizen was to vote for the man best fitted to lead America through the world crisis. They also failed to recognize that the so-called Rooseveltian "friendliness to Jews" was not a token of pro-Jewishness but of his Americanism.

1. He had not failed to appoint to high office Jews whom he regarded as extraordinarily fitted for the post—for example, Justice Frankfurter. Frankfurter was not appointed because he was a Jew, or despite his being a Jew, but because the President regarded him as the best man in the country for the Supreme Court at that particular time, irrespective of every other consideration.

2. Roosevelt's so-called "friendliness to Jews" consisted in nothing more than his championship of the cause of human freedom as against the aggressor nations. If that constituted friendliness to the Jews, it merely meant that we Jews were the first under attack.

The campaign was a bitter one, and many ugly issues were raised on which I felt deeply and therefore spoke out. These included the unworthy tactics of some of my possessing fellow Jews, who sought to frighten poorer Jews into abandoning their support of Roosevelt, whom they conceived to be the very symbol of democracy. I attacked the uncleanness of the campaign against President Roosevelt, including, for example, the attempt to punish him among the Italian voters because he had had the courage to speak out at Charlottesville on Mussolini's stab in the French back, and the attempt on the part of Willkie leaders to corral the Irish vote against the President because he was committing what might have seemed in some Irish eyes the crime of giving aid to Britain. So it went all down the line, including the nasty allusions to one of the ablest and finest women in the nation—the wife of the President.

One delightful letter following the campaign expresses the tenor of many that I received:

DEAR DOCTOR:

It is a question in the minds of many of us as to whom may be said to be the worst enemy of the Jews, Adolph Hitler or Rabbi Wise.

Perhaps it is your desire to be classed as one of the masses. Dr. Hirsch once said from the pulpit that this should be pronounced "them asses," which of course was not intended for you, but did include the masses.

SADLY
[signed] E.M.N.

This was but one of many of the bitter denunciations that followed my support of Roosevelt in 1940, and my denunciation of an article in a Republican daily consisting of excerpts from a booklet of the Republican National Committee, purporting to show how Jews supported Willkie. This was ghettoism at its worst, on the part of those who thought or claimed they were anti- or nonghettoists but who, the moment of necessity, from their point of view, arose, set out as pure ghettoites to act in behalf of their political candidate.

Even the deep and affectionate admiration of millions of Americans for Franklin Roosevelt was a minor factor in his re-election in 1940. The country voted on two policies as embodied in a candidate—the policy of concern at every cost for the well-being of all the people, including those temporarily disabled by economic circumstances, and the policy of leadership in such hemispheric defense as would stay the aggressors against the democratic nations, small and great. Here two affirmative decisions were reached, although the bitterest election contests since 1896 raged around the head of Roosevelt.

After four years—despite the continuing bitter assaults of such persons as the Bridgeport ex-congresswoman whose alliance with *Time* and *Fortune* had made her forget eternal values—Roosevelt emerged as the man who had made every possible preparation between 1939 and 1941 for the war that was forced upon us by the Axis powers, so as to make victory inevitable. He had also done what one man could, to prepare for the peace of the common man. This he did through the Four Freedoms and the Atlantic Charter.

In 1944, the choice confronting us was Roosevelt for a fourth term, or Dewey. At the Madison Square Garden rally preceding election I said:

> Let us not forget that we are not electing a man to prosecute England, Russia, and China—to prosecute and put in jail the leaders of these countries—but to do as President Roosevelt has done, namely, cooperate with them in order to secure a just and rightful and enduring peace.

> Some of our Republican friends seem to feel that President Roosevelt will not live or survive the term of office to which he is on Tuesday to be elected. What they really dread is not his mortality, but his immortality—that he will live immortally after a glorious career, this very great American—in the fellowship of Washington and Jefferson, Jackson and Lincoln, Cleveland and Wilson.

When last we were together on March 15, 1945, just before he left for Warm Springs, from which he never returned, he told me at great length the story of his purpose to make the Near East leaders understand the miracle the Jewish rebuilders had wrought in Palestine. He said to me at that time that nothing but good would come of the continuance and the emulation in neighboring lands of their toil and sacrifice for a great ideal. If, as he said, he felt a sense of failure in respect to his most recent mission to the ruler of Saudi Arabia to secure his assent to the development of Palestine, it was only because he attached too much importance to the power of that medieval figure in determining the fate of Palestine on the poor advice of some counselors in our State Department and in the Colonial Office in England. While there was a momentary sense of failure, at the same time he had already planned for another and, as he believed, more effective method of approach to the problem, the solution of which was bound to be the establishment of a free and democratic Jewish Commonwealth in Palestine.

I do not wish to have it understood that Roosevelt was particularly a friend of the Jewish people. He was a friend of man and of men. No one was more genuinely free from religious prejudice and racial bigotry. He faced men as men, a man as a man.

It was the genius of F.D.R. to bring back to the thought of the American people "the forgotten man." There was no "forgotten man" in his life. Though himself a child of fortune, he never forgot the children of adversity. I remember as early as March, 1933, how his soul rebelled at the Nazi doctrine of superior and inferior races! More than any American since Lincoln he brought the common man back to the remembrance and the conscience of all Americans.

Within a month of our last visit together, our country was bereft as it had not been since April, 1865, when another emancipator passed out of the presidency into history.

XIV

The Nazi Onslaught

FOR nearly twenty years of my life, including a whole decade before Hitler's actual assumption of power, in January 1933, I dealt with Hitlerism. My first acquaintance with it in a real way I owed to a meeting with the then American ambassador at Berlin, later ambassador to London, Alanson P. Houghton. It was in the summer of 1922, and I was hunting for instructors for the Jewish Institute of Religion, which was about to open its doors. The Ambassador told me with deep feeling of the evening he had spent almost exactly a year earlier with Dr. Walter Rathenau, the German Republic's minister of foreign affairs.

It is most likely that Houghton brought up the incident because Rathenau, too, was a Jew. As the Ambassador told the story, Rathenau's evening together with him in the American Embassy was on the very eve of his assassination. Houghton related that Rathenau had unfolded his own vision of and plan for peace—for peace permanent and universal. Houghton added, himself moved as he told the tale, "Rathenau helped me that night to understand, as I had never understood before, the spiritual genius of the Hebrew prophets. We parted and Rathenau returned to his mother's home. The following morning, as he was about to drive to the Chancellery in the Friedrichstrasse, three or four ruffians shot him, killing him instantly." It is worth recalling that Rathenau's mother pleaded that the lives of the murderers be spared at their trial on the ground that they did not know the character of the man whom they slew.

When Hitler came to power, it will be remembered, he revived the name and fame of the assassins as pioneers of Nazism and adorned the streets in Berlin with the names of these murderers. Years before the Hitler blow fell, Houghton foresaw what was coming for Germany and almost prepared the way for the service of one of his successors at Berlin, Professor William Dodd of the University of Chicago. Dodd was years ahead of the State Department in his grasp of the political as well as of the moral implications of Hitlerism and paid the penalty of such understanding by being virtually removed from office for having the decency and the courage alone among ambassadors to decline to attend the annual Nuremberg celebration, which was a glorification of Hitler.

The American Jewish Congress was under the writer's presidency and for some years under the presidency of the Honorable Bernard S. Deutsch. A few years before the fateful January, I had induced him, as a younger man, to take over the office of president, which he ably filled up to the time of his death in 1935. Very early the Congress took the strongest possible position with respect to what we had come to believe was the rising tide of Nazism. I must cite two examples of the Congress' understanding of what was to come. Deutsch and I learned that Sidney Matz, a gifted and beloved young Jew, son of Israel Matz, scholarly Maecenas of Hebrew literature, was about to go to Germany. We requested him to take over the task of consulting a considerable number of leading Jews of the Berlin community about two matters: One, what, if anything, could we American Jews do to avert the dreaded rise to power of Hitler, then as we saw clearly threatening? Two, if he came to power, what could we do in order to avert the threatened hurt to Jews?

He carried out the mission in October, 1932, and reported as follows: He had interviewed about thirty leading Jews all of whom, with one exception, had declared that "Hitler would never come to power" (*"wird nie zur Macht kommen"*). A group of them with utmost sarcasm had sent me the following message: "Say to Rabbi Wise that he need not concern himself with Jewish affairs in Germany. If he insists upon dealing with Jewish affairs in Europe, let him occupy himself with Jewish problems in Poland and Rumania." Such was the shortsightedness and even snobbery, for such it was, of the German Jews, on the eve of what was to prove the undoing of a thousand years and more of Jewish life in Germany. They added, "Since Hitler will never come to power, say to Rabbi Wise that his second query is wholly superfluous." One exception there was among these invincibly unrealistic, or shall we rather describe them as superoptimistic, German-Jewish patriots. Only one, Georg Bernhard, famous journalist in his time, editor of the *Vossische Zeitung*, stood alone among his fellow Jews, saying to Matz, "The American Jewish Congress is right in addressing us. Hitler will come to power and will destroy German Jewry." Some months later he was honored, together with the greatest living Jew, Einstein, by being named in the first list of Jews who were reft of their citizenship, along with a small number of non-Jews expelled or cast out from the Third Reich.

I do not presume to find fault with the intentions of so-called Jewish leaders in Germany, but their lack of foresight or vision proved, as we shall see, to be followed by most fateful consequences. One of the closest of his friends quoted Hitler himself: "I will annihilate the Jews of Germany, and after I shall have annihilated them, I will annihilate the Jews of the whole world." Hitler, who never kept a promise but usually carried out spoken or unuttered threats, may be said to have triumphed wondrously herein, for he destroyed 6,200,000 Jews—between 37 and 40 per cent of the world's Jewish population. It is credibly, even verifiably, reported that in all negotiations in the last year of the war through neutral powers on the part of the representatives of the Nazi regime in 1944, the first demand of Hitler had reference not to territory or to reparations but to the handing over to him of the Jews of such countries as England and the United States.

Within ten days of Hitler's ascent, or descent, to power, with the help of wretchedly deluded old Hindenburg and the connivance of one of the most perfidious though unhung Hitler war criminals, von Papen, the President of the American Jewish Congress and I met with the representatives of the B'nai B'rith and of the American Jewish Committee. We pressed home again and again the question, "What shall we do if Hitler comes to power?" The chairman of the American Jewish Committee, Dr. Cyrus Adler, made the reply destined to become classic as an exhibit of unwisdom and lack of prescience on the eve of tragic events: "President Deutsch, we will cross that bridge when we come to it, not before." The penalty of foresight is always inflicted upon the foreseeing by the blind, whom foresight reproaches and exacerbates but never teaches.

It may be that I had learned my lesson at the 1925 session in Vienna of the World Zionist Congress. There I lived through the mournful experience of watching from a hotel window a parade of Viennese marching to one cry, *"Juden Heraus!"* "Out with the Jews!" This in the city of Theodor Herzl! I remember a brilliant young American, Daniel V. Thompson, Jr., since become professor of fine arts at Yale University, insisting, together with my son, James Waterman Wise, that I carry a stout stick like his own to defend myself in case of attack. He noted my depression, and I told him and my son, who shared with me the experience of having met with Ambassador Houghton some years earlier, "You find me depressed. I remember that Jews have lived in Vienna sixteen hundred years and more, and today the city's greeting to us is *Juden Heraus,* in a police-authorized procession."

But to return to the theme, however dread! The day of evil came despite assurances from those who bore with admirable fortitude and wondrous patience the afflictions visited upon others, who counseled the impatient not to cross bridges before it became necessary to do so. Having read diligently whatever had been published about Hitler in the press of many languages, mine was a minimum of surprise, withal a maximum of horror, at the news that on the night of January 29, 1933, Hitler had been summoned to be chancellor of the Reich. At once, the reign of terror began, with beatings and imprisonment of Jews—one need but reread the "Berlin Diary" by William Shirer.

I recall having gone to Washington to visit the German Ambassador, who, I knew, was not a Nazi and would not long be kept at his post by the new Nazi regime. I found that while mine was anger, his was chiefly sorrow over what was happening to his country. I went to Justice Brandeis and told him the story of my visit to the German Ambassador. I had found in the Ambassador neither defiance nor self-extenuation but a sense of only slightly concealed shame over the conduct of his country toward the several groups of its earliest victims. These included Jews, the workers and their leaders, the heads of the women's movement, and these most despised of all victims of the new order, the pacifists, running up or down from Freiherr von Gerlach to Ambassador von Bernstorff, loathed because of his impenitently active and creative leadership on behalf of the Third Reich in the League of Nations.

Categorically and almost too dogmatically, as it then seemed to me, Justice Brandeis, after learning my story of the meeting with the German Ambassador, said, "The Jews must leave Germany: There is no other way." I interposed the question, "How can 585,000 people be taken out of Germany?" Before I could again record my doubt about the unlimited difficulties, he more fully and less categorically added in explanation, "I would have the Jews out of Germany. They have been treated with deepest disrespect. I urge that Germany shall be free of Jews. Let Germany—" and these were his only stern words, self-respecting rather than vindictive—"share the fate of Spain" (which four centuries earlier had expelled and exiled its Jews). Once again with an equal sternness he repeated, "No Jew must live in Germany." Even he could not have foreseen the measure of the tragedy that was to reduce the Jewish population of

Germany from nearly six hundred thousand to less than ten thousand.

The greatness of this Jewish leader was best revealed by the certainty and the immediacy of his response as contrasted with the temporizings and expediencies of those who looked upon this dismal scene and were prepared to do no more than deal with it as if it were another fugitive anti-Semitic episode in a foreign land.

That insight and that moral strength were to prove of greatest help to us, the heads of the Congress and leaders of a Jewish mass movement of resistance. From day to day, atrocity stories reached us. The tempo of violent maltreatment of the Jewish population of Berlin was fast increasing. Some comfort and hope came to our hearts when a few weeks later Roosevelt, whose birthday coincided with the day of Hitler's accession to power, was inaugurated President, Saturday, March 4, the day prior to the so-called German "vote" of March 5, which confirmed Hitler as chancellor. Thus Hitler's rule and Roosevelt's presidency began together and even ended together. Though Roosevelt died some weeks before the unconditional surrender, which he was first to feel must be the only outcome of Hitler's war upon freedom, he did not die without knowing that Hitler and Nazism were about to be destroyed.

It pains me as a Jew to tell that while Roosevelt, from the beginning and even before the actual beginning, saw and understood what was happening, influences were at work to blur his vision and to confuse his understanding. Chief among such influences, one is grieved to admit, were some German Jews of status and wealth who constantly sought to reassure Roosevelt that things "are not as bad as Wise and others describe them," seeking thus to counteract not "the atrocity tales" but the atrocious facts that shook Roosevelt.

Serious differences arose between other Jewish organizations and the American Jewish Congress. The former for the most part favored not so much temporizing as the policy of seeking somehow to conciliate the Nazi regime and thereby doing what could be done to alleviate consequences. These groups were still under the influence of those who insisted that, while anti-Semitism had been a favorite and the winning plank of the Hitler platform, now that he was in power, he could be trusted to moderate the violence of his views. What these failed and we did not fail to see was that there could not possibly be any moderation of Nazi violence.

Occasionally, particularly after the American Jewish Congress together with the American Federation of Labor had launched the boycott of German-made goods and products, proposals were put forth for deals with Nazi Germany that would have enabled some Jews to salvage some of their property and possessions. Referring to some of these proposals which had reached us, I declared in 1936:

> We are resolved to make possible the transfer of the largest number of Jewish exiles from Germany into Palestine. But one thing we will never do. We will not take any step or adopt any measure or resort to any device or stoop to any subterfuge which shall bring financial help or any reinforcement of strength to the Nazi Reich. To do that were to betray the hopes of mankind, so far as these be in our Jewish keeping. . . . We will not become "Hitler's drummers." We refuse to act as Hitler's agents or commercial travellers. Not only do we reject out of hand with scorn and contempt any and every proposal which would ensure the security of some Jews through the shame of all Jews, but we declare that if any attempt be made in America or in England, or in any land, to facilitate the exodus of Germans through strengthening and reinforcing the financial status of Nazi Germany, we will do what men can do in order to wreck and destroy such proposals. The honor of Israel, the values of civilization, the ideals of mankind are even more precious than life itself.

Here again we had the support of the unerring wisdom of Justice Brandeis. "Any arrangement," he wrote me, "which results in making a market abroad for German goods strengthens Hitler. His weakness because of the absence of a market [the result in part of our boycott] is Jewry's and the world's hope. To thus relieve Hitler's economic distress in order to save by emigration some of Germany's Jews—and notably the rich ones—would be very serious,—and deplorable 'statesmanship.'"

Having no faith in the possibility of affecting the Hitler regime, the Congress felt that nothing short of pitiless publicity could avail, particularly in view of the millions of German-descended Americans, including not a few Jews, who refused to believe that the German Fatherland could under any regime do the evil deeds imputed to it. Some of the groups vainly imagined negotiations might ease if not heal the situation. The Congress was determined to bring home the truth to the American people and in the spirit of that decision arranged to hold a mass meeting of protest at Madison Square Garden, Monday evening, March 27, 1933.

At once objections began to mount and multiply, including a considered plea by Judge Joseph M. Proskauer of the American Jewish Committee, who fairly and earnestly said the little that could possibly be said in dissent from the proposed protest. The Congress felt that American Jewry, largest in number among the world's Jewries, was bound to express itself with respect to the atrocities daily committed against Jews and other groups in Germany. We went on and prepared for the great protest.

Before the Madison Square Garden meeting I received warnings of caution, threats as to the result of such a meeting on the Jews of Germany if I persisted—but also information that silence would satisfy the Nazis that they had nothing to fear because they could also reach out and terrorize the Jews outside Germany.

Private letters smuggled out beginning March 23 told me of tortures, the cutting of *Hackenkreuze* (swastikas) into the flesh of Jews, imprisonment, and death, night visits and night rides from which Jews never returned—as well as of the economic and social outlawing of Jews from the professions, business, and all ordinary contacts with non-Jewish neighbors.

From one who had temporarily crossed the border into France I got the message: "Do not believe the denials. Nor the Jewish denials."

From an American I received a description of a meeting addressed by Goering:

> No one who heard Goering talk; no one who heard the texture of his voice when it uttered the word "Jew," could fail to know that if the government of which Goering is an essential feature survives for six months more, German Jewry is doomed. I heard him address thousands of brown-shirted Nazis, and his violence of speech found an echo in the cries of his audience, which literally screamed approval, and interrupted him for minutes at a time with cries of "hang them now"; "do it now";—mingled with laughter.
>
> It is idle to imagine that any amicable adjustment of the problem can be effected with Goering and his regime.

Through the diplomatic pouch came a letter from the man whom I most trusted in Germany that gave facts which would have made silence at this time the greatest of crimes:

MARCH 14, 1933

DEAR ——

I have just completed all my pouch work for the Paris courier and have only one half hour to write this letter in order that it may go in the pouch. I shall therefore confine this letter to a hasty account as to what has been going on in Germany since the National Socialists (the anti-Semites) have taken charge of the Government. In view of the censorship which the Nazi government has put into effect, it would be dangerous to write freely about conditions here in a letter going in the open mail.

You have doubtless been reading a lot of stories about the conditions here. What you have heard is only a small part of what actually happened. The Left newspapers have all been suppressed and the democratic and liberal papers are afraid to write the truth because the Nazis are determined to keep on prohibiting them for longer periods until they are ruined financially and are forced to close down. Like Mussolini and Stalin, the Nazis want a press completely dominated by them and are determined to root the other papers out. Even the foreign correspondents in Berlin are constantly under pressure from the Nazi-controlled government press bureau to modify their attitude toward the present regime in Germany and to abstain from reporting facts detrimental to the interests of the Government. They are especially after those newspaper boys who are Jews; one of them, the local representative of the United Press, finally had to leave the country a few days ago when he learned through his secret agents that members of Hitler's Brown Army were laying for him and were determined to "take him out for a ride" because he kept on reporting the truth.

A number of American Jews have filed affidavits with the American Consulate in Berlin giving accounts of how they were taken out of their homes at night by uniformed Nazis, beaten senseless and then left out in the woods after a written statement had been extracted from them that they would leave Germany immediately. While the Embassy, on instructions of the State Department, has made representations to the Foreign Office, unfortunately our diplomatic secretaries tend to tone the matter down in their reports to the State Department in order that the latter may have something to show to representatives of Jewish societies who complained to the Department "that will pacify them instead of alarming them" as one of the secretaries had put it.

One of my Russian friends, who is a refugee and has lived through the days of Bolshevist terror in Soviet Russia, told me that, aside from the fact that political opponents are not officially and openly put against the wall, the conditions here, at least during the week following the election of March 5, which resulted in heavy Nazi gains, are far worse. They are worse because the numerous crimes against Jews and political opponents are committed quietly under cover of night and those victims who are not nationals of another country are afraid to go to the German police which is dominated by the Nazis and will not do anything for them. We hear only of outrages committed against foreigners. The newspapers are afraid to report what they know, but these reports spread quickly and the result is that the Jews in Germany are terror-stricken, for they do not know when their turn is next, when several uniformed Nazis may knock at their door at three or four in the morning and take them out for a ride. Often victims of Nazi violence are so intimidated that they are afraid to talk of their sad experience, having been threatened with death if they say a word to any one. Hitler has finally issued an emphatic command to his followers to abstain from acts of violence but will it have effect? Only a few days ago, the Nazi Prussian Minister of the Interior in a public speech which was broadcast over a national hook-up practically incited his followers to further acts of violence, declaring openly that the task of his police was not to protect Jews and political opponents.

I am writing you this letter not merely to tell you as to what is going on here. I understand that the Nazis are planning to engage in propaganda on a large scale in England and in America in order to win adherents to their Fascist philosophy, which is far worse than anything that Mussolini has ever attempted. I am afraid that if their activities abroad are not counteracted at once, and very energetically, the result will be a growth of anti-Semitism in America from which the Jews may suffer for generations. Dr. Schacht, the former President of the Reichsbank and at present Hitler's economic and financial adviser, is an especially dangerous person in this respect because I understand that he is the one who is largely interested in swaying American public opinion towards Hitler. I have only a few more minutes, and the next courier pouch leaves in two weeks, and I shall therefore come to the main purpose of my letter. You must discuss this matter with some prominent Jews in Washington, who take an active interest in Jewish life, and urge upon them the importance of a speedy and energetic counter-propaganda before it is too late. The American Jews must not make the mistake of the German Jews who trusted to the intelligence of the German people and left the work of combatting the Nazis to the Social-Democrats. If they had spent a few thousand dollars during the past years, they probably would have been able to avert their present plight.

Of course, you realize the importance of keeping the contents of this letter absolutely secret, for if any of the persons with whom you may discuss this matter should inadvertently permit the information to leak out that I wrote you all this, I would be promptly discharged, and if the Nazis should get hold of this information you would probably never get to see me again. Otherwise you need not worry about me. I am ex-territorial and the Nazis will not dare to touch me. However, I am very careful and never discuss politics outside of the shop, on the telephone or in letters. Anything you write me through the open mail must not contain any reference to the subject matter of this letter. If there is anything you wish to ask me in this connection, transmit the letter to the State Department and be sure to seal it carefully, preferably with wax and obtain the assurance from the mail room of the Department that it will not be thrown into the open mails.

I am sorry that I am forced by lack of time to write you such a rotten letter, but sentences don't mean anything now, though I am ashamed of the queer grammatical constructions which I have been using in my haste.

Yours,

—

Before the meeting, something of deepest moment occurred. Deutsch and I went to the State Department, as I recall it, upon its invitation, and throughout the day, the Friday preceding the meeting, by the courtesy of the State Department, we were in constant touch with the German Foreign Office, that is to say with the representatives of Freiherr von Neurath. Again and again we were told that, if the protest meeting were abandoned and there were no more telling of atrocity tales, there would be some moderating of anti-Jewish measures.

The conversations went on, as the State Department records will show, throughout the day. Deutsch and I and our associates were unshaken and resolved to go forward. Sunday morning, however, I was called to the telephone from Washington, the speaker being from the German embassy, who again urged us not to hold the meeting the following night, repeating the offers of amelioration provided the protest meeting were abandoned.

This happened just before the Free Synagogue service at Carnegie Hall. I felt a sense of terrible responsibility and that I ought to consult the wisest head in Jewry.

Over the telephone I put the matter before Justice Brandeis. His reply was, "Go ahead and make the protest as good as you can."

XV

Resistance to Hitlerism

ON March 12, 1933, the Nazi swastika was proclaimed the official flag of the "New Germany." On March 27, the American Jewish Congress mobilized the first broad resistance movement to Hitlerism at a mass meeting held in Madison Square Garden, New York. That night, Bishops Manning and McConnell, Alfred E. Smith, John Haynes Holmes, Dr. S. Parkes Cadman, and William Green nobly uttered their abhorrence of Nazism, and together we lifted our voices seeking to forewarn Germany of what Hitler would inevitably mean. As chairman of the meeting, I pointed out:

A leader who sets out to divide his national home against itself may have election triumphs for an hour, but he is bound to go down in the end in moral defeat and in spiritual disaster.

If it be true that we Jews stand among the objects of Hitlerite displeasure and ill-will, it is because you and I know that Hitlerism aims not at a change of government, but at a complete change of regime. He aims at the end of Democracy. He aims at the overthrow of Republicanism. He aims at the destruction of the parliamentary system, and Hitler is understanding enough to know that Jews are not fitful, expedient servants for an hour of Democracy and Republicanism. He knows that we Jews, after centuries of fire, have come to believe with all our hearts in the sacredness and in the perpetuity of democratic institutions and the democratic ideal.

At the mass meeting I sought to make clear that neither the Jews of the world nor the Jews of Germany demanded exceptional treatment or privileged position. We affirmed certain elementary axioms of civilization: the immediate cessation of anti-Semitic activity in Germany, including an end to the policy of racial discrimination against Jews and of their exclusion from the economic life of Germany; the safeguarding of Jewish life and the human rights of Jews; the revocation of all special measures already taken against Jewish nonnationals (East European Jews) and their equal treatment with all other nonnationals in Germany.

The protest of America on the Nazi terror against Jews was countered by the Nazi government with the announcement that the boycott against Jews in Germany was ordered because of the "atrocity propaganda" by Jews in America. However, as we soon learned from Germany, the opposite was true. One letter from Berlin dated April 2 reached me giving details of the horrors of April 1 for Jews throughout Germany. It added:

> Over here they have made the Jews and everyone else think that this boycott was only a retaliatory measure because of the action of the Jews in England and America and that nothing would have occurred otherwise. Lies—all lies. It was prepared months ago. I know! ...
>
> They claim that all this was done in retaliation of what was done to Germany in foreign countries. Could any country in 48 hours have a complete list of every Jewish shop in Germany? This, mind you, included seamstresses, little shoemakers, tiny shops in basements that sell vegetables, and all this in the smallest hamlets and towns. You have no idea how all this was organized to the nth degree. They had speakers in every factory throughout the country telling workmen and the masses that through a boycott instituted by the Jews against Germany they, the workmen, would be the ones to suffer and so they must help in rooting out these people and hitting them in their most vulnerable spot.
>
> Thank God that the other countries know and, despite what this country is preaching that the mass meetings of the Jews in England and America has reacted injuriously to the Jews in Ger-

many, I tell you this is not so. No matter how much they suffered in humiliation and insult last Saturday it is not one-hundredth of what we are all convinced was REALLY planned. According to their real program [the Boxheim documents and others] they had intended not only to close the shops but to plunder them everywhere and do a lot of other things far worse than what they did, and which they brag about as having been carried out in strictest discipline.

Hitler made the statement that the "People" wanted to carry all this through themselves and that only by organization and by their storm detachments and the regulations which they carried out to the letter were atrocities averted. That wasn't it. They were *afraid* now that the outside world knew to completely carry out what they had so systematically planned and organized—a huge program. They had to let their troopers loose but they limited their dirty work to only one day, ordering that the boycott should be over by 7 P.M.

And again from a Berlin lawyer who sent this message from Zurich:

It was only foreign protests, especially that of America, which prevented even more happenings, a greater number of kidnappings and bloody beatings and possibly one big general pogrom.

In contrast to these letters, on March 30, I received a cable from three former presidents of the German Zionist Federation stating that the situation was most serious and urging that I issue a statement denying that the anti-German boycott had been proclaimed by Jewish organizations.

The violence and insolence of a lengthy cable signed by the editors of a Jewish paper in Hamburg was such as to make me feel sure it was either sent under duress or directly by agents of the Nazi government. My suspicion about several such messages was later proven correct. This one, dated March 31, read:

... German Jews accuse you and associates to be fools of outside political influences. Your senseless overrating of own international importance and lack of judgment damage largely those you pretend to want to protect.... Better shut off your own limelight and useless meetings as surest means against anti-Semitism. German Jews who feel one with our great national ideas and keep tactful are treated with pronounced consideration from Gentile neighbors and present government officials. Please enlighten everyone about foregoing. This is your most important duty to repair your crimes against us.

We understood the plea and the plaint of our brother Jews in Germany. They were German patriots who loved their fatherland and had reason to love it. Some of their leaders were under the impact of panic and terror, others under some form of compulsion, in any event the compulsion of a great fear if not actual coercion. We had no quarrel with our Jewish brothers in Germany and their leaders, but their policy of uncomplaining assent and supercautious silence had borne evil fruit. They who had virtually been silent through the years of anti-Jewish propaganda could not be regarded by us as the wisest of counselors.

To those leaders of German Jewry who declared that the anti-Jewish situation in Germany was a local German question I called attention to the words of Abraham Lincoln. Defenders of slavery urged and excused slavery on the ground that it was local. Lincoln's answer was, "Slavery is local, but freedom is national."

One thing more must be told. Students of the period will recall that one or two days before Boycott Day, April 1, 1933— the day on which the Nazis decreed that an absolute boycott of all Jews was to go into effect—it was reported by cable out of the Reich that a nationwide pogrom was being planned throughout Germany. The pogrom did not take place. The Nazi boycott, of course, was the real beginning of years of Jewish humiliation and agony. But the mass pogrom reportedly scheduled for that day did not come off. A careful study as well as consultation with many German Jews and some non-Jews in the course of the Hitler years served to confirm the rumors of the closing days of March, 1933. It is more than probable that the boycott of April 1 was a mild and belated afterthought and that, in truth, a Teutonic St. Bartholomew's Eve massacre had been planned against the Jews of Germany. But when the Nazi regime considered the strength of the American Jewish Congress indictment uttered by leading American citizens, Catholic as well as Protestant, it took heed of that warning and realized that the Reich would endanger its position in the eyes of the world if it resorted to a Jewish pogrom.

Someday the record may give the answer to this debatable question. I personally satisfied myself on my trip to Europe that summer, which took me to England, France, Czechoslovakia, Switzerland, and elsewhere. The European protest movement against Hitler then was undertaken as a result of the inspiration and leadership of the American Jewish Congress. Representatives of the Jewish communities of Poland, Latvia, Czechoslovakia, and Rumania told me that they had been in the dark. They did not know what to do. They were waiting for a lead when the cables came from Bernard Deutsch and myself calling for action on March 27, the day we had set for our great protest assembly in New York. Then they felt that they could and must go ahead. They took it for granted that we, far removed from the scene, were sufficiently informed concerning the situation, to know whether it was well for them to strike out.

If my analysis be correct, the American Jewish Congress performed a very great service for German Jewry, for world Jewry, for civilization. In any event, cruel as the first Boycott Day, April 1, 1933, proved to be, it may have been an improvised and belated substitute for something far more bitter and terrible. But the Congress protest was proof that a great people, however awful the threat, would not "take it lying down" and could be trusted to stand on its feet and not crawl on its hands. This word of Josiah Wedgewood, British Labor M.P. and truest of our friends, was an English reminder of the example of Mordecai, who would not bow the head, nor bend the knee before Haman, the Hitler of an earlier Persian day.

In America, we immediately met the counterpart, though happily on a small and individual scale, of both Nazism and timid Jews who, without the excuse of Nazi persecution, lacked self-respect. William Dudley Pelley of the Silver Shirts published in *Liberation:*

> Hitler has a destiny to fulfill. . . . He has already set his hand against the so-called "Lord's Chosen" in Germany. . . . It is the order of things that those wicked and malignant spirits . . . should meet a fearful fate in this closing Cycle of Cosmic Event. That contest is on-the-make and Hitler's job it has been to do the advance work.
>
> But Hitler is not going to finish that work. *The finish of it comes right here in America.*

And a gentleman who carefully described himself in the *New York Post* "As a Hebrew—and as an American whose ancestors have fought in all our wars since that of 1812" (forgetting, if he ever knew, the delightful characterization by the great American humorist who said that those Americans who bragged of their descent often forgot how great the descent had been) fulminated against the American Jewish Congress for daring to hold a mass meeting in protest against Hitler's terror and solemnly announced:

> I predict that even in the Germany of Hitler a patriotic, self-respecting citizen of the Hebrew religion will experience very little difficulty, and will suffer no hardship.

Amidst the early mounting horrors as reported day after day we sought aid from our government. Silence at first both on the part of the American government and the Prime Minister of England filled our cup of woe. We went ahead, pressed forward by the Jewish masses who could not be expected to understand such silence. About mid-April we planned a protest march in

New York, on May 10, the day of the ordered burning of Jewish books in Germany. And a great march was held and reported throughout the world. For reasons still inexplicable, the American Red Cross took it upon itself to publicize a statement of the German Red Cross to the effect that: "the reports of atrocities which have been spread abroad for reasons of political propaganda are in no way in accordance with the facts."

Within a few weeks after the mass meeting, members of both the House of Representatives and the Senate voiced their desire to do whatever they could to express America's abhorrence of the conduct of the Nazis.

Day after day and week after week, reliable reports of the breaking of all resistance by the Nazi Brown Shirts came through from many sources. The use of terror had been extended to destroy pacifists, labor leaders, liberals, socialists—in fact any resistance to the Nazi dictatorship. Although, as the *Manchester Guardian* reported on July 21, 1933, the terrorist wave had shattered all actual resistance, the terror had not ceased—but on the contrary had become more universal and more systematic. Priests of the Catholic Church had been arrested and the Protestants were not being spared. The measures against the Jews continued to outstrip in systematic cruelty and planned destruction the terror against other groups. Trade unions were closed to non-Aryans—so that the early prospect for Jewish workers seemed starvation. Clinics managed by Jewish doctors were closed. Farmers and peasants in western Bavaria were prohibited from having any business relations with Jews, under penalty of being officially classified as traitors; Jewish writers were excluded from the Union of Dramatic Writers, thus eliminating their work from the German stage and motion pictures; segregation of Jewish youth in schools, streetcars, and universities was decreed; and sterilization of the unfit was announced—with reports that the unfit would include Jewish children!

That summer (1933) my wife and I went abroad, first to

Prague, still the democratic land that Masaryk had re-created, although I saw Hitler youths walking through the streets at night singing their songs of hate. I wanted to go to Germany, but our Ambassador said he would not be responsible for what would happen if I should come and that it might well cause serious complications. We traveled on to the lands surrounding Germany—Austria, Switzerland, and France.

Everywhere I went I visited the asylums or shelters for German Jewish refugees, and through their eyes looked into the depths of hell. When I spoke to one man who became hysterical, I turned to his wife asking if she could not control him so I could understand. She replied, "If you knew what my husband has lived through, what he has seen and heard and experienced—you would not ask that question."

I met an old friend from Munich, who told about Siegel, whose picture had been in the press throughout the world bearing the placard, "I am a Jew. I am a treasonable German." Later he was shot to death at Dachau "trying to escape." My friend, in tears, could only say, "He was a fine, outstanding, honorable member of the Munich bar." The Germans denied that this picture was genuine, said it was nothing but an atrocity fake. But a representative of the *Brooklyn Daily Eagle* told me that he had himself taken the picture from the tower of a Munich church and, when told by a representative of Goebbels that the whole thing was a fake, had the original of the photograph in his pocket!

A physician from Munich and his wife called on me in Paris and said that their little girl of eleven had come from school, her face tear-stained, and asked them: "Is it true that we Jews are all *gemein* [base]? That is what they tell us in school." I learned how the children were compelled to memorize passages which say vile things about the Jews, how they were denied milk and bread when Aryans were fed.

The deepest concern of the Jews in Germany was "our children." Always the greatest joy of Jews was to live with their children. Now, their one hope was to send their children away to safety. Over and over, I heard, "We can endure it, but our children ..."

I wrote to a friend in July, after having spent days with refugees in London and Paris, that they were living in hell. "I feel this so deeply that if I were to read tomorrow of a pogrom, which may come at any hour, and the murder or suicide of thousands of victims, I could hardly be any sorrier or unhappier than I am over them excepting for the shock and tragedy of their manner of going."

From Zurich, I again begged Ambassador Dodd by telephone to make possible my air flight to Berlin. He was adamant in refusing, insisting that my picture had so often been published in the *Voelkische Beobachter* and in Streicher's *Stuermer* that I might be recognized, particularly because of my unmistakable passport, and give rise to an "unpleasant incident" at a landing place such as Nuremberg.

It was in Germany's neighboring lands that we got our first glimpse of the human desolation that was being wrought by Hitler. In Paris, as well as Prague and Vienna, we met with scores of the earliest homeless refugees, who gathered from time to time amid the necessarily scant hospitality of the hostel, called into being by the French Jews. My wife said at once, "Many of these unhappy beings will soon, they say, come to America. As soon as we return I shall establish a home for refugees, where they may dwell in security and comfort, and thus fit themselves for American life." She was better than her word. Within a few months, three houses of the Jewish Institute of Religion had been refurnished by the Women's Division of the American Jewish Congress under her leadership. Here Mrs. Wise and her associates made homes for eighty to one hundred refugees, young and old, at a time. Some of the most distinguished of the refugees, from 1934 to 1939, lived for a time in these houses, which Mrs. Wise had exquisitely furnished with the help of her friends and comrades. Largely in jest, Professor Einstein, visiting the houses and delighted with their charm and comfort, lamented, "Why cannot I live here? *Ich bin ja auch ein Refugee!*"

I must not omit to tell of a minor victory of the Women's Division of the Congress. At one of their annual luncheons, the speaker was Mayor LaGuardia, who, like President Roosevelt, was from the beginning a clearsighted foe of Nazism. In the course of his luncheon address, the Mayor had made the rather startling suggestion that, after the capture of Hitler, he be brought to this country and exhibited in a cage at the World's Fair, then being held in New York. The Berlin press reported the meeting, stating that "the mad Mayor had made this irresponsible speech before a company of a thousand or twelve hundred loose Jewish women." Despite the idiocy of the remark, the President of the Women's Division of the American Jewish Congress felt justly pained over the insult. In this spirit Mrs. Wise promptly telegraphed to Secretary Hull, insisting that he demand an apology from Germany. The Secretary forwarded the protest to Von Neurath, who promptly tendered an apology for his government, the only occasion, as I recall it, that apology was forthcoming, however grievous the offense committed.

The spirit that moved Mrs. Wise as head of the Women's Division of the congress to act without delay when the honor of Jewish womanhood was assailed led her some years later to act with the same dispatch and dignity when the British government, by its ambassador to Washington, offered her a decoration, the Order of the British Empire, in acknowledgment of the service she and the congress had rendered British soldiers through the Congress Defense Houses. To a quarter million of men the congress had offered shelter and hospitality during the war years. She felt so deeply about the conduct of the British mandatory government in Palestine and the grievous wrong it had done to Jewish refugees, many of whom could have been saved by opening the doors of Palestine, that without one moment's delay, she declined the honor, of which she never spoke again.

That summer in addition to meeting with and hearing first-hand accounts of life in Germany from hundreds of refugees, I met with leading statesmen of many lands, conferred with the representatives of Jewish and non-Jewish communities, and studied the activities of various relief agencies. At that early period in the Hitler regime, it still seemed possible that effective action by the League of Nations through a commission and economic pressure by enlightened public opinion, if secured promptly, might bring about the end of the Nazi government and its policy of persecution. And so I strove toward achieving these two objectives, desperately working against time and the unwillingness or inability of statesmen of many lands to see that not to end the Hitler regime would mean war or the destruction of all that civilized men held dear.

In Geneva, the World Jewish Conference was convened on September 5. I introduced and urged the unanimous adoption of a resolution calling for a world Jewish boycott of Germany. The resolution was unanimously adopted. I had been urged to call for such a boycott for many months. While I had believed from the beginning that the boycott was a natural, inevitable weapon in the hands of individuals against the war of extermination launched by the Hitler regime against Jews, I was firmly convinced that a world Jewish boycott could only be declared by a world assembly of Jews.

In answer to a question by the press at that time as to whether this was to be solely a Jewish boycott I answered:

> One of the most grievous disappointments of my life would be the failure of non-Jews, especially of Christian men and women in all lands, to stand by our side and join with us in wielding this weapon of defence against the Third Reich on behalf of the Jewish people. The truth is that tens of thousands of Christians feel exactly as we do about the crimes planned and perpetrated against Jews by the Nazi government.

The conference that September decided not only that there must be a continuance and an intensification of the world boycott against Germany but that the boycott must be moral as well as political. Even at that time I thought and said that moral and economic boycott ultimately would develop into political action:

> For my part, I cannot believe that liberty-loving countries such as England and France and our own will permanently endure the liberty-destroying, the justice-violating conduct of the Hitlerite Reich toward its own people—

and I added:

> Germany is in truth become a menace to world security and world peace.

A second decision of the World Jewish Conference was that a World Jewish Congress must be held, and it was then scheduled to be convened the following March.

In the months that followed every effort had to be bent toward getting financial help to feed the refugees of Hitler's regime, to move my country, which had been keenly disappointing in its failure thus far to enable German refugees to enter the United States, to strengthen through the World Jewish Congress a self-reliant democratic movement of Jews throughout the world in the face of what seemed relentless destruction, and to help America and other democratic lands to see and understand that their security and peace was in danger. On September 27, I said:

> When I speak of the menace to world security I do not mean that Hitler is going to smash and slash into France tomorrow or next day. He is much too shrewd and careful to do any such thing. The real danger is something much more subtle, much less overt, namely that he will carry the ideal of *Gleichschaltung* one step farther and that means insistence on uniformity. It means the over-ruling of other racial groups. It means the exercise of ruthless power in a ruthless way. It is all mildly and pleasantly put as *Gleichschaltung* which means little more than agreement or uni-

formity, but uniformity can be insisted upon only by those who are certain of their own superiority. After uniformity and superiority there will come the inevitable attempt to achieve world domination.

Within three weeks the German Reich had withdrawn from the League of Nations, and in doing so said to those who could hear, "Germany is against the world."

Germany still sought to put the matter as if it were merely a quarrel between Germany and the Jews, as if it were just a disagreement between Herr von Neurath and Sir John Simon, as if it were just a misunderstanding, with Dr. Goebbels on the one hand and Premier Daladier on the other. The truth was that something catastrophic had come upon the life of the world. One of the great, one of the mighty, one of the tremendous historic forces of the world had run amok, had fallen afoul of civilization.

It was only fifteen or sixteen months earlier that the Lausanne agreement had been reached, saying that if France, England, and Italy were lenient toward Germany we, the United States, would scale down the obligations owing to us from the nations to which Germany was a debtor. The world was with Germany then. With incredible naïveté the official organ of the Foreign Office of Berlin asked, "What has happened to change the views of the nations since July?" when Germany was permitted on terms of equality to meet with the nations at the London World Economic Conference, after which it was hoped there would be some abatement of the madness of the Hitler Reich. What happened? Everything happened. The everything was an affront, an absolute challenge to civilization, which civilization would have to meet or else be destroyed. The world was warned, and we Jews were—as we so often have been throughout history—the object lesson, the shock troops of civilization, first under attack. The challenge of each morning and night was how to make the world, our world, understand.

I must have sounded to many like a twentieth-century Cassandra when I spoke after my return from Europe:

> Men and women, remember my prophecy. Let the young people remember my words: you will see what will happen ten and twenty years hence, if this "Aryanism," this *Gleichschaltung*, remains within the Hitler Reich. You cannot have a people uniform, without differences, no variety, no dissent, no heresy, no racial heresy. You cannot have that inside of a nation without that nation finally wrecking itself in the effort to make that race or nation dominant not only inside but outside of the boundaries of that land. When will American civilization challenge Hitlerism?
>
> My answer, the answer not of a Jew but of an American, is: America will and ought to challenge Hitlerism, not with guns, not with arms, not by enmity, but by the voice of the President of the United States. It is a mighty voice, a magic voice, it is the one most potent voice in the whole world. God give it that for the sake of America's soul, that for the sake of civilization, for his own sake, the President's mighty voice may yet be raised in one of the critically decisive hours of human need in human history. Up to this time America has not yet ranged itself alongside of the forces of civilization. It cannot, it does not and it will not sympathize with Hitlerism and all that Hitlerism means. Someday, it may be soon, that voice *must* be lifted in no uncertain terms. And after it shall have been, with a new faith, and a new loyalty, we shall thank God for America, our country, and for its leader, our President.

In 1934, I returned to Europe to meet with leaders of Western European lands and to confer again in Geneva with my colleagues on the preparatory body for the World Jewish Congress. Difficult though it was to say certain things to Jews whose lives were in so precarious a state as those in Hitler's Reich, I felt impelled to express two fears: One was that our Jewish brothers in Germany might feel moved or compelled to accept a peace agreement or pact that might mean some slight amelioration or mitigation of their wrongs but that would in effect not alter their intolerable status of second-class citizenship.

There was still something graver to be feared. The Nazi Reich might decide to prevent some of the evil consequence to its regime by such palliative treatment of the Jews as would disarm world-wide Jewish protest. Against that menace to the integrity of Jewish life, we needed to be forewarned and forearmed. Insofar as the Nazi Reich had proclaimed war against civilization, to accept any terms of peace it might specially offer to the Jews would be to side with Hitlerism against civilization, indeed to betray civilization. At Geneva, I said to the World Jewish Conference:

> Our place is indubitably and unalterably in the ranks of those forces of civilization and freedom which cannot exist with Nazism. Grievous fate it is to be among the victims of Nazism without help and without redress. Infinitely more tragic it were to come to an understanding with Nazism. To die at the hands of Nazism is cruel; to survive by its grace were ten thousand times worse. We will survive Nazism unless we commit the inexpiable sin of bartering or trafficking with it in order to save some Jewish victims.
>
> This is not the unheroic or mock-heroic sacrifice of our fellow-Jews in Nazi Germany, but rather the refusal to purchase peace and security for some of us at the cost of the honor of us all.

At the beginning of the Hitler regime, the American Jewish Congress had been the only responsible Jewish body in America to call for and support the economic boycott of Germany. It was after, if not because of, our leadership that such mighty voices as those of S. Parkes Cadman, Harry Emerson Fosdick, John Haynes Holmes, Bishop Manning, and Bishop McConnell were raised in America. The aroused Jewish consciousness began the boycott, but the human conscience was now carrying it on. But it is painful to recall that the boycott was unapproved in certain Jewish quarters—and by those same self-appointed Jewish leaders who had urged silence at a time when silence on our part would have resulted in silence on the part of all the forces of civilization.

Thus, for example, as late as February 5, 1935, one of the leaders of the American Jewish Committee, in an interview in the *New York World-Telegram* denounced the boycott movement as "a vicarious sacrifice to one's own emotionalism." "Jews should see to it," he asserted, "that they do not fight Hitler with Hitlerism" because "historically bigotry always begets bigotry." Claiming that the boycott was contrary to the express wish of leading German Jews, he went on to add that the "destructive effects" of the boycott fell "squarely on many Jewish merchants and manufacturers" and that because of the millions of dollars in economic obligations involved in German-American relations, Jews had no right to "disturb the economic and diplomatic relations between America and a country with which America is at peace." The boycott, he concluded "is but the reaction of a small, highly emotionalized minority."

Thus, despite the tragic events within Germany, a Jewish leader was still able to regard firm and unafraid protest against unspeakable injustice as "bigotry" and to dismiss the millions of Jews throughout the world, the distinguished Christian churchmen, the American Federation of Labor, and other groups supporting the boycott as a "highly emotionalized and vocal minority." Nor could he understand that the boycott was not a form of attack but a moral and economic instrument of defense, that it recorded civilization's protest against Nazi Germany. Fortunately, neither the voice of America nor the conscience of the Jews was speaking through one who seemed to suggest that there were no higher obligations than those of the "tens of millions of dollars of German obligations held in America."

Nor was it coincidental that this leader in the same interview denounced the proposal for a World Jewish Congress at which Jews from all lands could meet to take counsel on their common problems as equals. For back of both attitudes, typical at the time of some conservative and wealthy Jews, lay two great unfaiths and distrusts. The first was a fundamental unfaith in the capacity of the Jewish people to manage their own affairs as Jews, an unfaith in the democratic ideal. Only a small number of substantial people, in their view, could guide the affairs of the Jewish people. The second unfaith was in America, and the fear that Americans would be ready to stamp as second-class citizens those Jews who raised their voices in protest and who chose to meet with their fellow Jews of all lands in democratic partnership in the moment of greatest affliction. America and Americans, I have been convinced all my life, respect the Jew who is unafraid and unashamed, who has the power of wrath against injustice, rather than the Jew who is nervous and fearful and who has little faith in the justness of the American people.

In the second half of 1932 the world had seemed to be ready not only for the beginnings of disarmament but for world peace. By March, 1938, the world had seen the mightiest massing of armaments in all the centuries of history. The world had become physically and morally prepared for war again. The world was even then divided into two war camps, led by Germany, Italy, and Japan in one. In the other were England, hesitating France, and possibly America, with an extraordinary passion for isolation and neutrality, which gave maximum help and reinforcement to the Nazi-Fascist world. One country after another had been overwhelmed by Nazi ideology. Treaties had been scrapped or just ignored: Italy in Ethiopia; Japan in China. Undeclared wars had been fought. Continents were being raped. Nazism and international morality had shown themselves to be incompatible. The democratic world was slowly being merged and fused together, alas by its enemies rather than by itself.

It was no accident that the carefully organized arrests of Jews for forced labor, confiscation of Jewish property, the closing of Jewish synagogues, and riots that were so carefully timed and planned as to be clearly government-instituted pogroms should have coincided in May, June, and July of 1938 with the trial mobilization of Hitler's Germany. The handwriting on the wall was made even clearer when the Italian Cabinet on September 1 prohibited Jewish immigration and ordered all foreign Jews and those who had acquired citizenship since January 1, 1919, to leave the country within six months. Other decrees followed. The Hebraic world was, I am not unhappy to recount, denounced as the chief enemy of fascism. And finally in imitation of the hostage system developed by Hitler, Jews throughout the world were told with attempted blackmail that the future of Italian Jews would depend on the future attitude of world Hebraism toward fascist Italy! The axis of death, the destruction of human freedom, and Jewish annihilation had indeed been welded. There could be but one answer to Mussolini as to Hitler:

> Jews in America are unready and unable to meet Mussolini's terms, namely not to oppose fascism as Americans. It is not enough for us to be the honest supporters of democracy, but we in America need oppose Nazism and Fascism as they oppose and do battle against democracy.
>
> One thing we cannot do for Italian Jews. We will not disavow our democratic faith in order to soften the vigor of the blows which may fall upon them. . . . To the Jew, democracy and all that it means is not a passing type or process of government. Democracy is the political faith of the Jew, and this were true even if it were not bound up with his fate. In an enslaved world, the Jew would not choose to live.

And the final terror against the Jewish people was let loose when a seventeen-year-old grief-crazed Jewish lad named Grynszpan slew a German official in Paris in November, 1938. On the day of the funeral in Düsseldorf, the Nazis took the rabbi of the town and broke his body to pieces and then carried his dead, mangled corpse to his wife, and his wife lost her reason. A thousand men died in Germany who had as much relation to Grynszpan as I. The collective reprisals against the innocent continued. A collective fine equal to virtually all that the German Jews still retained was levied.

The conduct of Hitler's government moved a former president, governors, senators, makers of public opinion, leaders of the Christian churches to speak, and the President of the United States not only spoke but acted in such terms as to make clear that the conduct of Germany placed it, in the eyes of America, beyond the pale of civilization. These were the words of President Roosevelt on November 15, 1938:

> The news of the past few days from Germany has deeply shocked public opinion in the United States. Such news from any part of the world would inevitably produce a similar profound reaction among American people in every part of the nation.
>
> I myself could scarcely believe that such things could occur in a twentieth century civilization.
>
> With a view to having a first-hand picture of the situation in Germany I asked the Secretary of State to order our Ambassador in Berlin to return at once for report and consultation.

Six years or nearly six years had passed since the burning of the Reichstag building by the Nazi leaders; four years had passed since the blood bath or purge of June 30, 1934; three years had passed since the organized and German-directed assassination of Chancellor Dollfuss; three years had passed since the Nuremberg decrees, which took from half a million Jews in Germany their German birthright, as precious to them as my Americanism is to me; less than three months had passed since the Nazi Reich, with the infinitely tragic concurrence and consent of England and France, had invaded and mutilated one of the dearest hopes of all mankind, Masaryk's and Benes' Czechoslovakian Republic.

Some of my people asked at this time why I who had led the protest against Hitler's Germany in 1933, had been silent during these weeks.

> I led the protest in 1933 and ever since. I led the protest and I spoke because the world was largely silent and the American

people seemed to be inert and apathetic to and unconscious of what was happening. At last, at long last, America has spoken and the world has spoken, overwhelmed by the barbarism of nationwide reprisals in recent weeks. . . .

How can that Government be expected to keep peace which wages new and savage wars against four hundred thousand because of the act of one youth, which wages new and savage wars against Catholics, Protestants, Jews, against religion, against labor, against liberals? England feels at last after less than two months that it has been tricked, duped insofar as it was led to imagine that peace would ever be the work of them that live by war and for war. . . .

I would be the last person in the world to minimize the act of the President, whose word and deed have been beyond our praise, but in all that has been said and done he has only expressed the heart and voiced the will of the American people.

. . . For the first time in six years the whole American people . . . have recognized in the horrors of suffering inflicted upon the Jews of Germany, an attack upon the sanctity of law and sacredness of justice itself, a violation of the ideals of civilization, a deliberate assault upon the foundations of democracy.

America seemed to stand united behind the President save for some handfuls whose hearts or investments were with the Nazis—save for the deluded who continued to listen Sunday afternoons to Coughlin's voice, though he represented neither America nor the Roman Catholic Church.

One thing more wrote itself out of my heart that day of the November disaster:

I would say this to the peoples of the world which at last face the monstrous things that have been done in Germany. Had the world felt in March 1933 as it feels today the awful things of the last five years would never have happened. Ethiopia would still be a free kingdom; Spain would not be devastated by civil war; Czechoslovakia would not be lost to the democracies of civilization; and the Nazi and Fascist regime would not sit supreme upon the ruins of what seemed like yesterday the promise of human civilization.

Late in January 1939, while again traveling to Europe, mine was the horror of hearing the voice of Hitler calling for the destruction of the Jewish people as warmongers. This hideous experience was a forecast of what I was destined to find throughout the London Conference on Palestine, which I went over to attend. One felt that craven decisions might be made in a world paralyzed by the specter of the dictator countries. Courage seemed to have ceased to rule the hearts of men. Fear had taken its place everywhere.

In those days and after I had a sorry and tragic vindication. Beginning in 1933, I had been warned that I was exaggerating, that things were not so bad as I imagined, that Hitler was just a passing phenomenon and not to be taken too seriously. By 1939 or 1940 the man with whom some Jews and the greater part of the Christian world was ready to compromise and against whom I had lifted my voice and labored with what power I had was become the enemy of mankind.

XVI

The Spirit of Warsaw's Ghetto

WHILE I live, I shall count as one of the fateful days of a long life the day of my first and only visit to Poland and to my fellow Jews of that land. I had long and often sought to visit and meet with Polish Jewry, for I had felt that, as president of the American Jewish Congress, it was my duty to learn the way of life of the second largest Jewish community in the world, its numerical strength being the least of its virtues. For Poland, wholly apart from numbers, had long been one of the *loci classici* of Jewish history. Polish Jewry has for nearly a thousand years served as asylum to Jews in flight. It suffered terrible persecution at different times, but—and this is supremely important—it was and remained the spiritual center of world Jewry century after century. It was the chief victim, too, of all Polish wars and divisions.

Its supreme Jewish distinction lay in its piety and its learning. No outward circumstance had impinged upon the piety or lessened the sacrificial zeal of its people and above all of its leaders, unequaled in learning. Beyond any other group it constituted a Jewish cosmos. Vilna—nominally Lithuania, but in spirit and truth, the Jerusalem of Poland—and its greatest son, Elijah ha Gaon, are enduring symbols of the glory of the Poland that was. The foremost schools of Jewish learning, the most famous Yeshiboth for the rearing of men for the rabbinate, these deeply enriched Jewish life and letters the world over.

I felt, rightly I believe, that I could not proceed to the World Jewish Congress, shortly to assemble in August, 1936, without at least getting a glimpse of that Jewry which was bound to take a leading part at its sessions. The journey itself was moving. From Vienna, where for the last time I was greeted by old Zionist colleagues such as engineer Robert Stricker, I journeyed overnight to Warsaw. Years later Stricker was to become one of the earliest and bravest of the Hitler victims. He had laid himself open to attack, for in his Viennese paper as well as on the platform, he had throughout nearly a decade been one of the sharpest opponents of Hitlerism. Sorrowfully I recall that Dr. Nahum Goldmann and I, two of his old friends and comrades, tried several times to secure his freedom from the Nazis. Either his captors were too perfidious or the intermediaries were too lacking in skill. Alas, this brave and honest man died, doubtless after suffering and unbroken heroism, in Nazi hands.

We reached Warsaw just before the noon hour. Before we reached our destination, I had chanced to note at a number of stations that large crowds were gathered. It did not occur to me that they were connected with myself until suddenly a distinguished New York lawyer, Louis Posner—who, at the merest suggestion of my wife in London, had volunteered to accompany me—called to me, "Stephen Wise, listen! The crowd is calling 'Stepan Weisz, Stepan Weisz' "—by which name Polish Jewry seemed to know me. At a wayside station, a committee entered the car, addressed me in Yiddish, which happily I understood, and handed me a paper, which, even if I still had it in my possession, with its generously meant and exuberantly uttered praises, I could not bring myself to put in this record. Evidently my name had preceded me, especially in relation to the great cause of Zionism and to the World Jewish Congress. This committee should have prepared me for what was to come at Warsaw. Without being unduly modest—

and no enemy will charge me with that—I had not dreamed that I would be honored with such a reception as fell to my lot there. Milling thousands were gathered at the railroad station, shouting my name. I made my way with difficulty through the crowd but only with the help of a committee made up of some of the most distinguished leaders of the country. I felt at once that the demonstration was so far beyond my deserving that I could not suppress my tears.

And it occurred to me, was ever a people on earth so grateful, so deeply and inordinately grateful even for the least? That is true of the Jew both in relation to his fellow Jew and to the non-Jew. Herzl enjoyed an almost Messianic experience when he journeyed, alas, in vain, to Russia and its unspeakable Minister Trepoff. The Jewish people is almost too grateful, if a people can be that, for the least of favors, for any act of decent kindness or civilized good will. So often and so cruelly have we been hurt, that a normally friendly act is regarded and rewarded as if it were a benediction.

It was deeply humbling to think that the little I had done for my people more than a continent away from Poland should be so fully remembered and abundantly rewarded. I could not walk through the Nelevski without being surrounded by friendly, sometimes cheering, throngs.

I have addressed thousands of meetings, great and small, throughout many years, but never such a meeting as was held in Warsaw to welcome me and hear the story of the World Jewish Congress, shortly to convene in Geneva. The hall was a veritable fire trap, with the audience standing and crowding every inch of it. I spoke to a most generous mass of men and women in "Kongress Deutsch," that is, imperfect German, with a sprinkling of Yiddish, Hebrew, and English. They heard me eagerly and shouted their approval even though I forebore to tell them that my visit to their country and city had come to be one of the most thrilling and enriching experiences of life. As I look back upon it, it became infinitely saddening in after years to learn that nearly all the leaders and speakers of that meeting were slain by the Nazis, in some cases with the help of Polish collaborationists.

I shall not seek to give in these pages even a summary of the impressions gathered over some days in Warsaw. These impressions were for the most part poignant and saddening though conveying a sense of indomitably mystic hope. I limit myself to one unforgettable hour and scene, which told me much touching the horror and the grandeur of the life of Polish Jewry.

To the Zionist organization offices came a group of men from Przytyk, a town become famous in later days. A number of the group had been under arrest, some of whom had been discharged and some only released though not discharged, pending appeal to a higher court. These were not beggars, nor even complainants, though there was bitterness in their accusing speech. Only a few months before, there had been six hundred Jewish families in Przytyk, living as Jewish families do for the most part in the smaller Polish towns, that is to say, in half-decent poverty. A day came when these people felt that, growing out of the general Jewish disorders in the land, an attack would be made upon them. A member of the group speaking with inward fire in his voice said, in Yiddish of course, "They thought they could do anything to us Jews, and that we would die like lambs in the hands of a butcher without offering resistance. But we did resist, and one of them, who rushed forward to murder our wives and children, fell."

They told of the unbelievable injustice of a quasi-judicial trial, which freed the pogrom-makers and sentenced to prison the Jewish defenders of their community. One after another spoke with passionate tenseness, their chief plea being to secure mitigation somehow of grievously unjust sentences imposed upon some of their kinsmen, one pleading particularly on behalf of a very young brother under heavy sentence. The crime of self-defense they admitted, self-defense provoked by fierce and murderous attack.

They asked for something more. And the Zionist party leaders who sat with me were no less deeply moved than I. The substance of their petition was: "We are not trying to make capital out of our misfortune; we are not like those Jews who begin to think of Palestine only after they are threatened with destruction or homelessness; we were and are, all of us, Zionists; we know that the still nearly five hundred Jewish families of our community cannot be transported to Palestine; we do not deserve it more than others, and we understand that if there were certificates enough for all of us, then all that the Poles would require to do in order to get rid of their Jews would be to begin pogroms in all the Polish cities and villages. We know that we must stay where we are, though we do not know how we shall be able to live through the winter. The police already get in the way of peasants who would, if left free, bring food to the hungry among us.

"But—" and here was the heart of their cry—"we are not *Gezwungener Juden* [Jews by compulsion] like some other Jews"—and they named these geographically. "If we lived in Palestine, we could defend ourselves. We are ready to die for the Jewish land, and to endure for Jewish honor. Let some of us go." A number was mentioned, and at once another named a lesser figure. "If ever so few—" and a most modest figure was mentioned—"we feel life is not so dear to us, and if we fall, it will be for Eretz Israel that we die." With tear-choked voice, I asked, "How long have you lived in Przytyk?" Swiftly the answer came, "There are *Mazevot* in our cemetery which are six hundred years old." Two things stood out, one, the tragic humility of the Jew, dating his history of centuries by gravestones, and, too, that moral grandeur which, with the patience of its eternal faith, "I shall not die but live," plans to tell the works of the Lord anew in his own land.

While in Warsaw, I discovered that there were the beginnings of a self-defense movement, underground, of course. And best of all, it was the offshoot of the Palestine self-defense. These self-defense beginnings were destined to have mighty and glorious consequences in the Jewish partisan movement of Poland, culminating in the tragedy and the glory of Warsaw's destruction. The defenders of Warsaw, who stood against the mighty Nazi hosts, have taken their place by the side of the Maccabean defenders of Judea, and anticipated the heroic feats of the Palestinian *Haganah.*

I have still to tell of the deepest impression made upon me by the Jews of Poland. For the first time I saw for myself something of the fabled piety and the unfabled misery of Jews en masse. I had many painful glimpses of the New York ghetto at a time forty to fifty years ago when standards of life were of the humblest. I have seen something of the crowded, poverty-stricken ghettos in the large cities of other lands. But nothing that I had previously seen or known threw any light on the life of Warsaw and its poorest denizens. I penetrated into and was shown subcellar homes, the darkest underground hovels imaginable. Many of these were tenanted by large families, and in some cases by two sets of families, alternating in their day and night occupancy. Making my queries as unoffending as I could, I learned that many of these families lived on fifteen to twenty zloty per week, the equivalent then of three to four dollars.

I ought perhaps to be ashamed to tell the story of my turning to one wretched, starved-looking family head and asking, *"Wie kann Mann mit so wenig auskommen?"* ("How can one survive with so little?") Quick as a flash and as confidently the answer came in Yiddish, "God will yet help." No complaining; no whining; no bitterness! Solely the declaration of unshakable faith: God will yet help. This was not the resignation of dumb piety. It embodied the full and unfaltering faith of such as accept the most awful trials of body and spirit as an expression of the divine will and purpose. I felt that I had come upon the embodiment of the spirit of Jewish piety at its truest, the piety of an uncomplaining martyrdom, the acceptance of such martyrdom as a phase of life's struggle. How pale and thin and anemic and externalized seemed the contrasting religious life of the haves, the possessing, whom I have known all my days.

I shall never cease to be humbly grateful for the revelation Poland—that is, Polish Jewry—afforded me of the inwardness of Jewish faith and life. I add life because, save for a few dissenting assimilationists, these Polish Jews were one in their misery, in their suffering, in their heroism, in the richness and nobility of their faith. Having caught a glimpse of them, I was not surprised at the defense of this city years later, valiant and wondrously prolonged. Nor yet at the courage of little, half-armed Jewish partisan-led groups against the proudest armies of Europe! My visit to Poland was more than a fateful episode. It was one of the most enriching experiences of all my days.

XVII

Death By Bureaucracy

ONE of the most tragic moments of my life came in the summer of 1942. We were, of course, in constant touch during the war with both the London and Geneva offices of the World Jewish Congress. On August 1, Dr. Gerhart Riegner, young and able director of our Geneva office, learned that a German industrialist had come to Switzerland in order to communicate the fact that a plan had been discussed in Hitler's headquarters for the extermination of all Jews in Nazi-occupied lands. These Jews, then totaling between three and a half and four millions, were to be deported to concentration camps in Eastern Europe and then exterminated through prussic acid and crematoria in order to liquidate the Jewish problem in Europe with one blow. The report would have seemed fantastic were it not for evidence Riegner had already received that mass deportations from France and Czechoslovakia had already begun. On checking, Riegner discovered that the industrialist, evidently an anti-Nazi, held one of the most vital positions in the German war economy, which gave him access to Hitler's headquarters and all Nazi war plans. Through intermediaries, he conveyed to Riegner the full details of the plan that was to result in the murder of millions of Jews.

Realizing the tremendous significance of his information, Riegner submitted it to the American and British consulates in Geneva, asking that they immediately inform me, as president of the World Jewish Congress, and Sidney Silverman, dynamic Labor member of the British parliament and chairman of the British Section of the congress. I did not receive the contents of Riegner's message until the twenty-eighth of August. I later learned from Riegner that throughout August he had waited desperately for word from London and New York. On August 24, he was finally informed by the American consul in Geneva that the substance of the message to me had been transmitted by the legation in Berne to the State Department and that the latter had indicated telegraphically that it was disinclined to deliver the message in question in view of the apparently unsubstantiated character of the information that formed its main theme. Fortunately, however, Silverman finally received Riegner's message through the British Foreign Office and transmitted its contents to me on August 28. I immediately communicated with Sumner Welles, then undersecretary of state, and then, as always, deeply understanding and sympathetic. Welles asked me not to release the information until an attempt had been made to confirm it.

During September and October, Riegner continued to receive first-hand reports from countries all over Europe that the plan for mass extermination was being rapidly implemented. All these reports he transmitted to the State Department through Leland Harrison, American minister in Berne. In November, four sworn statements reached the State Department through Harrison, fully substantiating Riegner's reports. Mr. Welles telegraphed that I come at once to the State Department. I went, sensing that I might hear the direst tidings and asked my son, James Waterman Wise, then in the service of the World Jewish Congress as its Washington representative for Latin American affairs, to accompany me.

In the office of Mr. Welles, we took our places and I shall never forget the quiet but deeply moving way in which he turned to us and said, every word etching itself into my heart, "Gentlemen, I hold in my hands documents which have come to me from our legation in Berne. I regret to tell you, Dr. Wise, that these confirm and justify your deepest fears." He handed me the original documents from Berne which confirmed our dreadful apprehensions. The documents' red seals suggested the blood of my people pouring forth in rivers. Mr. Welles added, "For reasons you will understand, I cannot give these to the press, but there is no reason why you should not. It might even help if you did".

We hurriedly called a press conference. To those present, I brought the startling and ghastly news that had just been imparted to us, that in addition to the two or three million Jews estimated already to have been slain in the camps and their gas—and even gasless—ovens, the Nazi regime was re-solved to annihilate the rest of the Jewish population of Eu-rope. I was free to mention the source of our awful tidings, namely the State Department.

The response was what might have been expected. There was general horror throughout the country, wherever the press dispatches carried, and heartbreak everywhere in American Jewry. When the facts were revealed in the British House of Commons, the House rose unanimously in token of its con-tempt for the doers and sympathy with the victims, an almost unprecedented act.

Riegner continued to forward information to the State De-partment, some of which was transmitted to me. On January 19, he sent a stark cable reporting that Jews in Poland were being killed at the rate of six thousand a day. Later he began to experience difficulties in sending his messages. The source of that difficulty was not revealed until the publication in 1947 of portions of Henry Morgenthau's diary, which revealed the amazing and almost unbelievable behavior of the State De-partment.

Annoyed by the public pressure and protest that had begun to mount as soon as the news of the Nazi annihilation pro-gram was released, the State Department bureaucrats, in Mr. Morgenthau's words, tried "to shut off the pressure by shut-ting off at the source the flow of information which nourished it." A few days after Riegner's cable which reached the State Department on January 21, 1943, the now notorious cable 354 was sent to Harrison in Berne ordering him in effect, again to quote Mr. Morgenthau, "not to send back any more of Riegner's information—any more stories of atrocities which might provoke more mass meetings and more public protest." Though the cable was signed by Sumner Welles, it is clear, as Morgenthau conclusively demonstrates, that Welles could have known nothing about it. For, apart from his well-known record on the subject, he cabled Harrison on April 10 asking him for further information from Riegner, in reply to which Harrison complained that such vital information should not be subjected to the restrictions of cable 354.

The crime of the bureaucrats, however, was far more serious than the attempt to withhold information. Early in 1943, we had learned from Riegner that some 70,000 Jews in France and Roumania could be rescued and some Polish Jews moved to Hungary, where there was as yet no organized campaign of destruction, if we could get funds into Switzerland. The money was to be deposited in the names of certain officials in Nazi-occupied Europe, who were ready to cooperate, and to be held till after the war. We needed, however, approval from the government and permission to transfer the funds, which were available. After we had made the initial approach to Washington, there was considerable delay. Finally, on July 22, I went to the White House to discuss the matter with the President. I may best be able to report what happened by setting down my talk with him.

"I hesitate a little," I told the President, "to bring the following to your attention. Even if you found that you could not comply with the extraordinary request I am about to make, you will understand and forgive. Word has reached us through the World Jewish Congress from our Geneva intermediaries communicating with our Geneva office. We are told that a group of Nazi functionaries are prepared to let a number of Polish Jews move into Hungary under certain conditions. And

now we come to the heart of the matter. They fully understand that we cannot let one dollar pass into their hands as
long as war continues. They therefore propose the following—
that for every considerable number of Jews permitted to move
out of Poland, there shall be placed in escrow with our American Legation at Berne a certain sum of money in their names.
These sums are not to be payable until after the declaration
of peace." I added, "Our armies will see to it that these Nazi
mercenaries shall not live to reap the benefit of their hostage-
holding, blackmailing plan."

The President's immediate answer astonished and delighted
me. "Stephen, why don't you go ahead and do it?" I hesitantly
replied that I had not even felt free to broach this to Secretary
Morgenthau, whose approval was indispensable until after I
had consulted with him. He lifted the receiver off the hook,
saying to Henry Morgenthau, "This is a very fair proposal
which Stephen makes about ransoming Jews out of Poland
into Hungary." My strange request had been heard on the
highest level and granted instantly. The next day I wrote the
President, "It gave me deep satisfaction to find while with you
yesterday that out of the depth of your understanding sympathy with Hitler's victims you welcome the proposal which is
now before the State and Treasury Departments."

Mr. Morgenthau has disclosed in his diaries that the President sent my letter to him, that he in turn sent it to Secretary
of State Cordell Hull, reaffirming the Treasury's approval of
the proposal, and that the latter had replied expressing his
agreement.

The subsequent shocking account of delay and sabotage by
State Department bureaucrats, abetted by the British Foreign
Office, has been told in detail by Mr. Morgenthau, and the
mere recital of them brings pain and grief to me as I write.
Suffice it to state that it was not until December 18 that instructions were issued by the State Department that the foreign
funds license was to be issued to Riegner in Geneva, *five full
months after the same license had been approved by the Presi-*

dent of the United States, the Secretary of State, and the Secretary of the Treasury. Let history, therefore, record for all time that were it not for State Department and Foreign Office bureaucratic bungling and callousness, thousands of lives might have been saved and the Jewish catastrophe partially averted.

A month after the issuance of the license to the World Jewish Congress, the War Refugee Board was created, which, first under John Pehle and later under William O'Dwyer, now mayor of New York, brought considerable amelioration, despite tremendous difficulties, to the Jewish captives of Hitler. And, throughout, Mr. Morgenthau and Mr. Welles shared the President's eagerness to do whatever could be done to bring some measure of succor to those who had been doomed to destruction.

XVIII

A Jew Speaks to Christians

IT was in Oregon that, with much and wide practice, I learned a difficult lesson—namely, how to speak to Christian congregations with entire candor about their faith as well as about my faith and my people. I learned the meaning of the Dantean phrase, to flatter by truth speaking. I came to feel rather early in my preaching that I would be unworthy of the privilege of standing in Christian pulpits if I failed to tell the truth as I saw it about Christian and Jew.

I had to tell what, of course, I knew, that Christianity was the daughter and Israel the mother, irrespective of the later repudiation of mother by daughter. I felt that it was incumbent upon me to say that Christianity was under unlimited indebtedness to Judaism—owing to Judaism the Bible Old and New, patriarchs, judges, kings, prophets, priests, apostles, psalms, ethical religion, the Sabbath, and prayer individual and congregate. I alway felt that upon me lay the holy duty of urging the establishment of such fellowship between Jew and Christian as would be worthy of both faiths. Often I saw fit to remind Christian congregations of the truth about Jesus, that he was above all a Jew in faith and life and practices alike. Whenever I felt there was need, I made it clear that the Christian attitude toward the Jew had through the centuries been a rejection of the Prayer on the Cross, "Forgive them, Father, for they know not what they do." Nothing, it seemed to me, could be more Christless than such unforgiveness.

It must be told with equal candor that I have rarely, if ever, come upon sharp dissent from the summons of one Jew to Christians to be equal to Christian penitence. Christian churches from end to end of the land have patiently and forbearingly, even gladly, heard the word of a Jew dealing with the highest and holiest concern of Christendom. From time to time I have had rather queer moments, none queerer than having a blessed old lady in a Christian church mildly protest, "Why do you say that the psalms are Jewish? Surely you know that the psalms are Christian and have always been sung in our Christian churches."

Because of such moments I have made it almost a rule to recite the Twenty-third, or the Nineteenth, or the One Hundred and Twenty-first Psalm, and to quote a phrase in its matchless Hebrew original of one or another of these psalms. I have found that Christians are ready, even eager, to hear the truth concerning Judeo-Christian relations and to listen reveringly to the psalms Jesus knew and loved and doubtless uttered in his worship.

Christian churches and their members made me feel that I must speak frankly and forthrightly lest they imagine I was repudiating Judaism and accepting Christianity in its place. Nothing could have been less true. On the other hand, I willed to correct a most grievous error that was common among the masses of Christendom in America, the idea that there was no basic relation between the Jews and Jesus other than that they had crucified him, as Christians would put it!

Jesus was a Jew, Hebrew of Hebrews. Whatever I believe with respect to the imputed miracle of his birth, his mother, Mary, was a Jewish woman. He was reared and taught as a Jew. He worshiped in the synagogue. He spoke no language save Hebrew, the harsher Hebrew of the Galilean country in which he grew up and of the synagogue in which he preached.

Jesus did not teach or wish to teach a new religion. His own word reads, "I come not to abrogate but to fulfill the Law." When he was asked which was the greatest commandment of the Lord, he replied in the words of the Torah, the Pentateuchal Scroll of the Law, still a major utterance of Jewish worship, "Thou shalt love the Lord thy God with all thy heart, with all thy soul and with all thy strength." This commandment is inscribed to this day upon the traditional doorpost of the Jewish home and in the phylacteries of the Jew. When he was asked about yet another great commandment of the Lord, he quoted once more from the Hebrew Bible, his and mine, "Thou shalt love thy neighbor as thyself." Thus taught and lived Jesus the Jew. In every courteous withal self-respecting way I tried to bring this home to the multitude of Christians who throughout the years have heard me with the attention worthy of the august theme.

One thing more I felt it my duty to say frankly at all times and under all circumstances to Christians. Time and again I dealt with the story of the crucifixion, saying that a people who heard Jesus gratefully one Sunday was not likely to slay him the following Friday, that, if some Jews had a part in his death, it should not be forgotten that power when threatened neither resigns nor yields. Moreover, it would be absurd to imagine that Judea, the little dependency of mighty Rome, possessed and exercised the power of slaying. Moreover I have felt it to be my sacred duty, in addressing Christian groups and committees, to remind them that even if it could be proven, as of course it cannot be, that Jews and only Jews were responsible for the crucifixion, those who called themselves his followers dare not overlook or ignore Jesus' last appeal on behalf of his persecutors.

I ventured to urge upon Christian bodies yet another truth that was not implicit in the relations between Jew and Christian, namely, that in stressing Christian doctrine of immortality, the life and teachings of Jesus the Jew were neglected, even minimized, in contrast with the maximum importance laid upon the death of Jesus. It seemed to me more urgent to dwell on the life and teachings rather than solely or chiefly on the death of Jesus.

Only once in nearly half a century of dealing with the relation of Jesus to Israel did a question arise and, when it arose, caused a very severe storm. Just before Christmas, 1925, I preached on Sunday morning at Carnegie Hall on "Jesus, the Jew." What I said that morning I had said before and said later, again and again. It was neither novel nor startling in any sense, save to such Jews and Christians as hold every barrier to be sacred. Simply and clearly I laid down the following, as I thought, undebatable theses:

1. Jesus was man, not God;
2. Jesus was a Jew, not a Christian;
3. Jews have not repudiated Jesus, the Jew;
4. Christians have, for the most part, not adopted and followed Jesus, the Jew.

The New York newspapers carried full reports of my address on Monday morning. Two incidents happened on the day of publication that made no end of trouble, not so much for me as for the United Palestine Appeal, the fund-raising agency of which I served as chairman. Monday afternoon, the President of the Orthodox rabbis' society of the country issued a blast against me and my heresy and proceeded to excommunicate me. The same day a denominational Christian Ministers Association met in Philadelphia and hailed me as brother. I know not which was more hurtful—the acceptance of me as brother and welcoming me into the Christian fold or the violent diatribe of a fellow rabbi.

The liberal rabbis of the country, for the most part, rallied to my support. One exception was an inveterate foe of Zionism; the other, an associate in the U.P.A., bade me refrain from sensational sermons about Jesus and Christianity and devote myself instead to the teachings of the Hebrew prophets, though he knew that no man in the rabbinate had sought more than the writer, not only to preach about the prophets, but to relate their teachings to the problems of our time.

The matter did not end here. An Orthodox religious group sought to displace me from the chairmanship of the United Palestine Appeal. Nothing could have been finer and more loyal than the attitude of virtually all the Zionist leaders, including that brilliant, withal occasionally circuitous, leader of the Zionist movement, Louis Lipsky.

In the midst of the excitement, a letter came to me from Nathan Straus, the grand old man of American Jewry, uniquely beloved both for his munificent philanthropies and for his warmth of heart. This letter had a profound, and to me very helpful, effect on the controversy, which was then at its height:

DECEMBER 25, 1925

DEAR DR. WISE:

I saw with the greatest sorrow in this morning's newspapers that you have offered your resignation as chairman of the United Palestine Appeal. I wish, as a Jew and a Zionist, who have given a great part of my life and large sums of money to Palestine and to all Jewish and non-sectarian causes, to protest against your action. I know that the United Palestine Appeal will never accept your resignation and I know that they should not.

Suppose you did say something with which some Jews did not agree! What of it? Is all your life of service for Jews and for America to be ignored by those people who take a newspaper headline and are prepared to destroy you and are ready to sacrifice your usefulness in connection with our great work for Palestine? I can hardly believe the newspaper reports that a lot of Rabbis, in good standing, should condemn a man like you, with your record and your position, without giving you a chance to explain what you meant. They should have known that no word would ever come out of your mouth that would not have the effect of making Jews still stronger Jews and better Americans. And that, if you said anything at all about Christianity, it would only be in order to remind Christians, as you and I always do, that the first thing for them to do is to be just to Jews. In order to show you how deeply I feel in the matter, I authorize you, as chairman of the United Palestine Appeal, to announce that, in addition to having created a trust fund of five hundred thousand dollars ($500,000), the income of which is being and shall in perpetuity be used for welfare purposes among all the people of Palestine without regard to race or creed, I herewith set aside an additional sum of one hundred and fifty thousand dollars ($150,000) of which amount one hundred thousand dollars ($100,000) shall be devoted to the early erection of the Nathan Straus Welfare and Relief Center of Palestine for all its needy people and for the housing of the administration offices of the Hadassah, and fifty thousand dollars ($50,000) to be devoted to the general purposes of the United Palestine Appeal under your leadership.

FAITHFULLY YOURS,

[signed] NATHAN STRAUS

There came the night, about a fortnight later, when, at a hotel, a special and prolonged meeting of the Administrative Committee of the Zionist Organization of America was held. Hours of discussion took place on my proposal that, in view of my "Jesus, the Jew" sermon, I withdraw from the chairmanship of the United Palestine Appeal. The vote was overwhelmingly in favor of my retention of the office. I was called to the hotel and informed of the decision. I was too moved to speak and limited myself to the utterance of two Hebrew words of the Book of Jonah. I did not even translate them; it was not necessary. I said only, *"Ivri Anochi,"* "I am a Hebrew." The incident was ended, and kindling enthusiasm followed throughout the campaign, which yielded the largest amount that had been collected up to that time, more than five million dollars.

In 1909 I proposed to my dear friends John Haynes Holmes of the Unitarian Church and Frank Oliver Hall of the Universalist Church that we together arrange a series of union services, which services, despite grave and sometimes violent opposition, were held. The purpose of these union services was not alone to show that Jew and non-Jew could meet from time to time in the spirit of common worship of the universal Father. It was designed to do more than that—to bring about on the part of the three congregations represented in the union service united or common action on behalf of those social ideals to which every one of us was separately committed, and for the furtherance of which we together set out to win the enthusiasm of our several congregations. In other words, we did not worship together solely or even chiefly for the sake of common worship, but rather that in the spirit of such common worship we might be fused together in the prosecution of a common purpose. That purpose was service to and furtherance of those high causes that all of us alike felt, and feel, were the central and essential things in our common religious aspirations.

When we arranged for our common service, each of us was mindful of the necessities of the case, each of us was meticulously scrupulous to avoid giving offense to the congregations of the others. We were of one mind and of one spirit in being utterly vigilant that no word be uttered, no prayer be offered up, no hymn be chanted that did not include within itself the spirit of the three congregations worshiping together. I must confess that I have been in attendance at and participant in other union services when, as it seemed to me, ministers, believed to be and believing themselves to be liberal, have failed to choose out of their rich hymnody such chants as it would be possible for Jews to sing without confusion or embarrassment, have used stereotyped formulae with respect to the triune God in invoking the benediction, or in offering petition in the presence of congregations made up largely or partly of Jews.

But the more important circumstance to be borne in mind with reference to the union services of more than three decades ago is that when we worshiped together none of us did or would abate one jot or tittle of our respective positions, of our several loyalties. Into our common worship, held for a number of years, chiefly in the interest of our common social ideals, there entered only those elements to which all of us together might without reluctance assent. We knew, as we worshiped together, that we would leave the place of our common worship and return to our various church bodies, each of us not less but more deeply and ardently loyal to his own heritage, because for an hour we had found it possible to link our hands in common worship. Each of us had gathered the resolution to move his people to make earnestly rather than laggardly, passionately rather than inertly, for those great social ends of life that, after all, are the final and supreme test of the verity of religious profession and the sincerity of religious practice.

If Jews and Christians are to worship together from time to time, we who are Jews can enter into the spirit of Christian worship, and Christians for a time can enter into the spirit of Jewish worship. But let me make it clear that I hold it would be an incalculable loss to the spiritual life of man if we Jews were to abandon, assuming such abandonment to be possible, our own particular type and form of worship. For that worship rests upon and has grown out of two thousand years and more of tradition, and it is compact of historical associations, of ancient traditions, of precious memories. It would be a most lamentable impoverishment of our common spiritual life if either the simplicity of the liberal Christian service, such as that which obtains in the Community Church, were to be given up, or the beauties and splendors of the traditional Jewish liturgy were to be abandoned.

Thus Christians worshiping with Jews might find the Shema, the affirmation of the divine unity, quaint and interesting, and might even hold the Hebrew Kaddish or memorial prayer, to be beautiful and moving, but to the Jew, the Shema and the Kaddish are infinitely more. When I speak the words of the Shema, I do far more than recite the Jewish creed. There comes before me, as in a vision, the spectacle of Israel suffering, of Israel triumphant. The storied martyrdom of Israel rises before me as in a dream, my people's soul lives in me again, and I live again the memories of my people as I utter those deathless words of the Jew's spiritual and eternal affirmation of God's unity. For I behold a mighty procession of priests and prophets and seers and apostles and martyrs marching on and on, pilgrims of the invisible, sustained by that unfaltering trust which moved the Jew throughout the ages to live by and for the truth of the Divine unity.

I can join in the Pater Noster or the Lord's Prayer, but the recital thereof stirs no memories in me. As I hear it or recite it, I frankly confess that I seek to reconstruct it, as it may be reconstructed, into that Hebrew tongue whence the form and spirit of it were in part derived by him who first uttered it. As I join in the Lord's Prayer, I think always and inevitably of its Hebrew original, and I think back to the time when Jesus first learned it from his Jewish mother, for in the century associated with Jesus brief prayers containing the spiritual yearnings of the people had, under certain circumstances, been prescribed for Jews. But in truth it is almost impossible for me to put into the Lord's Prayer, however rich I find it, all that it means to the devout Christian to whom it bears memories and traditions as does the Shema to me.

No one can be more bent than I am upon achieving perfect understanding and fellowship between Jew and Christian. But if in order to have the understanding of Christendom I must cease to be a Jew, or I must do that which will make for the minimizing of my Jewishness, then I must do without such understanding—as my fathers have had to do without it for hundreds of years, yea for more than a millennium. I crave the understanding and the reverence of the Christian world, but for myself as a Jew and not for me as a chameleon. I covet understanding of the Jew, not seeking to utter in accents that are not his own the Pater Noster but affirming simply and earnestly and everlastingly as did the holy mothers and glorious fathers of Israel—Hear, oh Israel, the Eternal is our God, the Eternal is one.

I must in truth add, and in sorrow, that the major trends of much interfaith effort throughout the last generation have been far from good. Most especially from the Jewish point of view, it is far from enough zealously to harp on the likeness or similarities of Judaism and Christianity. What alone matters is that there be understanding and mutual respect between those of different faiths, of religious viewpoints however divergent or even conflicting. This must be the goal and the chief goal of every interfaith undertaking, to make folk of different faiths, though zealously and passionately held, understand that, even when agreements and unities are impossible and undesirable without too great sacrifice, men and women must accord to each other the same understanding and respect as they covet for themselves.

With respect to the interfaith or religious-good-will movement, I have regretfully noticed certain trends. It has become so overorganized that it has lost freedom and spontaneity of attitude. It must not yield to the temptation to become, as it were, a church above and beyond churches. Let not the orthodoxy of higher organization kill the spirit.

Again, I have felt that there are and must be times when in scorn of consequences the interfaith movement must take great risks, as for the most part it has not done. For example, with respect to the infinite evil of every kind that stemmed from Nazism, neutrality was not the highest of virtues even for those who would be scrupulously just. The interfaith movement must be ready to lose a whole world of organization in order to retain or regain its own soul. More than six million Jews were killed by Hitler. How often and effectually did the interfaith movement seek to make itself felt? Would it not have been supremely fitting if a mighty interfaith and international organization—inclusive of Catholic, Protestant, Jew—had spoken out with directness and power against massive wrong?

Nor in our own country has the interfaith movement made itself adequately felt when the most urgent moral issues were at stake. Recently, for example, the freedom of the press has been gravely threatened by the arbitrary decision of an administrative body to shut out a respected organ of public opinion from the schools of New York, from teachers and pupils alike, because it had published a series of articles, in no wise defamatory, which criticized some practices of a great church. The most powerful interfaith body in our country refused to have part in the protest because, though these words were not used, that church is normally one of the interfaith constituents. "What do ye more than others?" may most fittingly be asked of a movement purporting to make for the basic verities of religious fellowship. Surely we of the House of Israel cannot long have part in a movement the aim of which, to foster interfaith unity, is, alas, permitted to neutralize the loftiest moral passion and the most commanding moral imperatives.

It may be that, because I have probably preached in as many Christian pulpits as any rabbi in history, I take Christianity seriously, indeed more seriously than do many Christians. They think of Christianity solely as creed or ritual. I, a Jew, think of Christianity not only as a faith but as a challenge.

There have been two or three great human crises in my lifetime, not primarily but only secondarily Jewish in nature or involvement. I write without passion or bitterness but not without sorrow that at least twice has Christianity tragically failed. Yes, and for the third time Christianity is tragically failing. It may be urged by way of explanation that not Christianity has failed but Christendom. But if Christendom fail in two or three mighty, successive crises, does not such failure include or involve Christianity, the faith of the confessors and disciples of Christendom?

Soon after World War I there was resurrected out of the ashes of the past (that is, the post–Civil War period) a movement that set up three objects of hatred for a nation. One was racial, the Negro; one was religious, the Catholic Church; one was racial and religious, the Jew. In the case of the Ku Klux Klan, the symbol of hatred became the uplifted and burning cross. The cross was lifted and burned in flames of fury and hatred by those who were members, in some cases even leaders, of Christian churches.

Though not a Christian, it seemed to me throughout the Ku Klux Klan years that the lifting up of the cross as a symbol of hatred and destruction of humans of other faiths and races was of the very essence of blasphemy. Christianity might, indeed would, have been spared the utter shame of this profanation if the leaders of the great Christian churches and these churches themselves had lifted up their voices singly and together and cried aloud against the shame of Christian hosts massed under the cross as a symbol of hatred. Save for a few, a very few, outstanding individuals, American Christendom was silent. Those few spoke for themselves, not with the power and authority of the Church or Churches of Christ. I do not say that violence should have been practiced even against the violent. But I could not help feeling that a thousand years of Christian missionary effort among Jews would not have been as effective as the gathering of groups of Christians, tearing the burning cross of hatred out of the hands of the Ku Klux Klan miscreants, and lifting in its place the Crucifix as the banner of Jesus, a Jew who preached and practiced the divine art of love.

It may have been a matter of strategy, but the Catholic Church was silent. This silence may have been in conformity to its tradition of remaining silent under attack, a tradition often observed in the breach when it alone or single-handed is under attack. But, after all, it was not only the Catholic Church that was being assailed, but a race as well as a people from whom the Founder of Christianity is come. The Negro race was not strong enough to defend itself with any effectiveness, and the Jews were left unaided and, for the most part, undefended, to bear the brunt of the attack until it died away.

In truth, it was Christianity which was under attack by its own professing sons and daughters. Still it chose to remain silent. Names and acts will be cited to prove the writer in error. He lived through those dark days and sorrowfully enough notes that Christianity, through its churches, failed to utter its soul clearly and overwhelmingly against the profanation of a name most sacred to it. It was no time for maneuver and strategy. It was a time for forthright speech, for united and resounding protest and action on the part of those who should have regarded Ku Klux Klanism as the sin of sins; who should have stood and lifted up the cross as their banner of justice, of healing, of love.

The second crisis came, and terrible, most tragic things befell, in the course of what may prove to be the greatest disaster of human history. If Hitlerism is imagined to be nothing more than Nazist anti-Jewishness, we fail to see the distinction between its ultimate purposes and its immediate methods or techniques. Now we know, though some of us fail to remember, that Nazism was above all a mighty and magnificently organized assault upon human freedom and democracy. The destruction of Jews was motivated on two grounds equally false, moreover equally evil. On the one hand there was the appeal to anti-Jewish scapegoatism, which flourished throughout European lands for many centuries. In *Nathan the Wise,* Lessing summed it up in the devastating line, "Do nothing, the Jew will be burned!"

But there was yet another and deeper, though not baser, motive that underlay the Nazi program against Jews. It was a far from mistaken intuition of Hitler that the mere existence of Jews on earth made more difficult his drive against liberty and democracy, and that, before freedom and the democratic way of life could be obliterated, the oldest champions and strongest defenders of these things must be destroyed. It is more than an accident of history that upon the outer rim of the Independence Bell in Philadelphia were inscribed the words of the Book of Leviticus: "And ye shall proclaim liberty throughout the land to all the inhabitants thereof." The truth is that since the days of Moses and Pharaoh, Jews as a people have sought to wrest freedom out of the hands of their oppressors. It was not the possessions of the Jews, it was not even racism, but it was their unconquerable dedication to freedom and to its truest political and collective form, democracy, which doomed the Jews of Germany and soon thereafter the Jews of many European lands.

Whatever the deeper motivations, Hitler seized power, and even before he seized power, he had, over a series of years, waged war against Jews. His racism alone should have sufficed to call down upon his head the deepest disapproval and condemnation of that church which purports to accept into its communion men of all peoples and races. Some prelates, such as Cardinal Faulhaber of Munich and later Cardinal Mundelein of Chicago spoke and acted courageously. But for the most part, Rome made its peace, which magnified the un-Christian doctrine of racism, and even effected a concordat with Nazism at a time when racist laws and anti-Jewish measures were well under way.

It should be remembered that, in addition to two thirds of a million Jews, the German population included some forty or forty-five million Protestants, and twenty to twenty-five million Catholics. Concentration camps were established and filled with Jews. True it is that there were others—political dissenters, labor leaders, above all pacifists— and needless to say those accused however falsely of Communism. But the brunt of the attack was borne by Jews, and, save for the fewest of voices, the two great church groups were silent, offering no guidance whatsoever to their communions. Let there be no mention of the names of Niemoeller and Barth. The former was at best a non-anti-Jewish Nazi, and the latter a theological juggler who was reduced or debased himself to silence rather than be disturbed in his higher verbal and theological gymnastics.

Thus the Christian churches and peoples bore themselves, many, though not all, of the people gleefully sharing in the depredations upon Jews. Cultivated and uncultivated alike, the unlettered and the most learned, joined in the dispossession and destruction of a people that had lived in Germany and become in the best sense of the term a contributor to and en-

richer of its civilization for centuries, even before Mendelssohn
and Heine, Einstein and Haber. But Christianity was silent
even aside from the problem of Nazi relations to the Jewish
people. The unspeakable crimes against Austria and Czechoslovakia were accepted by seventy million Germans without
demur.

If there was dissent among some, it was terrorized and voice-
less and made no impression on the totality of Nazi Germany.
No crimes of the men, who later were hanged as criminal war-
makers, seemed terrible enough to disturb the Christian conscience of the German people, Catholic or Protestant, as long
as there seemed the faintest hope of winning the war. The
penitence that comes after defeat is not penitence. It is the
guilt of self-reproach, the whining of unsportsmanlike gamblers
who have chosen the wrong side and, to their sorrow, lost.

Christian Germany did not stand alone in its abasement.
Christian Europe was little, if at all, better. Nor was the Christendom of our own country without fault. Occasionally voices
of protest were heard—the noble voices of Cadman and
Holmes and Atkinson, McConnell and Manning and Mundelein—but the dominant purpose of America was not to help or
save the victims of Nazism, who were most gravely wronged
or horribly threatened, but was limited only to the effort to
keep our country out of war. The wronged Jews were not alone
victims of the unconcern of our own country. For the most part
it seemed ready to permit English Democracy and French
Liberalism to be destroyed, if only we, the United States of
America, could be kept out of war by the Lindberghs and
like-minded Americans, who set racial quality above democratic equality.

The President of the United States, as is well known,
loathed Hitler and Hitlerism from the very beginning. Yet, with
a country that was divided and that only patience and some
terrible and immediately felt grievance could unite, he had to
postpone for three or four years his historic reference to the
aggressor nations and the need of quarantining them. This

was one of the most important statements ever made by an American president. The world will never know or understand how lonely and forsaken Jews felt throughout the years of agonizing suspense, with none to help and the Christian peoples too little concerned to seek to succor and to save.

That was the hour for Christian good will to Jews, in their direst extremity. Is it not the most melancholy testimony to Christianity that, had it not been for the Pearl Harbor disaster, the Jews of many lands would have perished in their affliction? It is because of my deep disappointment over the failure of American Christendom to bestir itself and to arise against the brutal foes and destroyers of the people of its Christ that my interest in the so-called interracial and interreligious goodwill movement has become attenuated. It failed, deliberately chose to fail, in the hour of our greatest need.

And there is a third and present occasion for the exercise of the power of Christianity, perhaps the most important of all, and Christendom seems oblivious to its import. The world of nations and peoples and races is in danger of war. How grave and destructive such a war, an atomic war, might be, it is not needful to tell. It might well be the last of wars, a war of universal self-destruction. But even if it be no more terrible than World War II, a third world war would have more and more terrible Nagasakis and Hiroshimas. What an atomic war would be in effect, no one can foresee but one knows that the wars of the past would be only the faintest prelude to the destruction that World War III would make inevitable. This is the prospect that lies today before mankind.

At such times have men not the right to expect that Christianity, the greatest religious force in the Western world, should make itself deeply, even decisively, felt? Is there not reason to believe or even hope that this might become Christianity's finest hour? The world is or appears to be divided into two camps of economic theory and practice. It is oversimplification and not too honest to hold that the division is between democracy and dictatorship, for much calls itself or is named democracy that is not democracy, and much is described as dictatorship that is not dictatorship. The contest is far from being undefiled democracy versus pure dictatorship. The real dichotomy is between capitalist democracy and communist dictatorship—the question being whether capitalism can permanently endure as democratic, and whether communism is bound to be permanently dictatorial. These are politico-economic problems that need not, cannot, be resolved by war. The truth is that war resolves no problems. War by intensifying problems makes them insoluble.

In this hour of almost world-wide conflict between these two systems of politico-economic theory and practice, what, if anything, is Christianity seeking to do, assuming, as I do, that Western democracy is for the most part Christian? I believe that the churches of Christendom are not for the most part intent upon averting the war of wars. Insofar as they support, indeed anticipate, every government plan and undertaking to stand against what is called communism, they are strengthening the war spirit of the nation.

Too many churches lightly assume that war must be, as if war were inevitable, as if there were no way out of the present situation but war. One understands that religionists cannot be sympathetic to a nation that exalts atheism and denies its people freedom of religion. But shall the Churches of God and their peoples in the Western world find atheism in communist lands more imperiling than the most godless of all things—the infinite wrongs, destructions, and defilements of war? If it be claimed that the churches and synagogues are not keen for war, the answer is, are they calling a halt to war plans and programs? Is it not the sin of organized religion to take yet another war for granted and to give no leadership, as it today gives no real and commanding and decisive leadership, to the most imperative of all causes, the cause of averting what may become world-destructive war?

XIX

Toward Israel's Independence

Dᴜʀɪɴɢ the past twenty-five years, I have had, alas, numerous occasions on which to be sharply critical of the conduct of successive governments of Great Britain as the mandatory power for Palestine. I felt at all times that I had such right to speak as is given to few Jews. My attitude to England is best expressed in the spirit of a word of my father, whose foot never rested on English soil, "While England lives, the Jew is safe." Such was my upbringing. Oft and again I have told that Herzl's last word to me in April, 1904, was, "Out of England will yet come great good for Zion and the Jewish people." In the earliest days of the first war, I gave my full support to the cause of Britain and France, and throughout my life I have loved Britain's people and their magnificent tradition of freedom.

But as the years passed, I could not but come to the conclusion that British governments were seeking to whittle down the Balfour Declaration and were increasingly violating both its letter and spirit. The Churchill White Paper of 1922 cut off approximately four fifths of the territory in which the Jewish National Home was to be established. There were the persistent attempts to limit if not to eliminate Jewish immigration and land purchase, to foist a permanent minority status on the Jew of Palestine—all culminating finally in the unspeakably tragic White Paper of 1939 and Ernest Bevin's vicious anti-

Zionism of the past few years. Indeed, British policy, as I declared at one Zionist congress, has too often appeared as if the
Balfour Declaration read, "The aim of His Majesty's Government is to hinder and to obstruct, to retard and to frustrate,
the establishment of the Jewish National Home." The officials
of the Colonial Office habitually treated the Jews as an in-
vasive and troublesome group in Palestine rather than as its
rightful rebuilders. Paradoxically enough, the status of the Jews
in Palestine, in British eyes, was neither the favored status of
a native population nor yet the position of a people with whom
a covenant had to be scrupulously observed.

At no time was I unmindful of the enormous tasks and the
overwhelming problems of the British government and its far-
flung commonwealth. But I could under no circumstances accept the oft-repeated plea of the British government that the
mandate could not be fulfilled, when only a minimum of effort
had been put forth by it toward such fulfillment. During those
years, it seemed not only that Britain had failed to try, but that
it had almost tried to fail.

My outspoken and vigorous criticism of British governments
during those years brought me into frequent and occasionally
sharp conflict with some of my Zionist colleagues, particularly
in Great Britain. They felt that such criticism of the mandatory
power would but serve to make our task of achieving satisfactory cooperation all the more difficult. Yet I felt that we
were not beggars who were pleading for charity or sympathy.
We were the sons and daughters of a great people exercising
our right of solemn protest against grave wrong and injustice.
No nation is great enough to be free to do wrong. It was honoring, not dishonoring, Britain to demand that it live by its highest standards, that it be equal to itself. It could not be wrong
to ask Britain to fulfill its solemn obligations.

American Zionists, I always held, had a particular obligation to voice that protest. For we were not, as I once put it,
under the compulsion of adjacency to the British seat of government. Officials from the Colonial or Foreign Offices could

not send for us from day to day with new proposals for whittling down the Balfour Declaration. We enjoyed a certain advantage, and we meant to make the most of it. Great Britain was the trustee not the possessor of Palestine, and it was our obligation to insist that she live up to the conditions of her trusteeship.

My heart has been filled with gladness since the Jews of Palestine by their own heroic effort and courage, and despite Mr. Bevin and the British government, brought Israel into being. I therefore have little desire to retell the story of our setbacks and disappointments, of the successive crises into which we were plunged by the proposals and policies of the mandatory government, of the sabotage and hostility of bureaucrats and officials, of violence and massacres launched on several occasions by the Arabs, which firm and resolute action by the British could easily have quelled at the outset. But I must speak of the most tragic of all episodes, the heartlessly cruel White Paper of 1939, which severely curtailed Jewish immigration to Palestine, which imposed serious restrictions on land purchase by Jews, and which was intended to prevent Jews from ever becoming the majority population of the land. This White Paper, issued shortly before Hitler was to begin his mass annihilation of European Jewry, was in effect a death sentence for scores if not hundreds of thousands of Jews who could have found life and safety in Palestine rather than death in Maideneck and Auschwitz.

The formal issuance of the White Paper was preceded by an unusual conference. On November 24, 1938, the then Colonial Secretary Malcolm MacDonald made a statement pointing to and forecasting the Arab-Jewish Conference of February-March, 1939, at St. James's Palace in London. I attended the conference as head of the American delegation. MacDonald's so-called Arab-Jewish Conference never came into being, for the Arabs refused to meet with us. Arabs met with the British officials. Jews likewise met with them. Arabs and Jews never met together.

I had never lived through four more difficult, more trying weeks. They were weeks and days that were not without compensation, however, for one lived in the midst of a new pride and a new dignity. Internal differences counted for less and Zionist unity for more than at any other Zionist gathering I had known. We thought together; we felt together; we acted together. And we acted together largely because of the compelling leadership of a man who won laurels at the London Conference, David Ben-Gurion, who was later to lead the Jews of Palestine with such unbreakable resolve and dauntless courage through the war of independence and to take his rightful place as the first prime minister of the Jewish State. Once again, Justice Brandeis was unerringly right in his judgment when he wrote me, "We have in Ben-Gurion and Shertok political leaders of great ability, men of understanding, vision and wisdom. We should give them unqualified, ardent support."

I recall one amusing episode during the session. At one point, the question of land sales was being discussed. Ussishkin, grand pillar of strength, turned to the British officials and said, "It will interest you to know that there are members of the Arab delegation here in London who tell you that land sales are prohibited by the Arabs. Some of these same gentlemen are trying to sell land to me as head of the Jewish National Fund." The Secretary laughed and asked if he could give him the names of these gentlemen. Ussishkin answered, "Mr. MacDonald, I won't give you the names because you might then buy the land."

On February 16, 1939, Dr. Weizmann, Ben-Gurion, and I met with the Prime Minister and Malcolm MacDonald in the Cabinet Room at 10 Downing Street. I found Mr. Chamberlain a simple, plain-spoken man, unsubtle and unsophisticated, whose fishy eye did not do him justice. He showed such understanding of the subject as could be gotten through a reading from day to day of the minutes of the conference.

The conference brought the most grievous hurt to the Jewish settlement in Palestine and to world Jewry. In the end, a plan was disclosed, subsequently known and hated throughout the Jewish world as the MacDonald White Paper. It placated the Arabs in order to appease Hitler's lieutenant, the Mufti. It proposed and later enforced an arrangement that was the complete negation of the Balfour Declaration. The scheme undertook drastically to curtail Jewish immigration into Palestine over a five-year period, to establish an Arab State in Palestine after five years, and to make any subsequent Jewish immigration conditional on Arab consent. It meant the acceptance of the terrible responsibility of keeping out of Palestine hundreds of thousands of Jews who might have escaped death in gas ovens if the MacDonald program, supported by Foreign Secretary Lord Halifax, had not become British policy for Palestine.

MacDonald, I may add, faced the thoroughly evil situation with ease and evasiveness. Halifax, somewhat more troubled, sought to defend it in the following words: "General Smuts at one time in his life said there are times when ethical considerations must yield to expediency," a confession of utter and unrelieved and unforgivable moral defeatism. The tragedy that was to ensue meant the complete surrender of the mandate and England's honor and the breaking of England's word to the Jewish people.

From April, 1939, until November, 1947, more than eight years, we suffered tragically under the White Paper. As a result of the elections of June, 1945, which placed the Labour party in power, the evil waxed greater and greater. The Labour government ignored and violated every pledge. The leadership of the Foreign Office fell to a man whose lack of sympathy, imagination, and tact did grievous hurt to the Jews and Jewish Palestine, but even more and cureless hurt to the honor of Britain. It seemed as if Bevin were resolved that the name of Balfour should be blotted out from the memory of

England. Balfour brought Britain honor. Bevin brought Britain shame.

That resistance to British policy would develop in Palestine was inevitable. The British measures against the admission to Palestine of hundreds of thousands of Jews who had fought the fight of free men aroused a spirit of unconquerable revolt. Only admirable restraint and national discipline kept the revolt within the bounds of resistance and kept it from taking the form of aggression. A people less firmly grounded ethically and spiritually would have reacted much more violently to British injustice than did the Jews in Palestine.

Fortunately, after years of the most lamentable and cruel injustice, the policy of Balfour was gloriously vindicated. But what a sorry, sordid, heartbreaking tale lay between the adoption of the White Paper by the British House of Commons in the spring of 1939, and the approval of partition by the United Nations, the declaration of statehood, the heroic defense of the state of Israel, and the world-wide recognition that has at last triumphantly come to the support of Israel!

My severely critical view of British government policy on Palestine during all these years, however, in no way lessened my life-long admiration and friendship for the people of Britain. Nor—and I believe I have the right to say this—did I ever allow my anger to blind me when other issues arose. This, too, some of my colleagues failed to understand, and I was castigated for being too friendly to Britain as frequently as I was condemned for being too critical. Thus, long before our country became involved in war with Nazi Germany, I had taken an active role in organizing aid for Britain. Immediately after the outbreak of the war, Dr. Weizmann, on behalf of the Jewish people, offered to place the man power and resources of Jewish Palestine at the service of Britain in its fight against the enemy of all mankind, an offer, I may add, that was brushed aside for a long time. Some persons felt that such offer of assistance should have been made conditional on the abrogation of the White Paper. At that time, I wrote to a colleague:

Far from being mischievous, I think it was an act of high wisdom for Dr. Weizmann to write to Chamberlain as he did. There was nothing else he could do. There was nothing else we ought to have done. He must have known perfectly well that England was bent upon the implementation of the White Paper which even from the Zionist point of view would be a petty evil compared with the defeat of England. Such defeat would be the one great irreparable disaster for all humanity in general, and most especially for us Jews, who always pay the price. It may interest you to learn that after we received final notice as to the decision of the Government in London in early March 1939, half a dozen men including principally Englishmen, urged Mr. Lipsky and me in the strongest terms to go back to America and to start a great fight against England. I said at the time and to the dismay of the group—and most especially to the English members of it— that I would do nothing of the kind; that I would speak out earnestly about the lamentable character of the British decision and would seek to characterize the perfidy of MacDonald. But that I could not bring myself to forget Hitler and Nazism; that we would be put in a most precarious position if we set out to move the American people against England when at any time we might be compelled to give our unmeasured and unequivocal support to Britain.

I still feel as deeply as ever that to act as if we had two enemies, Hitler and England, would be suicidal folly on our part.

If England fail, we are fallen. If England win, we have a chance, whether the implementation of the White Paper come or not. We still wish England to understand that we are with her, not because we must be but because we Jews choose to be; that we would not, if we could, live in a world from which democracy has perished.

Let none of us weaken the force of our united support of Britain by any diversion in any direction whatsoever.

A similar situation arose in 1946 when the Congress of the United States was giving consideration to extending a major loan to Great Britain to enable it to rehabilitate itself after the years of war. The British government was then in the most cynical and ruthless phase of its anti-Zionist policy. Bevin seemed determined to liquidate the Jewish National Homeland. Terror and intimidation were being directed against the Jews of Palestine. The survivors of Hitlerism were still languishing in the displaced persons camps of Europe, many of them after a decade, with their cherished hope of going to Palestine shattered by British ruthlessness.

In this country, as a result, anti-British sentiment was running high. The traditional isolationists and British haters were opposed to the loan. Many persons felt that the loan should not be granted unless Britain honored her obligations to the Jewish people and abandoned her shameful policy. There was serious doubt as to whether Congress would approve the loan. I determined to speak out. I recognized that the loan was not designed to be a matter of favor to the British government but that its primary purpose was to bring about a financially stable world and that its chief beneficiaries were to be the peoples of the British Commonwealth and the United States of America. I, therefore, issued a statement urging Congress to approve the loan, in which I said:

> The British Government has made it very difficult for me, as an American Jew and Zionist, to continue in support of the loan. Its conduct in Palestine has been marked by the most lamentable acts of aggression against the Jewish people. . . . No one, who is a friend of Britain, can fail to recognize that, in fact and even in the utterances of the Minister for Foreign Affairs, the British Government has pursued a course utterly unworthy of and irreconcilable with its best traditions of justice to oppressed peoples. Recently it has wrought grievous injury to the Jewish population of Palestine, entrusted to its care under the Mandate. Whatever be the wrong-doing of the British Government in Palestine cannot alter my conviction that the British loan is imperatively needed. I shall not permit my abundantly justified indignation against the British Government and its lawless practices to change the fact of my support, as an American, of the British loan.

Rabbi Wise, as president of the Jewish Institute of Religion, confers an honorary degree on Dr. James G. MacDonald, now U. S. Ambassador to Israel, on June 8, 1947.

With Mrs. Franklin D. Roosevelt at a conference of the American Jewish Congress held in Washington in 1940.

Opening the second session of the World Jewish Congress in Montreux, Switzerland, 1948.

My statement was issued a day or two before the vote on the loan was taken in Congress and the loan approved. Some of the country's leading newspapers, in reporting the passage of the loan, wrote that my statement was credited in Washington with persuading a considerable number of Congressmen to extend their support to the loan, whose negative votes or abstention might otherwise have proved decisive in defeating it.

I have never regretted this action, but it is interesting to record that the very same week Mr. Lipsky and I were denied visas to visit Palestine by the British government! As members of the executive of the Jewish Agency for Palestine, we were scheduled to join our colleagues in Jerusalem for an extremely important meeting. We requested the British Embassy in Washington to secure visas for our trip. After some hours, we were informed that London had refused to issue visas to us. The denial of the right to visit Palestine at that time was, of course, a confession of British guilt in relation to what was happening there. If there had been nothing to conceal, we would have been permitted to go. It meant confirmation of our worst fears —that the British government would seek, though in vain, to conceal behind an iron curtain the truth of its misconduct in Palestine. If Palestine had been a British crown colony, which it was not, we should still have had the right to visit our fellow Jews. But it was a territory under British mandate not ownership. And it was our right to visit the land in order to learn and tell the truth about recent happenings.

During the period between World Wars I and II, I participated actively in almost every Zionist congress that was held. Convened every two years, these congresses became a major institution in Jewish life. They provided the tribunal of the Jewish world, above and beyond all others, before which Jewish questions could be dealt with in the spirit of courage and truthfulness, at all costs and at all hazards. It was the platform from which we spoke to the Jewish people and to the world.

If to outsiders at the congress, Jewish or non-Jewish, the air seemed sometimes charged with tension, it must be borne in mind that the delegates, save for the Westerners, generally came from lands of political suppression, at least repression. Centuries of political and every other manner of oppression resulted, inevitably, in the freest play of self-expression and affirmation when Jews met at Basle and anywhere else as Jews and free men.

Several principles always guided the positions I took on Zionist problems at the congresses and elsewhere. I insisted at all times that there could be no compromise with the fundamental principle of Jewish peoplehood and the re-establishment of a Jewish commonwealth. I therefore opposed the formation of the Jewish Agency in 1928. Until then, the Zionist Congress and the executive it elected had represented the Jewish people in its relationship with the mandatory power and the League of Nations and had been responsible for the organization of the major portion of the work of rebuilding in Palestine. The agency was intended to bring into cooperation those non-Zionists who did not accept the idea of a Jewish commonwealth but who were ready to help build Palestine as a refuge for Jews, in much the same manner that they were prepared to contribute to Jewish colonization in the Argentine, in the Crimea, and other lands. While their help was certainly both desirable and welcome, I felt that admitting them to a position of political leadership and responsibility meant a serious compromise with the basic principle of Zionism. A philanthropic, economic, cultural, or spiritual interest in Palestine was laudable and helpful. But it was not Zionism. Accordingly, I was constrained to oppose a development that would, in my view, endanger the character and the heart of the Zionist movement. Though the agency was established, the struggle we waged ensured that the political direction of the moment remained in Zionist hands. I could not, of course, foresee that Hitlerism and all that it was to bring, would convert many of the non-Zionists to the Zionist ideal.

Another principle from which I refused to retreat was that we had continually to insist on the fullest implementation of the mandate and the Balfour Declaration. Any retreat from that position, at least until such time as Jews had established themselves as the majority in Palestine or were in a much stronger position than during the twenties and thirties, would have doomed us to permanent minority status. I therefore opposed at all times such suggestions as a binational state, limitation of immigration and land purchases, and similar schemes, which others were at times ready to accept. When the partition of Palestine was first proposed by the Peel Commission in 1937, I vigorously opposed it. For, its adoption at that time would have meant a pitifully weak state, limited in size and in population and threatened by hostile neighbors. By 1947 when partition was again proposed, the Jewish population had grown in strength and numbers. It was clear that a state, born in 1947 or 1948 out of the partition proposal, would be a viable and durable one, able to defend and secure itself, and capable of fulfilling the promise of providing a home for hundreds of thousands of incoming Jews.

There were times when colleagues counseled the acceptance of compromise proposals because their imposition by the mandatory power seemed inevitable. To them I always said, "It may be, alas, that we shall yet have to bow to the *force majeure* which is to be imposed on us. But that is a very different thing from our giving assent to such imposition. He who consents to evil becomes a doer thereof. He who resists evil alone is free from the sin of complicity. We will never assent to any denial of our inalienable and uncancelable rights to Jewish Palestine. Empires live in terms of centuries. Millennia have witnessed Israel's suffering and shall yet crown the triumph of Israel's hope." Israel had long suffered and mourned but never without hope. We had no right to yield one jot or tittle of our rightful aims or claims.

Finally, I sought inexorably at all times to help safeguard the democratic character of the Zionist movement. Occasionally, there were tendencies incompatible with that democratic character. Against those tendencies and the personalities who embodied them, I placed myself in resolute opposition. Zionism was the will of the Jewish people to re-create its life through a National Homeland. As such, Zionism had to reflect in its structure and in its procedures the democratic character of the experience and aspirations out of which it grew.

Because my adherence to these principles frequently brought me into conflict with the official leadership of the movement, I was at times accused of seeking office and power. I think that I can best express my attitude to office holding by citing a letter I wrote to my children several years ago when I was being urged by friends to stand for the leadership of the world Zionist movement:

> They are very anxious to have me meet with them before I go away. I am really not interested in the consideration whether or not I am to be the leader. I can tell you now that I will not be. I will fight in the leadership, but I think I ought now very clearly say that I will not accept the Presidency of the Zionist Organization or the leadership of the World Organization; that I am battling for a principle, for the purification of Palestine, and the cleansing of the movement both at home and abroad.

The Zionist movement and Zionist congresses provided for many who were later to assume major responsibility in Israel their only training in statesmanship and politics. The splendid performance of Jewish leadership in Palestine during the past several years and particularly in the brief period that has elapsed since the declaration of Israel's independence is the best indication of the quality of that training.

XX

The Jewish People Lives

THE history of the World Jewish Congress from
its prefounding days has been told well and in detail by my
colleague, Dr. A. Leon Kubowitzki, formerly secretary-general
and now chairman of the General Council of the Congress, in
a recent volume, *Unity in Dispersion.* There is, therefore, no
need for me to traverse again, in word and memory, the long
and arduous road that led finally to the organization of the
World Jewish Congress in Geneva in 1936 as a voluntary association of Jewish communities throughout the world for action and counsel on our common problems, as Jews.

But with the passing of the years, I have come more clearly
to understand the bitterness, the almost fanatical opposition to
it of certain primarily assimilationist Jewish groups. These were
under the influence, I regret to say, of certain sections of the
leadership of American and English, French and German
Jewries. From these there had long come not only a fantastic
denial of the existence of a world Jewish problem but the declaration or implication that Jews in all lands were united, if at
all, solely on religious or theological grounds. True it is that
religion is one of the elements in the life of the Jew, the chief
element. Perhaps the greatest thing the Jew has done is to strike
the note of religion in the world, to proclaim the moral sovereignty of the universe. But being a religious people does not
alter the fact that we are a people.

It was alleged and even possibly believed that the sole bond
of union between Jews of all lands lay in the affirmation, through
the *Shema Israel,* the classic watchword of Jewish life and faith,
of the unity of the Godhead. In very truth, this was no more
than an infinitesimal bond between, let us say, the late Chief
Rabbi of England, Dr. Joseph Herman Hertz, my boyhood and
lifelong friend, ardent and always helpful friend of Zionism, and
the saintly Claude G. Montefiore, who spiritually was a disciple of the great Benjamin Jowett, master of Balliol. It was not
a matter of self-deception as much as it was a matter of self-
protection. Subconsciously, it was felt by the enemies of the
concept of Jewish peoplehood that the position of the Jew
would be less hazardous and insecure if Jews in England and
America alike insisted that anti-Semitism was merely a fortui-
tous and fugitive anti-Jewish phenomenon and not a world-wide
problem related to the conditions of Jewish existence and
particularly the homelessness of the Jewish people.

Moreover, to deal with anti-Semitism as if it were a world
problem would have required grave and far-reaching changes
in the attitude of certain Jews to the oppressed and afflicted
among the Jewish masses in the East European lands, chiefly
Poland and Rumania and, before the revolution of 1917, Russia. It would have meant that the old methods and techniques
of benevolent intervention after the event and subsequent protection would need to be changed radically. It would have
meant, as I declared in my address to the first plenary session of
the World Jewish Congress in Geneva in 1936, the recognition
that "such service is charity, however vast; philanthropy, however boundless; kindness, however compassionate. Charity like
patriotism is not enough. Charity might suffice only if some were
in need and the rest secure and comfortable. Whilst Hitlerism
lives, for example, the time is not solely for charity but primarily
for self-defense, self-defense which is not physical nor violent,
but moral, political, economic."

One thing must be said by way of excuse or, in any event,
explanation of the reluctance of the *shtadlonim,* the self-ap-

pointed protectors of Jewish life, to face the facts and to deal
with them aright. It involved for these the very saddening confession of the failure of so-called liberalism as the solvent or
panacea of all human ills to which Jewish flesh was heir. Political and social liberalism was a cause to which Jews of the West
had given their deepest loyalty. It seemed disloyal to desert
that cause, even though it had long and perfidiously deserted
them.

I am far from seeking to imply that European and American
Jewish liberalism of the nineteenth century was nothing more
than a self-protective device. The Jew is a native and incurable
liberal, as well as idealist, and liberalism became a part, a very
considerable part, of his political faith.

Liberalism was no fleeting pastime in the life of the Jew.
Such it proved to be in the case of millions of Germans who
overnight, under the enticement or compulsion of Hitlerism,
literally put away the evil of their liberal thinking and doing
from before their eyes, to become passionate supporters of the
very negation and destruction of liberalism. Jews never were,
save for handfuls of camp followers, liberals by expediency.
They understood, as we continue to understand, that Jews,
viewing their temperament and conviction, have no place or
future in an antiliberal world.

The above serves to explain and in some part to extenuate
the seeming strange conduct of such Jews in Germany as for
years could not bring themselves to believe that Nazism would
endure for very long, that it was more than the most fugitive
of phenomena. These incorrigible liberals were not chiefly
bent on saving their possessions or even maintaining their long-
time status. They could not, would not, yield their intensive and
life-long faith that their country's and their personal stronghold
was an immutable liberalism. The final surrender of liberalism
in Germany came to pass, if at all, on the part of its Jews only
after being scourged like dungeon slaves out of the long-cher-
ished liberalism, which had become almost their religious faith.

Their error, not sin, was to take liberalism too seriously, to make a collective and enduring fetish out of what proved to be nothing more than a lightly held German political expediency or partisanship. Hitler, alas, understood that Jewish liberalism was not a pretense or affectation or pastime but a deeply rooted conviction. Hence, their fate! Hitler, alas, saw that only death could end their adherence to what Hitlerism was sworn to destroy—every last trace and vestige of liberalism. To their honor, it must be said that, whether Socialists or Democrats or even Communists, their undeflectable devotion to human freedom was the head and front of their Jewish offending. What a price they paid! Their sin lay not in their Jewishness. They loved liberty, as Jews evermore did and should, better than life itself.

But there was another type of opposition to the idea of a World Jewish Congress, particularly among certain sections of American and British Jewry, which had nothing to do with liberalism but which, quite the contrary, was based on fears, timidity, and moral cowardice. That opposition came from representatives of conservative, wealthy, and smug Jewish groups whose premises were that "Jews are not a people." They were in the main the same groups whose opposition to Zionism I had characterized as early as 1916 in a sermon: "The charge that Zionism is un-American is the charge uttered by perfervid Americanism, by that Americanism which is so doubtful touching itself and so fearful touching another that it dreads lest any departure from normality in Jewish life, as it conceives it, will be stamped and branded as un-American."

In the light of the tragic and costly experiences of the past decade and more, the basis of the opposition of these groups to the World Jewish Congress today seems utterly fantastic, belonging to past and remote centuries. Yet it is worth recalling, for example, that the American Jewish Committee, spokesman of some wealthy and conservative American Jews interested mainly in philanthropy, severely criticized the American Jewish Congress for calling a World Jewish Conference in Europe

in 1932 "to consider the calling of a World Jewish Congress for
the purpose of considering the world Jewish situation and the
welfare of the Jewish people and the adoption of such measures
as would alleviate it."

In its statement of opposition, a scant half year before Hitler
took power, the American Jewish Committee declared that "the
Jews had established national and local committees headed by
capable and distinguished men, many of whom hold important
posts in the legislative and administrative services of their
respective countries, and that these organizations are better
able to cope with internal problems than an outside conference."
"To call a congress of persons from many parts of the world,"
the American Jewish Committee further declared, "to discuss
the peculiar economic, political, and social conditions affecting
the Jews in the various countries, would be to furnish a spectacle that would be ludicrous and possibly tragic. There would
be no new information to be gathered, no new ideas to be suggested, no new action to be planned. There would be nothing
but speeches and there could be no advantage gained by Jews
anywhere by the passing at such a congress of platitudinous
resolutions." Nor did the increasing ferocity of Hitlerism teach
these groups very much, for their opposition to the World Jewish Congress persisted through its founding in 1936 and has
continued to the present day.

From 1920 until 1932, several preliminary conferences had
been held looking toward the establishment of a World Jewish
Congress. In May, 1932, the American Jewish Congress, which
throughout had taken the initiative for the formation of a world
body, invited Dr. Nahum Goldmann to organize a preparatory
world conference, and for that purpose Goldmann visited the
principal Jewish communities of Europe. Finally, on August
14–17, 94 delegates representing major Jewish organizations
from 17 countries met in Geneva. At that conference, I defined
the congress ideal as the "right of open and free assembly in
the sight of the world for full and complete public discussion of
Jewish questions and problems and tasks." "The Jewish people,"

I asserted, "has nothing to consider and discuss which does not invite and welcome and, indeed, require the light."

A second preparatory conference met in Geneva on September 5–8, 1933, with Hitler already reigning supreme in Germany. At this conference, we sought in vain to alert the world to the menace to world peace and security that Nazism constituted. Alas, however, the world failed to heed our warning in time.

The third and last preparatory conference took place in Geneva in August, 1934. At that conference, we were without the wise counsel and inspiration of Dr. Leo Motzkin, chairman of the *Comité des Délégations Juives* and one of the prime moving spirits of the World Jewish Congress idea. Twenty countries, including the Yishuv in Palestine, were represented. Once again, it was my task to speak bluntly to the nearsighted and timorous Jews who refused to join with us:

> Up to this time, it must be said that the shock of doom has awakened the Jewish people, but as a people we are not yet risen to a sense of collective responsibility and obligation in an hour of overwhelming peril. And at this time, self-deception is nothing more than self-anaesthesia. Even the boycott, as we have said, an instinctive, inevitable weapon of moral and material but not militant self-defense, has been put aside with the timidity of incomprehension and the delays of self-distrust. Every plan and purpose other than that of immediate relief, evokes such hesitations of prudence and such procrastinations of self-contempt as call themselves wisdom. Even when silence would have resulted in the absence of non-Jewish protest against this oceanic wrong, attempts still were made to silence protest.... World Jewry, not German Jewry, is under attack ... and there is an almost total absence of unity in world Jewry, and day by day tinkering has taken the place of long-view Jewish statesmanship.

Dr. Goldmann was elected president of the committee entrusted with the preparatory work for the organization of the World Jewish Congress. When, in 1935, he was appointed representative at the League of Nations of the Jewish Agency for

Palestine, I succeeded him as president. In January, 1936, Dr. Kubowitzki, then president of the Council of Jewish Associations in Brussels, was designated as secretary-general for the preparation of the first World Jewish Congress. That congress, an epochal event in Jewish history, met in Geneva in August, 1936.

In telling the story of the first congress session in Geneva, I revert for a moment, in lighter vein, to a rather queer incident that occurred on the eve of our assembly. The day prior to the opening, a stink bomb was thrown into the hall. Its aroma and flavor threatened postponement, but these were finally dissipated with one minor personal consequence. The Geneva police placed a guard over me and at my side day and night. Other delegates at the congress may have been so favored. I know only that, like Peter Schlemiel, I walked around with my shadow. But my shadow, an undisembodied Geneva policeman, was most obviously and expensively with me at mealtimes. Never before had I ordered two glasses of beer at one time, particularly after forty years of teetotalism, but my shadow shared my life in every sense, particularly during meals.

I might add that the Geneva stink bomb was not the first nor only reminder that the congress and its anti-Nazi convenor were not uniformly popular. In the late twenties and early thirties, whatever anti-Nazi word of mine, as president of the American Jewish Congress, was published, abusive and even threatening letters were certain to follow. My wife always wished to send these missives to the police. Only once did I permit an especially nasty, threatening letter to be forwarded to the police, because my wife was particularly disturbed over the red fluid with which it was written, the writer purporting that the crimson fluid was his own blood.

I had occasion to deal frankly with one such threat. Years before Hitler's accession to power, I warned again and again of the danger of his rise. One day, after announcing that I would speak the following Sunday on "The World Threat of Hitlerism," I received a note of warning that I would not live to deliver that address, that I would be shot while speaking. Entering the pulpit in Carnegie Hall that Sunday morning, I began by reading the letter, adding only this, "I prefer not to be interrupted while preaching by the writer of this letter. If I am to be shot, I venture to suggest that it be done now, at this moment, before I begin." I began and ended the address without a moment's interruption, and I have lived to tell the tale nearly twenty years later.

I go back to the first session of the World Jewish Congress. Two hundred and eighty delegates, representing the Jews of thirty-two countries from all parts of the globe, attended the session. As one who had dreamed of and labored for that hour for years, my first words to the delegates were those of the ancient benediction of our people, the *schehecheyonu*, "Blessed Art Thou, O Lord, our God, King of the Universe, who hast permitted us to live until and to attain unto this hour."

The representatives of two great Jewries unfortunately were absent from that founding session, those of Germany and of the Soviet Union. The Jews of Germany, we understood, were not free to meet with their fellow Jews, who spoke the language of free men. We regretted deeply the absence of the Jews of the Soviet Union, for we were reluctant to bring ourselves to believe that so large a portion of the Jews of the world would be lost forever out of the fellowship of world Jewry.

Out of that session there finally emerged the World Jewish Congress, uniting in voluntary and democratic association, the Jewish communities of many lands. At the time, I said that its functions would be:

> To bring Jews together of many different lands and many different views who do not meet together in any other way: to bring Jews together on a new plane, not that of giving and receiving, but for an interchange of views touching every manner of Jewish problems with a view to their solution; and to help Jews of one

land face the problems of Jews of other lands, to invite their counsel and invoke their experience.

At the same time, I adumbrated the principle that has remained the fixed policy of the World Jewish Congress. As a world organization, representing the Jewish communities of many countries, the World Jewish Congress, as such, had to maintain neutrality as among the nations of the world, but there could be no neutrality, I insisted, "vis-à-vis the moral law and its terrible violation. Jews throughout the centuries of their tradition have taken the position of defenders, furtherers, magnifiers of human freedom. Jews always have sought not only safety. They have striven for freedom."

May I be permitted, not in satisfaction, but in sadness over what the years subsequently brought, to recall two predictions I made at the founding session. Speaking of those who had refused to join the congress, I said:

> Its doors will remain open to the latest comers. We know that dubiety, even more than timorousness moves these, as it moved world Jewry for the most part to absent itself from the first Zionist Congress in 1897. But one does wonder why the absentees have learned little or nothing since the day of Theodor Herzl, that these suffer themselves to be ruled by lying Protocols rather than by the truth of their own being and collective necessity. What will history say to them, who in the presence of political uncertainty, cultural sterility, refuse to meet openly with their fellow-Jews, whether because of fear or any other expediency. History will judge. As for us who assume a great responsibility, history will say that we faced a great task and, as Jews, we were not afraid.

Speaking to the delegates and to the world, I gave expression to our abiding faith in the indestructibility of the Jewish people.

> Gathered in this first session of the World Jewish Congress, we have faith. We have faith in our capacity to make our own people understand; faith in our capacity openly to appeal to the con-

science of mankind. We have faith in that moral order which, under God, will not permit a people to perish, which through nearly forty centuries has revealed its capacity to suffer and endure as well as to achieve in the highest.

The world was to be thrown into war. More than six million of our fellow Jews were to perish. We were to be denied the opportunity of saving scores and even hundreds of thousands by bringing them to Palestine. Six Arab nations were to make war against the Jewish Homeland. We were to be sabotaged by Great Britain and its Foreign Secretary. Nevertheless, we have willed to survive and, through Providence, the Jewish people has not only survived; it has been reborn gloriously as a nation on the soil of our fathers.

One major problem, and some minor problems arose, as soon as the first congress began its sessions. The press concerned itself mainly with one of the minor questions—namely, whether some Americans who had somehow secured mandates should be admitted as delegates. These were thinly disguised anti-Zionists and Communist sympathizers. At the time, Jewish feeling ran strongly against Jewish Communists because of the pro-Arab attitude of the Palestine Jewish Communists at a time when the Arabs were waging a bitter and even murderous war against the Jewish community of Palestine. Regretfully, the congress shut out the tiny American Jewish Communist group almost with unanimity. One of the very few dissenters in favor of admitting them was Mrs. Wise, whose simple but significant statement was, "I cannot bear to see any Jews shut out of a Jewish Congress," a token of intense and catholic Jewish feeling, unspoiled by fears of misunderstanding.

The major problem was the future relation of the congress to the Zionist movement and organization. Some of us had come to feel what we had but vaguely known, that at the very heart of Jewish life in Eastern Europe there were those who, without being assimilationists in the Western European sense of the term, held themselves aloof from Jewish nationalism. Several of the Polish delegates adhered to this position. To those of us, who were long-time and ardent Zionists, this position was particularly trying, most of all in the presence of the Jewish fate in Germany; the Dachau concentration camp had already been established and was in terrible operation. A compromise was at least (but not, it is needless to say, until after the fullest debate) possible: namely, that Zionism become the creed of the World Jewish Congress, but it was to place itself under the regulations, perhaps I should say auspices, of the World Zionist Congress, and virtually to refrain from independent action in respect to the Zionist movement. That position has been faithfully and vigorously held resulting through the years in fullest cooperation with organized Zionism, but in turn, securing little more than lip service from the Zionist parties. There have been times, when as I see it, it would have been far better for the World Jewish Congress to have acted freely and independently and thus to have brought help when critically needed from a body committed to Zionism and yet standing somewhat outside of the Zionist organization.

Such a time may be the present when it seems impossible for the Zionist authorities in our country to deal effectively, for one reason or another, with the American government. We have loyally held to our position, and it is good to be able to state that the most reasonable and unprejudiced Zionists have come to see that there are areas in which, for special reasons, an organization, unidentified and even unaffiliated with the world Zionist organization or the Jewish State, can be most helpful to Zionist interests. For example, with the help of the first-rate advisors of the American Jewish Congress, I have, as president of the American and World Jewish Congresses, in these days, October, 1948, addressed a full memorandum to President Truman, covering the reasons and the precedents for the American government granting at last *de jure* recognition to the state of Israel in place of the *de facto* recognition extended on the memorable fourteenth day of May, 1948.

The history and achievements of the World Jewish Congress are admirably set forth in the volume to which I referred earlier, and it is not my purpose to repeat them here. Suffice it to say that, since its founding, it has rendered inestimable service to Jewry the world over in many vital areas of Jewish concern. Its intervention with international and governmental agencies before the war on behalf of oppressed Jewish communities; its work of rescue and relief in which it pioneered during the war and its immediate aftermath; its role as liaison with the underground movements in Europe; its share in such remarkable episodes as those revealed by former Secretary of the Treasury Henry Morgenthau; its vast research in preparation for postwar problems of war-crimes punishment, reparations, restitution, human rights, etc.; the status it has won as a consultant agency before the United Nations and other international agencies— all these have constituted a remarkable record of service. Probably most important of all is the fact that the World Jewish Congress today serves as a framework democratically uniting the Jewish communities of more than sixty countries throughout the world.

I should perhaps tell something of the more recent Second World Jewish Congress session, which did not take place until the summer of 1948, again in the neutral and hospitable land of Switzerland at Montreux. It was a congress of saddest memories, because of the ever present shadow of the mass slaughter of millions of our fellow Jews. Nothing less than the presence among the delegates of the representatives of the Jewish community of Israel and of a member of the Provisional Israeli Government, David Remez, and the thunderous welcome that greeted him lifted up our hearts and did what could be done to disperse the shadows. At the first session, twelve years earlier, the delegates from Poland represented a great Jewry, greatest of all Jewries in the things that matter in Jewish history—piety, learning, devotion, integrity—a Jewry as we then estimated of

Conducting an interracial Passover Seder service at the Free Synagogue School in 1948.

The last photograph of Rabbi Wise, taken with President Abram L. Sachar at Brandeis University.

three million, three hundred thousand. In 1948, barely one hundred thousand Jews remained alive in Poland.

And now after twelve years of cruelest and most devastating interlude, we were again met in Switzerland, not to plan for the fifteen or sixteen millions of the Jewish population of 1936, but after the unbelievable destruction of our people and of the loss of millions of our fellow Jews, once again to take up the problem of Jewish survival, without which no plea for Jewish unity would in the slightest degree avail. We faced the tragic truth that it must needs be the survival of the impoverished few, with two very special circumstances to affect every phase of the problem before us: 1. The state of Israel had come into being, and its representatives were at hand. 2. Eastern Europe had lost its large Jewish population, though the delegates from the survivors of the ghettos of Poland, Rumania, Hungary, Yugoslavia, and Bulgaria were present, sorrowing as we sorrowed, over the destruction of their nearest, but comforted and quickened by the new hope that, as they saw it, had come to these states under the leadership or dominance of the Soviet Union.

We were most disturbed, even unhappy, over the absence of delegates from the Soviet Jewish population, which was for many of us a gloomy foreboding of the total severance of Russian Jewry from their Jewish brothers the world over. Or, what might be of even greater import to our millions of brothers in the Soviet who could not join us in deliberations over Jewish survival and unity, we knew that the absence from the congress, whether voluntary or involuntary, marked a serious break in Jewish unity, might even be a portent of their final and indistinguishable absorption within the Soviet population.

The delegates from Eastern Europe, for the most part, united in their support of the newly established state of Israel in keeping with the consistently helpful attitude of the Soviet government during the past four years within the United Nations. But we of the West were disturbed by and resentful over the overtones of our Eastern comrades, everlastingly harping upon Anglo-American imperialism, though we old-time and unshakable Zionists were far from happy over the excuse for such insinuations and attack furnished by Bevin's anti-Jewish policy and the subordination of the American State Department to the divide-and-rule policy of the British Colonial and Foreign Office.

Inevitably, we had to face the problem posed by the acute political divisions of the world today. It had been feared by some, particularly by such as were hesitant about convening the congress. It did not wreck the congress, although it did give us some difficult moments. Having been welcomed into the conference, the East European delegates had the right to expect that they would be treated in every sense as were the delegates from all other lands. And they were. No discrimination against them was attempted or would have been tolerated by the congress. They were active participants in every phase and item of the congress' problems. They firmly held to their opinions and were hardly averse to endless and even exhausting repetition of their views, especially when these involved the all too familiar terms "progress and democracy," of which Eastern Europe is not quite the sole heir or solitary guardian.

We did approach a living and divisive issue as we neared the end of the session. The question arose on the election of the world executive committee. The congress was entirely ready to recognize the strength of the Communist groups where these had come to represent goodly numbers of the people, as in Poland. The delegates from the Eastern European countries, however, insisted that among the Americans to be named to the world executive there should be included a representative of a Jewish Communist organization in the United States. The American delegation, with my full agreement, firmly rejected this demand. We insisted that it was the responsibility of each delegation to determine who should represent its community. While scrupulously refraining from interfering with other countries in their choice of designees on the Executive Committee, we expected similar noninterference in our designations.

The group for whom representation was demanded, we

strongly felt, was so utterly unrepresentative of the American Jewish community and its contribution to Jewish life so negligible that it was not entitled to representation on the Executive Committee from the United States. Thus, we were forced to reject the demand, however tempting amid the warmth and good fellowship of the congress session and our utter unreadiness to give place to the faintest suspicion of red-baiting within the World Jewish Congress. Our position was overwhelmingly upheld by vote of the plenary session when nominations to the Executive Committee were approved.

Despite these difficulties, inescapable in a world rife with so much political and social tension, the second session of the World Jewish Congress was a momentous achievement and a gratifying success. The adherence to the congress of Jewries in more than sixty lands demonstrated unanswerably that the fears and timidities which we encountered during the years prior to and immediately following the organization of the congress had been largely dissolved. Alas, that it took a catastrophe of such unprecedented proportions to teach some of our fellow Jews the lesson of common action, of forthright speech, of dignified affirmation!

The session gave to Jewish communities the world over, the smallest together with the most powerful, a genuine and uplifting sense of equal and democratic participation both in the discussion of the problems that we face commonly as Jews and in the formulation of their solution. And, second only to the magnificent events surrounding the birth of the state of Israel, the Montreux session of the World Jewish Congress was a dignified and triumphant affirmation of the indestructibility of the Jewish people, of its will to survive, and of its determination to do all that one historic group can do to bring about a warless world of freedom and democracy, of justice and peace.